W9-BGT-737

CELEBRATIONS OF DEATH

THE ANTHROPOLOGY OF MORTUARY RITUAL

CELEBRATIONS OF DEATH

THE ANTHROPOLOGY OF MORTUARY RITUAL

RICHARD HUNTINGTON
Harvard University

PETER METCALF
University of Virginia

CAMBRIDGE UNIVERSITY PRESS

CAMBRIDGE

LONDON   NEW YORK   MELBOURNE

Published by the Syndics of the Cambridge University Press
The Pitt Building, Trumpington Street, Cambridge CB2 1RP
Bentley House, 200 Euston Road, London NW1 2DB
32 East 57th Street, New York, NY 10022, USA
296 Beaconsfield Parade, Middle Park, Melbourne 3206, Australia

© Cambridge University Press 1979

First published 1979

Printed in the United States of America
Typeset by The Fuller Organization, Philadelphia, Pennsylvania
Printed and bound by Vail-Ballou Press, Inc., Binghamton, New York

Library of Congress Cataloging in Publication Data
Huntington, Richard.
Celebrations of death.
Bibliography: p.
1. Funeral rites and customs.   2. Death.
I. Metcalf, Peter, joint author.   II. Title.
GN486.H84   393   79–478
ISBN 0 521 22531 0 hard covers
ISBN 0 521 29540 8 paperback

TO OUR ANCESTORS

CONTENTS

vii

Contents

Contents

LIST OF
ILLUSTRATIONS

FIGURES

PLATES

Illustrations

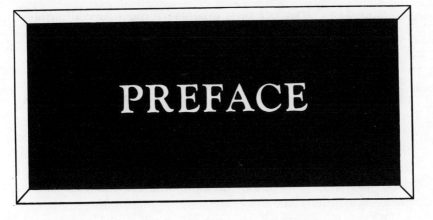

PREFACE

Death is receiving renewed attention in our society. After three generations of silence, our mortality is again a fit topic for public discussion. There are now seminars, courses, and television talk shows on death and dying. Psychologists, theologians, and social critics have all contributed to this new awareness of death. There is now even a profession of thanatology.

We, however, are not thanatologists. We are anthropologists, and each of us has spent years researching societies where death is celebrated in the midst of life. We were led to these societies (Metcalf to Borneo, Huntington to Madagascar) by an interest, not in death, but in certain aspects of social life. Our researches were aimed at the comparative study of social structures, but we were confronted with cultures that are startlingly open in their dealings with death.

Later, our individual ethnographic writings benefited from discussion of the similarities between Bornean and Malagasy funerary customs. Furthermore, for each region one is led to consideration of the same early theorists, Hertz and Van Gennep. These writers drew their examples from the peoples of this Malayo-Polynesian world and brought the understanding of the transcultural significance of their death rites to early heights. Anthropology

Preface

has tended to expropriate these insights for more general purposes and has integrated them into the heart of its theories of society and religion.

We return to the specific focus of these works in order to retrieve Hertz's and Van Gennep's insights on death. From this perspective, their works clarify certain current concerns among anthropologists and illuminate efforts to understand the changing role of death in modern society. The anthropology of these funeral rites has implications that go beyond the villages in which we conducted our researches. Therefore we use our knowledge of these societies as bases upon which to construct a broader anthropological synthesis on death.

This study is a joint effort in the fullest sense, and we have now spent over three years planning, writing, and revising this book. There is no part that has not benefited from the exchange of ideas and criticisms. However, there has been a division of labor according to our respective areas of interest and research experience. Huntington is primarily responsible for Chapters 1, 4, and 6; Metcalf for Chapters 2, 3, and 5. The Introduction, "The anthropology of death ritual," and the Conclusion, "American deathways," are products of close collaboration. Ultimately, only one hand can hold the pen; Metcalf wrote the Conclusion, and Huntington the Introduction.

Each of us owes many debts of thanks to our teachers and to those who have helped us in our researches. Due to the double authorship it would be unwieldy to list all these debts here. We have each thanked these people in other works and will do so again. Relating to the present book, we would like to thank Walter H. Lippincott of Cambridge University Press for his encouragement and help, and James Boon for his critical reading of earlier drafts. We also owe an obvious debt to the scholars whose works we draw upon for examples. We respectfully request their indulgence if we place their work in analytical contexts different from those which they originally intended.

Metcalf acknowledges support from the Wilson Gee Fellowship Program, University of Virginia. Huntington received support from the Teschemacher Fund, Harvard University.

Joint authorship is relatively rare in anthropology. This is largely a result of the highly personal and localized style of field-work in another culture. An additional result of this research technique is a strong tendency on the part of anthropologists to leap from minute and unique social fields toward global conclusions. Field research can also lead the anthropologist to put aside the cultural blinkers of his or her own society only to adopt in large measure those of the society being studied. Working together has expanded the empirical and experiential base for our study. Whether this has reduced some of the above-mentioned shortcomings while maintaining the sense of immediacy and human intimacy that derives from personal field research, the reader must be the judge. For our part, we have found this collaboration to be tremendously stimulating, challenging and enjoyable.

Cambridge, Massachusetts   P. M. & R. H.
May 1979

INTRODUCTION

THE ANTHROPOLOGY
OF DEATH RITUAL

MATTERS OF LIFE AND DEATH

What could be more universal than death? Yet what an incredible variety of responses it evokes. Corpses are burned or buried, with or without animal or human sacrifice; they are preserved by smoking, embalming, or pickling; they are eaten – raw, cooked, or rotten; they are ritually exposed as carrion or simply abandoned; or they are dismembered and treated in a variety of these ways. Funerals are the occasion for avoiding people or holding parties, for fighting or having sexual orgies, for weeping or laughing, in a thousand different combinations. The diversity of cultural reaction is a measure of the universal impact of death. But it is not a random reaction; always it is meaningful and expressive. This study is about the rituals by which people deal with death, and hence celebrate life. Anthropologists have no special understanding of the mystery of death. We can but recount the collective wisdoms of many cultures, the wisdoms that have been acted, sung, wailed, and danced at funerals through the ages.

For the funerals of a great many cultures are, in comparison to our own staid traditions, rowdy affairs. This is true in those areas that form the twin foci for this study, Madagascar and Borneo; true for many of the cultures we will be considering from Southeast Asia and Eastern Africa. Closer to home, one thinks of Irish wakes or the jazz funeral processions in old New Orleans. Though our custom calls for quiet, restraint, sympathy, and sorrow, it often happens that the pleasure of the reunion of family and friends bubbles up and almost eclipses the prescribed funeral behavior. Empirically, in many funeral rituals signs of life and community eclipse representations of death and separation.

The study of death rituals is a positive endeavor. In all societies, regardless of whether their customs call for festive or restrained behavior, the issue of death throws into relief the most important cultural values by which people live their lives and evaluate their experiences. Life becomes transparent against the background of death, and fundamental social and cultural issues are revealed. For example, in Madagascar, the pervasive opposition of maleness and femaleness that underlies the structure of that society achieves its most powerful and focused expression in funeral ritual. In Africa, the politically fragmented Nyakyusa and Dinka peoples reveal in their funerals basic survival values of warriorhood and cooperation. In centralized kingdoms everywhere – Africa, Europe, Asia – events surrounding the death of the king reveal most strikingly the nature of each polity and the structure of its political competition. In the United States, the individualism, materialism, and commercialism that characterize our national ethic seem to stand in particularly sharp relief in the context of our funeral industry. Peoples' customary responses to death provide an important opportunity for sensitive probing into the nature of human life.

THE "DEATH AWARENESS" MOVEMENT

Currently, there is a growing interest in all facets of death. It is now fashionable to deal frankly with this formerly taboo subject. The legal, medical, and moral issues surrounding death and our new abilities to delay it are discussed frequently in the general press and in professional journals. Courses on "death and dying" are being introduced into the curricula of our schools at every level from fourth grade to graduate seminar. The introduction of "death education" in the public schools is almost as controversial as the introduction of sex education. This is no accident: Some association of sex with death occurs in nearly every culture in the world. In another vein, a popular book (now made into a feature film) presents the reports of people who have "died" and then been revived to describe the nature of *Life After Life* (Moody 1975).

In many respects, this "death awareness" movement began with the enormous popularity and influence of Jessica Mitford's exposé of *The American Way of Death* (1963). Mitford attacked the American funeral industry for profiteering through selling unnecessarily expensive services and goods to a captive clientele under great temporary stress. She questioned the appropriateness of the funeral ritual itself, especially the elaborate treatment and display of the corpse. With this public reassessment of the ritual, there began a broader reconsideration of all aspects of the experience of dying and the significance of death in modern society.

Mitford saw the normal American funeral as irrational, and by the standards of most of the peoples of the world, native American funeral customs are indeed strange. So thoroughly have Americans sealed themselves off from death that many have never seen a corpse. Others have seen one only in the carefully stage-managed context of the funeral parlor, the body elaborately packaged and beautified. After delivery to the undertaker, the corpse

> . . . is in short order sprayed, sliced, pierced, pickled, trussed, trimmed, creamed, waxed, painted, rouged and neatly dressed . . .transformed from a common corpse into a Beautiful Memory Picture. This process is known in the trade as embalming and restorative art, and is so universally employed in the United States and Canada that the funeral director does it routinely without consulting corpse or kin. He regards as eccentric those few who are hardy enough to suggest that it might be dispensed with. Yet no law requires it, no religious doctrine commends it,

nor is it dictated by considerations of health, sanitation, or even personal daintiness. In no part of the world but in North America is it widely used. The purpose of embalming is to make the corpse presentable for viewing in a suitably costly container; and here too the funeral director routinely, without first consulting the family, prepares the body for public display. [Mitford 1963: 54]

Remembering the oddities of our own funeral practices, we can avoid any tendency to feel superior toward the other cultures we are about to examine. Conversely, the exploration of the death rituals of other cultures will allow us to observe American funerals with a new and more balanced perspective.

Study of Western attitudes toward death and dying began before Mitford's book. Most notably, sociologist Geoffrey Gorer (1965) compiled a detailed study of mourning practices in England and historian Philippe Ariès (1967) documented the changing Western attitudes toward death over eight centuries. Collections appeared containing numerous empirical studies of the social-psychological reactions of people to death, their own impending death, and that of others (Feifel 1959, Fulton 1965). Even as these academic studies multiply, our death customs are themselves undergoing changes. On the one hand, consumer groups have organized to procure simpler, less expensive, more "rational" funerals. Although this movement has attracted wide interest, few people actually choose these streamlined funerals for themselves or for their loved ones. On the other hand, many funeral businesses are shedding their traditional cloak of restrained respectability and are mounting more explicit promotional campaigns for a greater variety of funeral arrangements. Even these changes, however, tend to be variations on the classical American funeral themes of embalming and viewing. Innovations such as drive-in wakes and motorcycle funerals would not startle Mitford. In spite of such variations, or perhaps related to them, there is today a strong desire to confront the issue of death, to know better what it entails, and to place the structure of our institutions and emotions within the context of this more precise knowledge.

The Anthropology of Death Ritual

DEATH RITUAL AND THE BIRTH OF ANTHROPOLOGY

Paradoxically, although there is little in the way of a body of anthropological literature specifically directed to the topic, death-related behavior is of crucial importance to many of the central theoretical developments in anthropology since its beginnings. Positions regarding death have always been closely related to the anthropology of social life. In a roundabout way, anthropology has never been able to study humans seriously without considering the essential fact of their mortality. This is because death and its rituals not only reflect social values, but are an important force in shaping them (Geertz 1973: 94–8).

Data from burial practices and beliefs about death were of central importance to the early development of the study of human evolution, of the rise of ancient civilization, and of cultural and social institutions. In all three fields, direct concern with death-related material lessened as each began to make use of additional data and to investigate more specialized questions. However, the legacy of an early focus on death and burial customs continues to inform the important assumptions of our major scientific theories about human existence.

Research into the emergence of humankind has relied heavily on two kinds of evidence: tools and grave assemblages. This focus developed, not from any fascination on the part of archaeologists with the origins of work or funerals, but from the simple fact that skeletons and tools of bone and stone can survive for millennia to serve as data for researchers. The arrangement of these items in a specific pattern at a burial site is often the only indication that remains of symbolic activity among these early bands of our forebears. For example, in a comparison of Mousterian and Upper Paleolithic burials, Binford (1968: 148) finds evidence of "greater corporate awareness and increased social differentiation" in the latter, symptomatic of the development of a "fully modern" community. Her formulation goes beyond an inventory of artifacts to make deductions about the social meaning of the lives and deaths of individual human beings.

5

Introduction

Just as the evidences of burial are often the only data surviving from early paleolithic cultures, mortuary constructions are often the most impressive and revealing remains of early civilizations. The importance of ancestors in the religions of the Greeks, Etruscans, and Romans makes tombs and burial jars important sources of data for classical archaeology. In Egypt, archaeologists made startling discoveries about an ancient way of life revolving around a national death-oriented cult that reached its most lasting representation in the huge pyramids. Students of ancient civilizations are not restricted to excavating burial places. There are also temples, palaces, and cities. However, the structures designed for the dead seem to provide a special fund of information about the ideologies and values of ancient societies.

In social anthropology, the theme of death has moved in and out of vogue. Early nineteenth-century writers tended to be uninterested in the topic of death and death-related behavior. Social anthropologists such as McLennan, Morgan, Lubbock, and Wake wrote about the evolution of sexual morality and its relation to the evolution of social structures. Toward the end of the century the emphasis changed. The anthropology of Tylor and Frazer focused attention on beliefs about death and existence thereafter. This approach is often labeled "intellectualist" because it tried to reconstruct the solutions devised by early humans to questions presented by natural phenomena. Frazer and Tylor asserted that early humans' contemplation of death and deathlike states such as sleeping and dreaming was the origin of the concept of soul and hence the origin of all religion. To the extent that religion was viewed as an early and largely erroneous attempt at science, the entire human intellectual enterprise was seen to be specifically rooted in early humans' musings on the theme of their postmortem fate.

DURKHEIM AND THE SOCIOLOGY
OF RELIGION

The work of the great French sociologist Emile Durkheim directly opposed this intellectualist emphasis of the English tradition of anthropology. Durkheim, a founder of modern sociology, emphasized that the moral cohesion of society and its expression in religion could be explained largely in reference to sociological factors and not as a result of the fears and imaginations of individual personalities. As we shall see in Chapter 1, funeral rituals and the expression of fear and anguish in confrontation with death were important data for Durkheim's theory. But such data were marshaled to support a sociological theory, not an intellectualist explanation.

Whereas for Frazer and Tylor primitive beliefs relating to death provided easy solutions to questions about the origins and nature of religion, for Durkheim conceptions about death were part of the problem, not a solution. This is because, from his approach, the very nature of the individual as an entity differentiated from the group is the central problem to be investigated. Durkheim's theory focuses on the integration of individuals into communal life. In this process, beliefs and ideas play a role that is much more complicated than that envisioned by Tylor and Frazer. Durkheim devoted much of his career to investigating the complexity of collectively held beliefs and concepts, and exploring how such "collective representations" unite individuals even while simultaneously specifying their separate identities. Throughout Durkheim's work, there is a dynamic tension between the autonomy of the individual and the individual's identification with society; between the physical separateness of human organisms and the necessity to transcend it through the use of language and symbols. Within this theoretical framework, the event of death is an important but difficult topic that brings to the fore the ambiguities and contradictions of human social existence and definition.

During the first decade of this century, Durkheim and his students produced a remarkable series of essays on the sociology of religion, many of which were published in their journal, the *Année sociologique*. One by one these essays took up the topics of sacrifice, symbolic classification, magic, sin and expiation, and body symbolism. They reformulated these classical theological issues within the sociological framework established by Durkheim's work. This was truly a cooperative effort, and most of

7

these essays are collaborations of two authors. English-speaking anthropologists have only recently begun to accord these works the attention they deserve. It was the belated translation and republication of these essays that was largely responsible for the great florescence of studies of symbolic forms that has been one of the chief developments in social anthropology during the last fifteen years.

One of these essays, Robert Hertz's 1907 study of secondary burial, provides the primary point of reference for our analysis of death ritual. In 1909, another Parisian scholar, Arnold Van Gennep (who was conversant with but not associated with Durkheim's group) published *The Rites of Passage*, which dealt with funerals as one of a large class of rituals. Both appeared in English translation in 1960. Together these two works provide a forceful and truly original perspective on the nature of death ritual in human affairs. It is with the ideas of these two men that we must begin our exploration of the significance of funerals.

VAN GENNEP'S RITES OF PASSAGE

We begin with Van Gennep. His study was of a broader scope than Hertz's and its influence has overflowed the disciplinary boundary of anthropology to play an important role in other fields, and has even seeped into the general press and popular consciousness. Van Gennep's thesis is that all rituals involving passage from one state to another share in a single tripartite structure defined by the necessary function of separation from one status and reincorporation into the new one, with a marginal or liminal period in between. There is a deceptive simplicity to Van Gennep's notion, which at first sight seems to amount to little more than an assertion that rituals have beginnings, middles, and ends. However, Van Gennep was the first to notice just how similar are the beginnings, middles, and ends of an extraordinarily wide range of rituals. As he commented, others had noticed recurring themes in rites of marriage, initiation, and funeral rituals. Van Gennep emphasized that these similarities are not random analogies but part of a single general phenomenon. The general structure underlying a huge variety of ritual behavior relates to the social function of recruiting and incorporating individuals that mature, age, and die into a fixed system of culturally defined roles and statuses. This function is made necessary by the fact that society outlasts the individuals that comprise it.

The importance of Van Gennep's ideas and the influence of his book go beyond these sociological applications. Van Gennep also makes a contribution to the study of the nature of social classification and the logic of categories. His theory rests on the awareness that a single distinction creates two classes, and that any such duality implies a tertiary structure. Van Gennep uses this one–two–three logic of structure (so familiar to us now through the work of Lévi-Strauss) to understand social process (see Figure 1).

Because of his emphasis on process, the structuralist aspects of Van Gennep's work tend to be forgotten. But he makes it clear that his tripartite arrangement is rooted in a binary distinction (between two social statuses) and that it is not always visible on the surface of particular rituals or performances.

> Our interest lies not in the particular rites but in their essential significance and their relative positions within ceremonial wholes – that is, their order. . . . Their positions may vary . . . but the differences lie only in matters of detail. The underlying arrangement is always the same. Beneath a multiplicity of forms, either consciously expressed or merely implied, a typical pattern always recurs: *the pattern of the rites of passage.* [1960: 191]

Van Gennep's essay, like much that was written in Paris during the first decade of this century, is strikingly modern. Its style contrasts sharply with the anthropology that preceded it. Nineteenth-century anthropologists had been absorbed in tracing, according to various schemes, humanity's rise through a series of

death	ONE DISTINCTION	marriage
alive / dead	TWO CATEGORIES	single / married
alive → dying → dead	THREE STAGES	single → engaged → married

Figure 1. Schema of Van Gennep's rites of passage

social stages, each more complex, moral, and rational than the previous stage. The chief form of evidence for the nature of these past stages consisted of those bizarre and irrational surviving customs found in historical and contemporary societies. The "doctrine of survivals" assumed that all seemingly irrational practices and beliefs were relics of, and evidence for, past social forms. Such an approach drastically impoverished anthropology's capacity to make sense of either the past or present eras, or of the nature of their common inhabitant, the social person.

The data for the doctrine of survivals were frequently aspects of ritual behavior. This inability to view ritual as anything other than an anachronism was a peculiar development of nineteenth-century rationalism, and Van Gennep's achievement can be fully appreciated only against this background. Franz Steiner (1967) provides a succinct insight into this odd but prevailing Victorian view of ritual.

> The Victorian era was a rationalist age which differed from the previous Age of Reason in that it attributed importance not only to the various attempts at rational explanation, but also to the residual context which did not yield to the solvent of reason. This was particularly true of religion, which was then being adapted to the needs of an industrial society. Now the ground held by religion could be covered by various ethical theories, but there remained, unaccounted for, some very important attitudes which were not susceptible to the same kind of treatment and which, indeed, seemed irrational under such examination. These attitudes and contexts, which had thus been divorced from their background and from institutional functions, became isolated to a degree which was new in human history. The more the links, props and joints of the socio-religious thought structure were absorbed into theories of rational ethics, the more isolated became the little islands of prescribed ceremonial behavior. . . . [Steiner 1967: 50–1]

This attitude colored nineteenth-century anthropologists' assessments, not only of current ritual practices, but of all ritual. Customs such as the mock battle in ancient marriage rituals were seized upon as evidence for elaborate reconstructions postulating primitive stages of marriage-by-capture overlaid upon stages of

matriarchy and followed by patriarchy [McLennan 1970 (1865)].
Van Gennep's 1909 study proposed a radically different assessment
of the meaning and function of ritual behavior, one subversive of
the entire project of ethnocentric evolutionism. Elements of ceremonial behavior were no longer the relics of former superstitious
eras, but keys to a universal logic of human social life. Mock battles in marriage rituals were dramatic representations of the function of "separation," not leftovers of a rude past.

With Van Gennep's thesis, some of the fear and arrogance of
ethnocentrism vanish from transcultural study. For Van Gennep
takes precisely that aspect of ancient and primitive societies that
first appears so odd, foreign, senseless, and bewilderingly various,
that is, ritual symbols and behavior, and transforms it into that
which is simple, logical, and universal. The concept of the rite of
passage stands close to the center of three major issues in modern
social anthropology: the integration of the individual into society,
the nature of symbolic meaning, and the moral and intellectual
relativity of cultures.

LIMINALITY

It is not this emphasis on structure, classification, and cultural relativity that has had the most influence on the recent study of symbolism, but rather Van Gennep's concept of liminality. Turner's
(1967) brilliant expansion of this concept is largely responsible for
the wide circulation enjoyed today by Van Gennep's theory and
terminology. Building upon Van Gennep's insight that the transi-
tional phase sometimes acquires a certain autonomy from the rest
of the ritual, Turner develops a view of "a state of transition"
(1967: 94), the inhabitants of which are "betwixt and between"
normal social roles, and close to some transcendent and sacred
core of social and moral value. Turner follows Van Gennep's lead
in exploring the characteristic ways humans represent change with
symbols drawn from biological processes such as menstruation and
decomposition. Turner's focus on the autonomy of liminality
eventually leads him far afield from specific rituals of transition.
As he notes, with self-deprecating humor, it is

a hypothesis that seeks to account for the attributes of such seemingly diverse phenomena as neophytes in the liminal phase of ritual, subjugated autochthones, small nations, court jesters, holy mendicants, good Samaritans, millenarian movements, "dharma bums," matrilaterality in patrilineal systems, patrilaterality in matrilineal systems, and monastic orders. Surely an ill-assorted bunch of social phenomena! [1969: 125]

Turner's development of the theme of liminality extends far from its initial application to Ndembu initiation rituals. But Van Gennep's original emphasis on the autonomy of the liminal derives most strongly from his consideration of death rituals. The chapter titled "Funerals" opens as follows:

On first considering funeral ceremonies, one expects rites of separation to be their most prominent component, in contrast to rites of transition and rites of incorporation, which should be only slightly elaborated. A study of the data, however, reveals that the rites of separation are few in number and very simple, while the transition rites have a duration and complexity sometimes so great that they must be granted a sort of autonomy.
[1960: 146]

Van Gennep's survey of death rituals throughout the world emphasizes the ways this theme of transition seems to dominate funeral symbolism. Water journeys and islandlike afterworlds appear over and over again. Additionally, Van Gennep noted that, surprisingly, the theme of regeneration and growth expressed in symbols of agricultural and human fertility is equally common. Where Turner has emphasized that the symbolism of growth and fertility, on the one hand, and degeneration and putrescence, on the other, are a function of liminality per se, Van Gennep was cautious. He noted that this liminal phase of funerals is not entirely autonomous, not entirely interchangeable with liminal phases of other rituals. He carefully left room for a special relevance of these highly charged and sensuous symbols to death itself.

In Van Gennep's formulation, liminality is never divorced entirely from its ritual context. Where it most nearly approaches autonomy is in the context of funerals, perhaps because death is so much more profound a mystery than other transitions such as marriage and initiation. Additionally, Van Gennep's concept of liminality is never separated from the notion of change, process, and passage. Never is it extended as a fixed complementary category, as in some of Turner's developments. Although such an extension enables one to explain a staggering array of phenomena, it makes the concept of liminality too static, it seems, to relate with any force to people's needs in the face of death.

HERTZ'S STUDY OF SECONDARY BURIAL

As Van Gennep himself noted (1960: 190n), the only other writer to appreciate the importance and character of the liminal phase of ritual was Robert Hertz. This is not surprising given that Hertz's special concern was with death rituals. Funerals provide only a part of the data of Van Gennep's wide-ranging survey. They are, by contrast, the sole concern of Hertz's essay "A Contribution to the Study of the Collective Representation of Death" (1907), one of the most original analyses pertaining to death written in this century. This book is largely an extension of and a tribute to the precocious insights of Robert Hertz.

Hertz discussed those societies that do not see death as instantaneous. Although such a view of death is not uncommon in much of the world, Hertz drew much of his material from Indonesia, particularly the island of Borneo. In this region, many peoples conceive of a period when the mortal is neither alive nor finally dead; this Hertz called the "intermediary period." The end of this period is marked by the "great feast," during which the remains of the deceased are recovered, ritually processed, and moved to a new location. Hertz noted that the length of the intermediary period may be prolonged by several factors, such as the need to accumulate a surplus for the feast. But the irreducible minimal duration is the time required for the bones to become dry and free of decaying flesh.

The fate of the corpse is to suffer putrescence and formlessness, until only dry bones remain, hard and imperishable. It was Hertz's insight that, in Borneo, the fate of the body is a model for the fate of the soul. As the corpse is formless and repulsive during the intermediary period, so the soul of the dead person is homeless and the object of dread. Unable to enter the society of the dead, it must lead a pitiful existence on the fringes of human habitation. In its discomfort, the soul is liable spitefully to inflict illness upon the living. Elaborate observances are required to divert its hostility. The "great feast" terminates this miserable period by honoring the now dry bones of the deceased, confirming the soul's arrival in the land of ancestors, and marking the reestablishment of normal relations among the survivors.

Such an explanation is hardly a general postulate comparable to Van Gennep's schema of the rite of passage or of the nature of liminality. Hertz used a different but equally powerful lens through which to focus on death, viewing the issue through one type of burial custom. Yet there is no question that Hertz's concerns were no less general than those of Van Gennep. The difference is largely one of sociological style. Hertz followed Durkheim's method of the special case. Rather than survey all forms of a phenomenon, one example is chosen, the analysis of which will illuminate a wide range of related forms. The classic example of this is Durkheim's choice of the topic of suicide as the special case on which to test his theories of the integration of the individual into the larger social group. In studying the representation of death, Hertz chose the custom of secondary burial – an elaborate form of the general tendency toward representing death through manipulation of the corpse.

Hertz's treatment of general issues wholly within a single ethnographic context was, in this way, a forerunner of the modern tradition of social anthropology. Whereas the value of Van Gennep's approach can be appreciated in comparison with the style of anthropology that preceded it, Hertz's work makes sense only in the context of what followed. As a student of Durkheim, he shared in the development of comparative sociology.

Hertz's essays exemplify this descriptive integration, the meaning of the facts being shown to lie not in themselves, considered as separate facts, but in their interrelation; the art of the anthropologist being to reveal this and hence their meaning. We do not understand what the double disposal of the dead in Indonesia means till we know also about the beliefs held about the ghosts of the dead and also about the rules of mourning, but once we have grasped the pattern of these three sides of death – corpse, soul and mourners – we see that each expresses the same idea of transition; and we further understand why a ruler's death cannot be announced, why widows may not be immediately inherited or remarried, why corpses of the very old and of small children are treated differently, etc. [Evans-Pritchard in Hertz 1960: 15]

Central to this approach was a new and more exact form of comparative analysis. Hertz was careful to concentrate on a limited range of facts from one area of the world, and not to lift facts out of context from widely divergent societies. The representation of death is a problem of universal scope and even the seemingly bizarre practice of secondary disposal of the corpse is more widespread than is generally realized. Examples could be cited from Central Asia (Lopatin 1960: 90–114), North America (Driver 1961: 450), South America (Crocker 1977), Melanesia (Haddon 1908: 149; Tuzin 1975; Wagner 1972: 147–50), and elsewhere. Reburial was a part of the Jewish tradition (Meyers 1971) and is still practiced in Greece (Alexiou 1974: 47–9). But Hertz stuck for the most part to the rich material from Borneo and Indonesia. It is upon this empirical base that his analysis, whatever illumination it might cast on behavior elsewhere in the world, must stand or fall. One could search the world for confirming parallels or doubt-casting exceptions, but in the context of Bornean ethnographic facts, Hertz's analysis possesses the modern characteristic of falsifiability.

In his analysis of the symbolism of the decaying corpse, Hertz borrowed from his colleagues' account of the nature of sacrifice (Hubert and Mauss 1899). What connects secondary disposal with sacrifice is the conception that objects must be destroyed in this world in order that they may pass to the next. Hertz saw that what applied to the sudden destruction of sacrifice also applies to the slow one of decomposition. In this way, he placed himself in the tradition of Smith (1889) in exploring the subtle interaction between the nature of a concept and the "material husk" within which it must be wrapped in order to have form (Beidelman 1974: 56–7).

MODERN DEVELOPMENTS
OF HERTZ'S THESIS

Although Hertz's essay is often cited, with praise, there are few places in the anthropological literature where it is discussed in much detail. The most prominent of these discussions (Goody 1962; Miles 1965; Bloch 1971) draw their inspiration from the sociological side of Hertz's analysis. For example, Goody's study of *Death, Property and the Ancestors* discusses Hertz's analysis of the problem of restoring the social fabric after death has rent it. This approach provides an effective base for Goody's emphasis on the transformation of economic, social, and emotional relationships wrought by the funeral rituals of a West African people. But the symbolic aspects of Hertz's argument have been passed over.

Meanwhile, those anthropologists responsible for the revival of interest in Hertz's symbolic analyses have paid little attention to his essay on death. By translating and publishing the essay together with Hertz's "The Pre-eminence of the Right Hand: A Study in Religious Polarity," Needham highlights Hertz's concern with body symbolism (Hertz 1960). The introduction to that volume, by Evans-Pritchard, is a general discussion of the *Année sociologique* with but a few lines specifically referring to the death essay. Needham's development of Hertz's work has built mainly on the essay on the polarity of the human body rather than on the essay relating to its mortality. The former was again reprinted in a large collection of articles on left–right binary symbolism (Needham 1973). The older volume containing the death essay is now out of print. Other anthropologists, notably Douglas (1971), have also expanded upon Hertz's insights regarding the body as a "natural symbol" for moral phenomena. The complex issues raised by the death essay have yet to be discussed.

The elaborations of Hertz's insights wrought by scholars such as Goody, Needham, and Douglas have been fruitful and stimulating. However, the separate developments of the sociological and symbolic aspects of Hertz's work serve to point up how specialized anthropology has become in recent decades. In his short essay, Hertz tried to encompass a problem larger than those that exercise his successors. He tried to cover the whole range of human activity: the symbolic, the social, the pragmatic, and the emotional. Perhaps it was his situation as a young man working in a new science during its formative years that permitted him to be so ambitious.

Certainly Hertz's essay is flawed in several respects, largely due to its attempt to achieve grand aims based on limited and second-hand data. At times it seems as though he is attempting desperately to bridge this gap with every analytical device available in the first decade of this century. Explanations drawn from studies of Hindu pollution and Hebrew sacrifice are applied directly and sometimes inappropriately to the cultures of Borneo. Exceptions to his thesis are argued away with the same utilitarian reasoning that he elsewhere rules out as inadmissible. But no one has ever claimed that Hertz's death essay is a measured and mature piece of work. Indeed, it is his intellectual daring that makes Hertz so rewarding. His crucial insight remains: Close attention to the combined symbolic and sociological contexts of the corpse yields the most profound explanations regarding the meaning of death and life in almost any society.

THE FORMAT OF THIS BOOK

It is not our intention in this book to provide either an encyclopedia of the world's funeral customs or a history of the anthropological study of death rituals. We limit ourselves to a few outstanding cases that provide striking illustrations of the major themes deriving from Hertz's study. Our interest in these cases lies in the details of cultural practices relating to death and the treatment of the corpse. In order to keep close to the poignant human drama of death, we supplement these cultural descriptions with several vivid eyewitness accounts of specific funerals in these societies. Our study is divided into three main parts, each of which consists of two chapters that explore complementary sides of the issue at hand.

In Part I, "Universals and culture," we look at some of the attempts anthropologists have made to establish universal theories about responses to death.

The undeniable and often-noted universality of death suggests the attractive possibility of an uncomplicated panhuman explanation of funeral rites and death-related behavior. Anthropologists have often stressed a certain "psychic unity of mankind," so postulating that whatever different beliefs people have, whatever different types of societies or environments they inhabit, they nonetheless share the same type of emotional and cognitive qualities. However, the question remains: Can these kinds of universals, if they can be identified, serve to explain mortuary practices?

The strong negative emotions of fear and sorrow that seem naturally to accompany death are candidates for a universal cause of funeral rites. Chapter 1 explores the attempts of Durkheim and the English anthropologists who adapted his ideas (including A. R. Radcliffe-Brown) to base a theory of society on the ritual expression of emotion. We conclude in this first chapter that the strong emotional aspect of funerals, although nearly universal, is too malleable and too various to provide a general explanation for the forms of funeral ritual.

Universal symbols based more on logic than on emotion have also been postulated by anthropologists. An important example is provided by Hertz in his essay on the nearly universal association of the right hand with good and the left hand with evil. Given the natural binary form of moral evaluation (good/bad) and the fact of human two-handedness, it is logical that this means of moral representation should be utilized by most of the world's peoples. Throughout this book, we regard the corpse as a similar sort of natural symbol. In Chapter 2, we examine the significance of two widespread practices: the use of loud noises in association with the presence of the dead; and the application of mundane techniques of processing to the corpse. As with emotional responses, these symbolic quasi universals prove too ambiguous to provide a general explanation for the forms of funerals.

In the chapters of Part II, "Death as transition," we look at the kinds of ethnographic case material that led Hertz and Van Gennep to stress that death is a gradual process. If death is to be seen as a gradual transition from one state of being to another, then it must be placed in the context of the period that follows and the period that precedes the cessation of breath.

Hertz noted that in much of Borneo, Indonesia, and Melanesia, the extended ritual of burial, exhumation, and reburial relates directly to beliefs about the afterlife. In Chapter 3, we test Hertz's analysis against the data of modern field research among a particular ethnic group of Borneo. We also make some comparisons with other Indonesian groups outside Borneo.

In Chapter 4, we focus on death as a transition from life, rather than to death. Van Gennep noted that of all the rites of passage, funerals are most strongly associated with symbols that express the core of life values sacred to the society at hand. Turner has also demonstrated how the symbols of liminality tend to be drawn from the biology of growth and decay, of sexuality and fertility. Because much of Van Gennep's writings before the appearance of *The Rites of Passage* concerned the religions of the peoples of Madagascar, it is appropriate that we should return to these data and analyze how the links between death, birth, and the values of life in one Malagasy society are revealed by Van Gennep's analytical construct of a rite of passage.

The chapters of Part III, "The royal corpse and the body politic," examine two sides of the socio-political question of the death of kings, under which rubric we include all manner of leaders, chiefs, pharaohs, and headmen. In Chapter 5, we examine the uses that royal relics are put to by their successors in the dramatic arena of political competition. We examine the ways construction of elaborate death edifices such as pyramids in Egypt and tomb-towers in Borneo can be instrumental in the establishment of more centralized authority.

Chapter 6 explores various uses of the corpse as a symbol of the corporate continuity of the kingship and polity even though royal incumbents come and go. How can a mortal represent a supposedly eternal polity? We look at the classical case of ritual regicide among the Shilluk people, who inhabit the Upper Nile region.

Introduction

The Shilluk postulate that their king must be killed before his body, the symbol of the nation, becomes weak with age. Elsewhere effigies are used to replace the imperfect king. We explore the different uses of royal effigies in Renaissance England and France and relate these differences to the political philosophies of each culture.

Finally, in our conclusion, we turn back to our culture, and to corpse symbolism in modern America. We note that from our wider comparative perspective American deathways no longer seem as exotic and irrational as they appeared to Mitford. Although our death customs, like those of others, are characterized by certain unresolvable paradoxes and ambiguities, they make sense within their cultural context. The elaborate preparation of the corpse so that it appears natural, healthy, and comfortable for its last public appearance relates directly to important American cultural values concerning the nature of the individual and of life.

PART I

UNIVERSALS
AND CULTURE

I

THE EMOTIONAL
REACTION TO DEATH

Surely one of the most prominent aspects of death is its potential for intense emotional impact on the survivors. The reasons for the strong response are almost as numerous as they are obvious. There is the simple but often searing fact of separation from a loved one. There is emotion at the realization that he or she will no longer enjoy the fruits of life. There is shock at the suddenness with which death often strikes out of nowhere. There can be fear for one's own life, and fear of the power of death in general. There may be anger at the persons or powers supposedly responsible for the death. Finally, there are numerous strong reactions to the corpse itself.

The interpretation of emotional states presents special problems to anthropologists because the discipline focuses on culture and society, on communal ideas and corporate structures. The emotions within individuals are largely beyond our purview. We have learned that we must be cautious in attributing particular emotional configurations to members of other cultures. Because we know that notions of such seemingly simple things as space, time, and color vary in complex ways from one society to another, how could we assume a constancy for such complicated moods as sorrow, joy, love, and hate? For all the importance of the emotional aspect of human experience, it is an area fraught with difficulties for a discipline that attempts to escape systematically from the biases of its own culture. As we shall see with this brief look at the emotions expressed in the funerals of some of the world's peoples, we can assume neither the universality of particular modes of feeling nor that similar signs of emotion correspond to the same underlying sentiments in different cultures.

RADCLIFFE-BROWN'S THEORY OF SENTIMENTS AND SOCIAL INTEGRATION

Although the funeral customs of many of the world's peoples can seem strange to us, there are aspects of their practices that strike a chord of familiarity. One such familiar practice is weeping. In our own society, it is quite permissible to cry at funerals. It is common for some individuals, especially some of those close to the deceased, to be overtaken with emotion and shed tears, sob, or occasionally cry out loud. In many societies, crying at funerals is not merely tolerated, it is required by custom, and at predetermined moments the entire body of mourners will burst into loud and piercing cries. Just as suddenly, the weeping halts and the tears that had just been running so profusely cease. An early attempt at understanding this custom of ceremonial weeping is found in Radcliffe-Brown's *The Andaman Islanders*. We turn to this work not only for the interesting analysis of ritual weeping, but also because Radcliffe-Brown based his entire theory of society on the ritual expression of sentiments.

It seems simple enough to explain why people cry at a funeral. After all, it is a sad occasion. But this fails to explain a number of features of Andamanese weeping. Radcliffe-Brown insists that any explanation of ceremonial weeping must cover *all* its manifestations in Andamanese culture. There are, it appears, seven different occasions when an Andamanese "sits down and wails and howls and the tears stream down his or her face" (Radcliffe-Brown 1964: 117). This is not a spontaneous expression of feeling. It is mandatory, and the individual is in complete control. Radcliffe-Brown reports how he once asked some people how it was done, and they immediately sat down and provided a demonstration, effusive tears and all. The occasions for such a display are as follows:

1 When two friends or relatives meet after having been for some time parted, they embrace each other and weep together.
2 At a peacemaking ceremony.
3 At the end of a period of mourning, the friends of the mourners (who have not themselves been mourning) weep with the latter.
4 After a death, the relatives and friends embrace the corpse and weep over it.
5 When the bones of a dead man or woman are recovered from the grave, they are wept over.
6 On the occasion of a marriage, the relatives weep over the bride and bridegroom.
7 At various stages of the initiation ceremonies, the female relatives of a youth or girl weep over him or her.

In examining this list, Radcliffe-Brown notes that there are two varieties of weeping. In the first three instances, the weeping is reciprocal; two parties cry over each other and embrace each other. In the latter four examples, the wailing is one-sided; one person or party weeps over a passive person or object. Radcliffe-Brown insists, then, that in order to understand the weeping at Andamanese funerals, one must take into account all seven instances and also explain their division into reciprocal and one-sided varieties.

Radcliffe-Brown's explanation, in keeping with his theory of society, is that this ritual weeping is "an expression of that feeling of attachment between persons which is of such importance in the almost domestic life of the Andaman society. In other words the purpose of the rite is to affirm the existence of a social bond between two or more persons" (Radcliffe-Brown 1964: 240). In those cases of reciprocal weeping, then, it is obvious enough that a social relationship is being mutually stressed. Reunions between friends, former enemies, or between mourners and their non-mourning friends, are all occasions for stressing and affirming social ties. Radcliffe-Brown insists that although participants may not actually feel the sentiments that bind them, participation in this mandatory rite will strengthen what positive feelings they do have, and create such sentiments where they were previously absent. As a general theory of weeping, this is perhaps rather shallow, but he points out that the Andamanese also refer to such situations as ones of intense emotion, calling for some act to cover the "shame" of reaffirming ties.

For the reciprocal weeping that marks the end of mourning, Radcliffe-Brown shows that, according to Andamanese custom, the mourners are associated with the world of the dead, and hence separated from the rest of society. At the end of the period of mourning, they are reunited with the rest of the community. This mutual weeping stresses that in spite of the death, and in spite of the temporary seclusion of the mourners, they now renew their bonds with the community of the living.

The second variety of ceremonial weeping, in which one party cries over a passive person or remains, serves to express the continued sentiment of attachment in spite of the fact that social bonds are being altered and lessened. Radcliffe-Brown maintains that such weeping cannot be explained as due to the sadness felt at the weakening of a relationship. Such weeping, when looked at in the total context of Andamanese weeping, is also a positive affirmation of the continuity of social ties even though they may be modified by initiation, marriage, or final reburial.

Much of this explanation can be neither demonstrated nor disproven. But there are a number of positive aspects to Radcliffe-Brown's approach that take us beyond the obvious and uninformative observation that people cry because they are sad. For one thing, Radcliffe-Brown separates sadness and the expression of sadness. These are not spontaneous outbursts. Sadness and its expression are related, however, and this relationship is the reverse of what we might expect. For Radcliffe-Brown, the sentiment does not create the act, but wailing at the prescribed moment and in the prescribed manner creates within the wailer the proper sentiment.

What makes Radcliffe-Brown's analysis stimulating is that he takes a seemingly obvious item, weeping, and places a number of sensible methodological constraints upon his analysis, and hence arrives at conclusions that are illuminating of Andamanese culture

Andamanese wailing at funerals, we can see, has a very different meaning and takes a very different form from the expression of grief in, say, American funerals. Radcliffe-Brown's contextual analysis of all the situations calling for weeping, combined with his interest in the native explanation, leads away from a simple but plausible analysis based on the universality of sorrow and toward an investigation of the symbolism of wailing in Andamanese ritual.

This path is, however, cut short by Radcliffe-Brown's tendency to revert to universals. In his grand theory of persons and society, these ritual expressions of emotion hold a central place. The wailer comes to feel the appropriate sentiment, and, as we have seen, this sentiment is not merely a negative sentiment of sorrow and loss, but a positive emotion of social bonding:

> ... ceremonial customs are the means by which the society acts
> upon its individual members and keeps alive in their minds a cer-
> tain system of sentiments. Without the ceremonial those senti-
> ments would not exist, and without them the social organization
> in its actual form could not exist. [Radcliffe-Brown 1964: 324]

This global claim for the function of ritual is based on the assumption that all participants of all rituals in all cultures come to feel positive sentiments of social bonding through joining in the prescribed behavior.

That Andamanese ceremonial weeping is a symbol not only of sorrow but of social ties seems valid given the range of occasions when weeping occurs, the two varieties of weeping behavior, and the statements of Andamanese informants.

Ritual wailing in other societies follows very different patterns. For example, the Bara of Madagascar perform such on-cue crying only at funerals, and only at two times: while the body is lying in the women's hut before burial, and just before the secondary burial of the exhumed bones. Also, weeping is absolutely prohibited during the preparation of the body for burial and during the exhumation of the bones for reburial. Only the women are expected to cry, although it is tolerated where closely related boys and men join in briefly. Also, such wailing is done only by day. As another example, consider the ritual lamentation for the dead in Greek villages. For this event, female specialists are hired to sing heart-rending laments as part of a highly theatrical performance. The examples could go on. In each case, if we follow Radcliffe-Brown's method of (1) noting carefully the range and variation of social contexts of ceremonial weeping, (2) remembering that this weeping is a symbol with meaning and not a spontaneous show of emotion, (3) relating the weeping to indigenous beliefs, and (4) collecting indigenous explanations of the weeping, then we will discover much about the meaning of this practice in each culture.

If, instead, we follow Radcliffe-Brown's more general notion that all ritual activity, including wailing, in whatever form and style serves to channel sentiments of social bonding and support the organization of society, then the careful contextual analysis of the ethnographer is for naught. All roads lead to preserving the social system.

It was Radcliffe-Brown's insight that expressions of sentiment in ritual are not merely reflections of feeling, but symbols whose meanings can be discovered through careful analysis. It was Radcliffe-Brown's mistake immediately to forsake this sound view for the meretricious charms of an instant universal theory.

FUNERAL SENTIMENTS AND DURKHEIM'S THEORY OF SOCIETY

The universalistic theory of Radcliffe-Brown was greatly influenced by the work of Durkheim. For this reason, and because of Durkheim's enormous influence on the anthropological study of religion, it is instructive to examine how he dealt with the problem of the emotional aspect of death rituals. Durkheim discussed the ritual expression of sentiments in terms similar to those later used by Radcliffe-Brown. However, there is a crucial difference in emphasis. Where Durkheim was seeking to understand the integration (or nonintegration) of the individual into society, Radcliffe-Brown took the problem to be the solution. He assumed, as a starting point, that society is based on a system of shared sentiments. Durkheim, on the other hand, was involved in a lifelong search to know to what extent society could be defined in relation to "collective representations," what might be the nature of such representations, and how might we discover and demonstrate their nature. Within the framework of this search, the material on the funeral rituals of the native Australians presented Durkheim with a unique rhetorical opportunity.

First, let us observe the rites, for they contain an intensity of emotion that, although not entirely beyond our abilities of empathy, seems far more bizarre and shocking to our sensibilities than does the custom of ritual wailing. Durkheim opens his discussion of funerals with this vivid description.

Here is a scene which Spencer and Gillen witnessed among the Warramunga. A totemic ceremony had just been celebrated and the company of actors and spectators was leaving the consecrated ground when a piercing cry suddenly came from the camp: a man was dying there. At once, the whole company commenced to run as fast as they could, while most of them commenced to howl. "Between us and the camp," say these observers, "lay a deep creek, and on the bank of this, some of the men, scattered about here and there, sat down, bending their heads forward between their knees, while they wept and moaned. Crossing the creek we found that, as usual, the men's camp had been pulled to pieces. Some of the women, who had come from every direction, were lying prostrate on the body, while others were standing or kneeling around, digging the sharp ends of yam-sticks into the crown of their heads, from which the blood streamed down over their faces, while all the time they kept up a loud, continuous wail. Many of the men, rushing up to the spot, threw themselves upon the body, from which the women arose when the men approached, until in a few minutes we could see nothing but a struggling mass of bodies all mixed up together. To one side, three men of the Thapungarti class, who still wore their ceremonial decorations, sat down wailing loudly, with their backs towards the dying man, and in a minute or two another man of the same class rushed on to the ground yelling and brandishing a stone knife. Reaching the camp, he suddenly gashed both thighs deeply, cutting right across the muscles, and unable to stand, fell down into the middle of the group, from which he was dragged out after a time by three or four female relatives, who immediately applied their mouths to the gaping wounds while he lay exhausted on the ground." The man did not actually die until late in the evening. As soon as he had given up his last breath, the same scene was re-enacted, only this time the wailing was still louder, and men and women, seized by a veritable frenzy, were rushing about cutting themselves with knives and sharp-pointed sticks, the women battering one another's heads with fighting clubs, no one attempting to ward off either cuts or blows. Finally, after about an hour, a torchlight procession started off across the plain, to a tree in whose branches the body was left. [Durkheim 1965 (1912): 435–6, with the permission of Macmillan Publishing Co., Inc. and George Allen & Unwin Ltd.]

Durkheim's description continues in this vivid fashion to portray the mourning obligations of various categories of kin. The reports from several areas of the continent are the same: People (according to rather precise formulae) gouge their faces, slash their thighs, burn their breasts, and attack their friends. Much of this activity is so ferocious that it is not uncommon for mourning to add to the death toll. Women, in particular, are enjoined to considerable displays of suffering. They are reported to be the most prominent victims of some of the physically aggressive melees; they lead in much of the howling and lamenting, and, to highlight this, they are prohibited normal speech during mourning. Sometimes whole villages of women are under sentence of speechlessness for long periods. The habit of communicating by signs develops and grows as mourning rites follow mourning rites, and it is not uncommon for some women to cease speaking altogether for the remainder of their lives. All in all, the rites are marked by extreme displays of anguish, anger, and aggression, tinged with sexual implications and destructive tendencies.

When Durkheim confronted the reader with this startling material, he had already outlined his basic theory emphasizing the positively cohesive effects of public celebrations. He has already suggested that a certain renewal of common values, a firming-up of communal conceptions, and a strengthening of social bonds is the unique function of ritual. This famous demonstration (Durkheim 1965: 385–92), however, pertains to rites of joy, to annual calendrical rites in Australia, when groups gather together after the dispersal of the dry season. That such rites performed by people reuniting as a group even as they unite themselves to the rhythm of the earth's seasons should promote a positive mood of solidarity is plausible. Indeed, it seems likely that this is, in a sense, the obvious purpose of this particular rite in the eyes of the participants. But Durkheim wishes to demonstrate not just that a calendrical celebration has this positive function but that it is a feature of ritual in general. How can he claim that the violent, destructive, unplanned-for, and negative behavior surrounding a death fulfills this sociologically pollyannalike function?

Durkheim must face the same difficulty that Radcliffe-Brown brushed aside. On the one hand, we cannot assume that people actually *feel* the sorrow that they express; and we certainly cannot claim that the ritual expression results from inner emotions. On the other hand, for the rites to fulfill their supposed sociological function, these acted sentiments must become real. Radcliffe-Brown claimed that people participating in the ceremonial weeping come to feel the emotion. But the emotion he said they feel is not sorrow but togetherness (Radcliffe-Brown 1964: 240). Durkheim is quite clear, however, that the emotions that develop and are amplified by participation in the funeral rite initially are feelings of sorrow and anger.

> If he weeps and groans, it is not merely to express an individual chagrin; it is to fulfill a duty of which the surrounding society does not fail to remind him. . . . Sorrow, like joy, becomes exalted and amplified when leaping from mind to mind, and therefore expresses itself outwardly in the form of exuberant and violent movements. But these are no longer expressive of the joyful agitation which we observed before; they are shrieks and cries of pain. Each is carried along by the others; a veritable panic of sorrow results. When pain reaches this degree of intensity, it is mixed with a sort of anger and exasperation. One feels the need of breaking something, of destroying something. He takes this out either upon himself or others. He beats himself, burns himself, wounds himself or else he falls upon others to beat, burn and wound them. [Durkheim 1965: 446]

Obviously, the sentiments expressed and amplified in this ritual do not automatically transform themselves into social solidarity.

Durkheim stresses, however, that although the mood of this rite is different from others, the fact of emotional arousal is common to rituals of joy and of sorrow. A death is a shock to the family group. Its members feel the family lessened and weakened, and so they gather together in reaction to the loss and to comfort one another. However, this coming together of the relatives, this sense of oneness they seem to develop in the face of bereavement, is only the reflection of their grief. What Durkheim finds important to his sociological theory is the way that other members of society feel moral pressure to put their behavior in harmony with the feelings of the truly bereaved. Those who feel no direct sorrow themselves will nonetheless weep and inflict suffering and inconvenience upon themselves. How can it be other than a positive affirmation of their commitment, not only to their suffering neighbors, but also a commitment to an abstract value of neighborliness, of society?

One need not join Durkheim in answering in the affirmative. But let us be clear how important this funeral material is to his theory. The two most important criticisms of Durkheim's explanation of how the "external" society is inculcated into individuals through ritual are both weakened in the face of this material. First of all, it has been suggested that Durkheim bridged the gap between individual and society with a crude use of crowd psychology. But the funeral material, as Parsons (1968b: 437) noted, provides a crucial demonstration that crowd psychology was not what Durkheim intended. The power of crowd behavior derives from the fact that the crowd is an unorganized, ad hoc assemblage. The rituals that Durkheim describes are, by contrast, minutely organized. Intense emotion and tight organization go hand in hand even in these funerals where the obligations of slashing one's thighs or burning one's abdomen are precisely determined by kinship (mother's brother and mother, respectively). The funeral material makes it clear that emotional "effervescence" does not replace structure but results from structure. Durkheim's approach stands in contrast to later debates in anthropology that saw explanations based on "structure" and those based on "sentiment" as mutually exclusive.

The other important criticism is summed up in Lévi-Strauss's aphorism that Durkheim's theory of religion "starts with an urge, and ends with a recourse to sentiment" (Lévi-Strauss 1963: 70 – 1). The circularity of Durkheim's theory is quite obvious regarding the calendrical rites, for there can be no source to explain the welling up of the urge to perform the ritual that produces the sentiment of solidarity. Durkheim's case regarding funerals is stronger, rhetorically and sociologically. One can readily accept that, at a time of death, some people genuinely feel the great emotions that are expressed. This provides a source for the sentiment that is transformed in ritual. Durkheim's claim that a broad sense of social solidarity derives from ritual is stronger in this funeral case when those who personally feel no sorrow are nevertheless compelled to put themselves through such extreme discomfort. In his analysis of the calendrical rites, Durkheim has the sentiment of solidarity bubble up naturally out of the expression of joy. But the dialectic between sorrow and comfort, loss and gain, real emotion and obligatory display that emerges from the discussion of these terrifyingly intense funerals provides a more solid grounding for his theory of the social function of ritual. One does not know Durkheim's intentions, but it is characteristic of his style of argument that this strongest evidence is presented last, and cleverly introduced as a supposed negative case.

There is perhaps another advantage to presenting this funeral material toward the end of *The Elementary Forms of the Religious Life*, and that is that Durkheim wished to dissociate his theory from those that viewed primitive man's contemplation of death as the source of all religion. Durkheim was constructing a sociological theory with an empirical base and not an intellectualist theory like that of Tylor, who argued that primitive man developed ideas about the soul and devised rituals from contemplating death. This sort of theory of the origins of religion was in vogue at the end of the last century. Durkheim, following Robertson Smith, turned the relation between belief and ritual around. The ritual is essentially due to sociological factors, and men create eschatology to rationalize their ritual behavior at mourning. "Men do not weep for the dead because they fear them; they fear them because they weep for them" (Durkheim 1965: 447). We do not wish to review here the long history of chicken and egg arguments about the relation between religious beliefs and practices. It is, however, important to note that although death rites provide Durkheim's strongest evidence, he carefully avoided any implication that they might be the source of religion and ritual and hence, in his framework, of society. To this, we concur. Death rituals often provide the most interesting and challenging material for the understanding of people and their cultures, but in spite of our devotion of this book to the topic, we see no reason to add unnecessarily to the claims death makes on the shape of human institutions.

There is in Durkheim's approach the possibility for illuminating analysis of particular ethnographic situations. This would demand, of course, the sort of intimate knowledge of the people and culture that Durkheim, writing from Paris, lacked. His theory suggests a subtle dynamic of social interaction that could be apprehended only through the type of sustained personal field research that became the hallmark of anthropology in the generation following Radcliffe-Brown. Unfortunately, that generation largely turned away from the study of religion. When anthropologists returned to the study of religion, the analytical emphasis had shifted so that studies were focused on systems of belief with little direct reference to the intimate social interaction that would provide the locus for a truly Durkheimian analysis.

THE NYAKYUSA OF TANZANIA: EMOTIONS AT AN AFRICAN FUNERAL

One of the first anthropologists who attempted a systematic analysis of the emotional aspect of funerals based on firsthand experience was Godfrey Wilson (1939). In his essay "Nyakyusa Conventions of Burial," Wilson demonstrated how illuminating a cautiously Durkheimian approach can be for understanding the expression of sentiment in a ceremonial context. Emotions may be vague and irrational, but when the analyst knows the culture and the particular participants, and has him- or herself shared in the events, and furthermore, is extremely scrupulous of the level of verifiability of each piece of evidence, then the study of the emotional aspect of life yields great dividends.

Wilson asks three general questions through his exploration of the Nyakyusa conventions of burial. First, noting that Nyakyusa burials are jolly affairs in comparison to English funerals, he asks why the emotional tenor differs from one culture to another. Second, he questions why it is that the normal emotional response of people at a funeral is never random, but falls within an obligatory pattern. One *must* dance and flirt at a Nyakyusa funeral just as one *must* wear black and be solemn at an English funeral. Third, he asks what are the social dynamics that preserve the conventions of funeral behavior or lead to their modification. One can begin to answer these general questions only by taking a detailed look at another society's customs in contrast to our own. We shall do this several times in the course of this book, and for this first case, we restrict our investigation to the emotional dimension as analyzed by Wilson. Godfrey Wilson's essay refers only to the burial ceremony. For an analysis of the full funeral cycle, see Monica Wilson (1957).

To begin with, we need some basic information about Nyakyusa society. Social relationships are determined by membership in three groups: family, village, and chiefdom. These social relations are largely established, expressed, and maintained in two ways: exchange of cattle and attendance at funerals.

The most important factor in all social relationships pertaining to family, village, and chiefdom is the attendance at ceremonies, especially burials. As soon as the death has occurred, messages must be sent to all kin, affines, villagers, and the chief. If anyone is overlooked, he or she will be extremely angry at the affront. On the other side, should anyone receive the message and then deliberately not attend, this act will be considered a serious breach of the social relationship. This obligation to attend the burial ceremony holds not only for representatives of each family; but men, wives, and all children over the age of ten must attend, for otherwise they would be accused of having helped cause the death through witchcraft. Many other people come voluntarily, to enjoy the feasting and dancing, and they are welcomed. The size of the crowd depends on the amount of meat made available by the sacrifices.

The main activities of the burial ceremony are divided according to sex: The women wail and the men dance. The women begin their ceremonial wailing at the time of death and continue intermittently until the end of the burial activities three or four days later. The "owners of the death" among the women spend most of their time inside one of the houses, which is the center of the wailing. The rest of the women sit and wail just outside the house, or else they enter and wail upon arrival and then move to the group outside. Men and boys may wail once, and then they join the male "owners of the death." Old women are the most persistent wailers, providing around-the-clock support for the grieving women in the house. The corpse is kept in the house until it is buried later on the day of death or the next morning. Until burial, the women hold the body in their arms and the wailing is extremely intense. One Nyakyusa told Wilson that they like to delay burial long enough for the women "to weep and assuage their grief, for they always wail more before the body is buried, when they can see the dead man" (Wilson 1939: 8).

In addition to grief, Nyakyusa reactions to death express several elements of fear: fear of the afterworld, fear of the spirits, fear of not performing the ceremony properly, fear of contagious disease, and fear of witchcraft. It is within this particularly Nyakyusa framework of explicit fears that the purpose of the various funeral rituals is to be understood. The stated purpose is "to drive the spirit away." The Nyakyusa fear further contact with the spirits of the deceased, which are believed to send misfortune and insanity upon their survivors.

Many Nyakyusa had converted to Christianity by the time of Godfrey and Monica Wilson's field researches, and the comparisons between Christian and non-Christian Nyakyusa are instructive. One of the chief attractions of Christianity in this area was its reassurance on the topic of death. Christian preaching about heaven is seen by old Nyakyusa as a strong threat to the traditional social order. The old men complain that fear of death no longer motivates the young people to attend properly to burial ceremonies. These changes and laments only serve to highlight the prominent role of fear in Nyakyusa concepts of death.

Women bind one another's bellies with strips of bark-cloth during the wailing ceremony. Relatives and friends provide a woman mourner with numerous cloths. They explained to the Wilsons: "I give them these to tie round their bellies because they are all atremble, they are full of fear." The men don't wear belts, say the women, because "They are not afraid like women, they do not tremble much" (Wilson 1939: 12).

Gradually the focus of activity shifts from the women to the men, from the decreasing wailing to the increasing dancing (see Plate 1). Dancing is led by young men dressed in special costumes of ankle bells and cloth skirts, all holding spears and leaping wildly about. Women do not dance, but some young women move about among the dancing youths, calling the war cry and

Plate 1. Nyakyusa men dancing at a funeral. Though stylized,
the postures of the dance are extremely energetic
(from Wilson 1951: 131, with permission
of the International African Institute).

swinging their hips in a rhythmical fashion. The number of dancers slowly increases, as does the number of drummers and the
crowd of onlookers. The noise and excitement grows and there
are no signs of grief. Yet when Wilson asked the onlookers to
explain the scene, they always replied, "They are mourning the
dead" (Wilson 1939: 12).

This burial dance is traditionally a dance of war. Nyakyusa
state that they do the war dance to honor the deceased, who was
also a great warrior, a powerful man of the spear. If the deceased
is a woman, they honor the fact that she gave birth to warriors.
The dance, of course, also expresses the virility and courage of the
dancers themselves. And there is a strong sexual component to the
dance, which, as the era of interchiefdom raiding recedes, is rapidly becoming the dominant motif. In either case, male strength
and courage is emphasized in contrast to female fear and trembling.

Additionally, Nyakyusa men state that the dance helps them
express and overcome their grief and anger over the death of a
kinsman. "This war dance is mourning, we are mourning the dead
man. We dance because there is a war in our hearts – a passion of
grief and fear exasperates us. . . . A kinsman when he dances he
assuages his passionate grief; he goes into the house to weep and
then he comes out and dances the war dance; his passionate grief is
made tolerable in the dance [literally, 'he is able to endure it there,
in the dance'], it bound his heart and the dance assuages it" (in
Wilson 1939: 13). Wilson's careful translation of these statements,
especially his renderings, "passionate grief" and "exasperate,"
demonstrate that the Nyakyusa view these acts as expressing and
relieving certain unbearable emotions.

This dance is a vehicle for the expression of a considerable
range of emotions; grief and exasperation fade into an act of honoring the warlike qualities and virility of the dead man. This leads
into feelings of pride and exhilaration of the dancers' own courage
and virility, and this leads easily into fighting among the young
men and lovemaking between some of the youths and the girls.
Traditionally, the outbreak of violence was common at burials
because the endemic raiding among chiefdoms left many open disputes waiting for the sort of provocations that the war dance

afforded. Now that the emphasis has shifted more to the sexual aspect of male prowess, violence is less common. But in a society in which almost every girl is betrothed at puberty, these romantic and sexual conquests can also produce social turbulence: "So far from ceremonies having the sole function of promoting social integration, as some would have us believe, the burial ceremonies of the Nyakyusa were occasions on which existing antipathies continually found overt expression in fighting and new antipathies arose" (Wilson 1939: 14). One cannot assume that rituals automatically fulfill some socially integrative function. This must be demonstrated, and the precise nature of the performances' effects on social life must be carefully delineated.

The Nyakyusa, like so many peoples, seem to feel the need to confront death with an assertion of life. They express a desire to turn their attention away from the contemplation of death, which holds only fear, sorrow, and uncertainty for them, and gradually toward "a realization of present life in its most intense quality, to the war-dance, to sexual display, to lively talk and to the eating of great quantities of meat" (Wilson 1939: 24). This transfiguration of the sorrow of the chief mourners requires, in the Nyakyusa view, the active and sympathetic celebration of others. That transformation of mood, with its interaction between those whose grief runs deep and those whose sympathy for the mourners leads them to dance, is a subtle process, the action of which escapes a general description of the Nyakyusa conventions of burial. It is, however, poignantly evident in Wilson's description of a particular burial.

Here is a description of one of the pagan burials which I observed. It is the second day; the man, who was quite young, died yesterday afternoon and was buried early this morning. I arrive at 7:30 a.m. to find that the wailing is the dominant activity. The dead man's house is full of weeping men and women, shedding tears and wailing in the conventional high-pitched voice. His sister, his young wife, a step-mother, a classificatory brother and two half-brothers, with many other women, are inside the house. The noise is considerable. The rest of the women, fifty or more, are seated just outside, in and around an unfinished bamboo house which he died leaving half-built; they too are weeping and wailing. A few men are seated in a group on the opposite side of the swept place facing the women; they are either silent or talking soberly.

The emotion pitch is very high. The classificatory brother leaves the house and walks about round the new grave with his hands to his head, shedding tears and calling: "Alas! Alas! What kin are left? Alas! What kin are left?" He is a mature man about forty years old. Then he takes by the hand a half-sister of the dead man, a woman of thirty or more, smothered in mud and pot-black, her belly supported by many bark cloths, and with a baby on her back; together they walk over the grave weeping and wailing, addressing each other in words that I fail to distinguish, and stumbling about as though blind with grief. The baby sleeps quietly all the time. Then comes an old woman, stepmother of the dead man, leading a daughter in each hand (his half-sisters), all wailing, shedding tears and calling out indistinguishable words. They sit down on the newly-filled grave, first making towards it gestures of extreme grief; and there they sit with their arms on one another's shoulders rocking to and fro' and weeping. More people keep arriving and in the background now is the insistent wailing of seventy or a hundred women in and outside the house.

For the first hour after my arrival the drums are only occasionally beaten, and a few young men rush across the grave brandishing spears, but only spasmodically.

The two half-brothers, after wailing in the house, come outside and walk up and down together still weeping. Then they each take a spear and run back and forth several times wailing the dead man's name. One of the half-sisters, meanwhile, rolls over and over in the fresh earth of the grave in passionate contortions, with the tears running down her cheeks. Gradually a group of women relatives collects on the grave, eight or nine of them; they sit huddled up together with their arms on one another's shoulders wailing. One woman, before she sits down, makes a series of trembling gestures towards the grave, crying out "Avaunt!" in fearful grief.

Then, at last, the drums begin in earnest and the young men start to dance. To me, as well as to the Nyakyusa, the insistent vital rhythm of the drums and the sight of the leaping dance fall on the senses gratefully, bringing relief from the almost unbearable tension. [Such a subjective account of the observer's feelings is, of course, quite valueless in itself; but we have already proved that the Nyakyusa protagonists have feelings of which these are but a sympathetic image (Wilson's note).] The situation begins to change. Still in the house the wailing is loud and continuous, but the women on the grave give place to the dancers and return to the house, while the group of women outside gradually ceases wailing and turns all its attention to the dance. The conversation among the men changes also, none are silent now and the talk is more eager than before. Soon the dancers begin to cut the bananas; one stem falls full on a young man's head, causing loud laughter among the onlookers. But at first the dance, though lively, is by no means wholly gay. The male kinsmen dance with grief in the looks, calling out "alas!" as each shakes his spear.

No women are yet dancing at all; two or three kinswomen wander about distraught, and one of the half-sisters in particular seems quite blind to the dancers, who have to get out of her way. The situation is, however, a lively one, and it becomes livelier still as the young men from another village come to join in, bringing three more drums with them. Six drums are now being beaten and about thirty young men are dancing. Two hours have passed since I first arrived.

At four-thirty p.m. I am back again to find the scene changed once more. There is no sound of wailing, not even inside the house, and the dancers are having a glorious time. About a hundred men are either dancing or standing round looking on, with a number of girls walking rhythmically about among the dancers. These girls are non-relatives and adorned with great finish.

The young men leap and dance, some with more agility than others; they stamp, roll on the ground, leap in the air, turn somersaults, hurl their spears into the earth and fight invisible enemies. All the spectators, save the chief women mourners and one or two of the men, seem lively and excited. I see the young wife [She will die herself four days later. There has been a series of deaths in this family which gossip attributes to the sorcery of an enemy (Wilson's note).] of the dead man looking tired and sad, and she and the other women mourners spend most of the time in the house; but one of the half-brothers, on the other hand, who appeared to be so greatly affected seven or eight hours before, is laughing gaily as he dances.

Two cows have been killed and are now being cut up. As the sun sinks and the dancers go away home, taking their meat with them, the relatives and near neighbors gather round fires and begin to roast and eat the meat. Some is given separately to the groups of friends from other chiefdoms; and by the next morning the whole of the two cows is finished. "It was a grand burial," people say afterwards, "we have seen him on his way (to the place of the spirits) properly." [Wilson 1939: 24–7, with the permission of Witwatersrand University Press.]

CULTURE AND SENTIMENT

The examples we have presented in this chapter are from societies whose customs seem violently emotional in comparison to the norm in our own society. Throughout the world, death is generally a time for the expression of strong emotional response. There are societies, however, that surprise us in just the opposite way by the seeming equanimity with which death is greeted. Geertz describes the funerals of the Javanese as "a calm, undemonstrative, almost languid letting go, a brief ritualized relinquishment of a relationship no longer possible" (Geertz 1960: 72). Geertz mentions the case of a young girl who was crying slightly after her father died suddenly. Her relatives hushed her gently into a show of composure by telling her that she could not continue participating in the ritual if she cried, that such crying made it hard for the deceased to find his path to the grave. The proper emotional state to be achieved is called *iklas*, a "willed affectlessness," an evenness of feelings from which the peaks of elation and the troughs of despair have been eliminated (Geertz 1960: 69–74). For the Javanese, mortality does not seem to hold any great terror and they discuss it with little show of anxiety. In part, this calmness is due to a pervasive fatalism about dying: It is all in the hands of God. In part, death is often asserted to be a good state, empty of desire and striving. But although the emotions and beliefs of the Javanese and Nyakyusa are very different in content, both are enforced by subtle social pressures.

It is clear that the emotional representations of the social pressures that lead people to place their behavior in sympathetic harmony with their fellows in times of loss is amenable to the analysis of an experienced and sensitive field researcher. Such an analysis is exceedingly difficult, however. It demands an intimate knowledge of the society and the language; it calls for many observations of burial rituals so as to become attuned to the elements of social interaction, to appreciate the importance of slight variations, and to be certain that some key aspects hold true in spite of the uniqueness of each event. Additionally, when dealing with sentiments, the temptation toward unwarranted universal conclusions and/or assumptions is particularly great. The temptation is also great to attribute to the participant feelings that he may well not experience. Far from providing some kind of universal explanatory framework for analysis of death-related behavior, the emotional aspect demands from the researcher the most subtle awareness of cultural variations.

Cultural difference works on the universal human emotional material, just as it does on universal modes of reasoning or requirements of institutional arrangement. Although we clearly recognize emotions that are familiar to us, the range of acceptable emotions and the precise constellation of sentiments appropriate to the situation of death are tied up with the unique institutions and concepts of each society. The Australian aborigine, the Andamanese, the Nyakyusa, the Javanese, and the several cultures we have yet to examine in this book all express different emotions at funerals and, as a result, they may experience feelings that are somewhat different in each case. Uniformity of human emotion does not explain the rituals of societies. The baffling combination of the familiar and the strange, the universal in the cultural particular, confronts the anthropologist even when examining human sentiments, even human reactions to death.

II

SYMBOLS OF DEATH
AND TRANSITION

Though often intense, emotional reactions to death are too varied and shifting to provide the foundation for a theory of mortuary ritual. A recent cross-cultural study by a group of psychologists concluded that grief is shown at funerals in most societies, but not all. Even this weak result was achieved only by defining grief so widely as to include virtually any emotion, namely, "sorrow, mental distress, emotional agitation, sadness, suffering, and related feelings" (Rosenblatt, Walsh, and Jackson 1976: 2). These authors approach funeral practices assuming that they fulfill certain panhuman needs to perform "psychological work." But the need to release aggression, or break ties with the deceased, or complete any other putatively universal psychic process, does not serve to explain funerals. The shoe is on the other foot. Whatever mental adjustments the individual needs to make in the face of death he or she must accomplish as best he or she can, through such rituals as society provides. No doubt the rites frequently aid adjustment. But we have no reason to believe that they do not obstruct it with equal frequency.

Despite the perennial appeal of such theorizing, something more is needed to explain the remarkable richness and variety of funeral rituals. In succeeding chapters, we turn away from emotion in order to explore the meaning of these rites in social terms. But we are not yet ready to leave behind the nagging issue of universal, or at least general, features of behavior. Are there not regular features of funerals that crop up again and again?

Indeed there are. One obvious example is color symbolism. Although it would be an error to assume that our cultural association of black with death and mourning is universal, there is a very wide distribution among the cultures of the world of the use of black to represent death. Turner (1967) suggests that there exists an almost universal color triad of red, white, and black. In many societies, white relates to such things as purity and fertility, red to both good and evil aspects of power and life, and black to decomposition and death. Turner suggests that the wide distribution of this symbolic color triad may relate to the association of these colors with bodily fluids; especially white with milk and semen, and red with blood. Black, he notes, is rarely associated with a bodily excretion, but tends to be associated with loss of consciousness such as when one faints or "blacks out" (Turner 1967: 89). Throughout the world, black often provides the funeral hue. But there are many exceptions. White is sometimes appropriate in Christian funerals to symbolize the joy of eternal life, which the Resurrection promises to each believer. Some of the peoples of Madagascar provide another exception: Their funeral color is red. An important item in their funeral rituals is a large number of expensive, brightly colored, striped shrouds. These come in many colors, but they are always called the "red cloths." Red is used in these funerals to represent "life" and vitality in opposition to death. In both these exceptions, the funeral use of white or red is in symbolic opposition to the blackness of death. But in parts of Borneo white is the color of mourning because it is associated with the pallor of death and the whiteness of bones. (Plate 2 below shows mourners wearing white cloths and headbands.)

A second widespread feature of funerals pertains to the mourners' hair. As Leach (1958) notes, practices involving special cutting of the hair have a worldwide distribution, and they are particularly prominent in funeral ceremonies. Frequently survivors are enjoined to shave their heads as a sign of mourning. Elsewhere, the custom is reversed; the mourners, especially men, forgo their usual habits of shaving and trimming beards, mustaches, and hair and hence emphasize a hirsute dishevelment for the time of mourning. And it need not be one way or the other. Often in a single society, even within a family, some mourners shave while others put away their usual razor. Hence there is a universality about the use of such practices, but not about their significance from place to place.

In this chapter, we examine two additional symbolic items having a wide distribution and association with death rituals. The first is what we may call a purposeful noisiness, the second relates to symbols of rotting. At first sight, these two items appear dissimilar, and their selection consequently arbitrary. Whereas the former seems mysterious and unaccountable, the latter seems obvious. (Although we must remember that it is possible for decay to be cheated, for instance by cremation of the corpse.) But however dissimilar, it is an empirical fact that din and corruption are constantly associated, as Lévi-Strauss has demonstrated in his monumental mythological studies (1973: 296–475; specifically 310, 396).

DRUMMING: SYMBOL OF DEATH, LIMINALITY, OR DIVINITY?

In many parts of the world, funerals are noisy affairs. This is already apparent from our examples in Chapter 1. It is also very much the case among the Berawan, a small ethnic group of central northern Borneo, whom we shall turn to for case material at several places in succeeding chapters. The Berawan comprise just four communities, each of several hundred people and occupying a single massive wooden longhouse. Great tracts of dense rain forest separate the villages from one another, and in precolonial times each was a sovereign political unit. The Berawan gain their livelihood by growing hill rice in clearings made anew each year, by foraging in the jungle, and by fishing in the great rivers that also provide the only means of transportation in the interior.

During funerals, the Berawan gather great crowds of people into their longhouses. Drinking and socializing are enjoined upon

the guests, and all but the close kin are encouraged to enjoy themselves as gustily as possible. The general hubbub can be heard
half a mile away through the quiet forest. But not satisfied with
that, the Berawan have additional ways to make noise at funerals.
There is the great brass gong that is used initially to announce that
a death has occurred. A special tattoo is used, and the deep rever-
berations can often be heard several miles away, summoning
people from their farms. Then there is the large drum that can
only be played during funerals. Its boom can be heard day and
night, producing rhythms that are proscribed at other times. The
same rhythms are played on gongs large and small, which together
make up an orchestra with several players. The larger gongs are
hung vertically, and struck with a padded mallet to produce a
deep, resonant sound. The smaller gongs are strung horizontally in
descending order of size on two strands of rattan stretched across
a frame. The player holds a piece of firewood in each hand and
plays rapid tinkling figures, further augmented by the staccato
clatter of children beating on bamboo slit gongs.

But even the music of the gongs and drums is lost in the din of
games in which noise is supposedly only a by-product. Tops are
played outside, in an arena overviewed by the veranda of the
longhouse, which provides a grandstand. Men compete to see who
can fling their own top in such a way as to knock a target top set
spinning in the center of the arena out of the area of play. The
men jostle for position to take a shot, holding their heavy hardwood tops in their upraised hands. When they throw them, a dull
moaning whirr is heard. If the shot is well judged, the two tops
make a loud clack on impact, and the target goes flying out of
the ring. Then a great roar of approval goes up from the veranda.
The men must remain alert to avoid being hit by a ricocheting
top.

Meanwhile, another game is played inside the house using rice
pestles. This is a game in which women excel, though men may
play. The pestles are hardwood poles about five feet long and
three inches wide at each end, tapering slightly to the middle.
Normally they are used to pound rice free of its husk, in conjunction with a mortar that consists of a heavy slab of hardwood with
a hemispherical indentation about six inches in diameter. In the

game, two pestles are placed side by side across two bulks of timber such that they are about four inches above the floor. A woman sits on each side, grasping the adjacent ends of each pestle in either hand. They begin to beat the pestles, two strokes downward onto the bulks of timber, then two sideways, clashing the pestles one against the other. The player stands off to one side, flexing her knees and bobbing her head to get the rhythm. Then she dances nimbly across the clashing poles, trying to execute fancy steps without getting a blow on the ankle. This game is invariably played indoors on a raised plank floor of the longhouse, which provides a massive sounding board for the crashing of the pestles. This activity is in addition to the regular pounding of rice, which is a continuous chore during funerals due to the number of guests to be fed.

Finally, when the corpse is moved out of the longhouse to the barge that will carry it to the graveyard, a series of shotgun blasts punctuate the wailing of the womenfolk.

All this cacophony at Berawan funerals would come as no surprise to Rodney Needham, whose paper "Percussion and Transition" (1967) first pointed out how widespread this phenomenon is. He expands upon an idea originally stated in a paper entitled "The Origin of Bell and Drum" by Maria Dworakowska (1938), who argues that the use of bells and gongs at funerals derived from the use of drums, which in turn originated from "coffin-logs." Hence the association of these instruments with the dead. Needham accepts this association, shorn of its historical speculation, but criticizes it as too narrow. First, the list of instruments is too restricted: drums, gongs, bells, xylophones, metallophones, rattles, rasps, stamping tubes, sticks, resounding rocks, clashing anklets, and other objects are all used in these contexts. Berawan funerals could add a couple more items to the list, as we have seen. Needham shows that the only feature shared by these instruments, if such they may be called, is percussion. Not all of them are capable of producing a melody, or even a rhythm, so these attributes are not the relevant ones. Second, he shows that such percussive noise is not restricted to funerals. It is found at weddings and birth feasts, initiations and harvest festivals, and all manner of rites of passage.

Needham states his conclusion as follows: *There is a connection between percussion and transition.* As to why this connection exists, Needham is unable to offer an explanation, and he is pessimistic that anthropology is capable of finding one. So universal is the phenomenon, he believes, that its grounds must be sought in the "general psychic character of mankind" (1967: 394).

Concerning the association that Needham points out, we can easily make surmises similar to our musings about color and hair symbolism. A percussive noise seems to punctuate and divide time ("mark time") the way a line or a wall demarcates space. Hence it is a natural symbol for marking a temporal change in status, especially one as irreversible as death. Furthermore, the drumbeat has an obvious affinity with the heartbeat and rhythm of life. Or equally, it can resound with the hollow finality of death. There is a universal potential for multiple symbolizations appropriate to the funeral situation. The drum and the bell can toll for death, beat and ring to affirm life, or neutrally mark the progression and transition of the event.

One other noticeable aspect about the drum, in addition to its percussive and rhythmic characteristics, is that it makes a relatively loud noise. Great noise or extreme silence, individually or in alternation, provide, like white and black, shaven and hairy, several opportunities for symbolic representation and heightened drama. In another well-known and intriguing paper, Needham (1964) traces the connections that hunting peoples of Malaya and Borneo make between "Blood, Thunder, and the Mockery of Animals." Thunder in Malaysia, he writes, is "an appalling natural phenomenon, seeming to crack and reverberate menacingly on the very surface of the forest canopy and shaking the guts of the human beings cowering underneath" (1964: 281). Naturally, the great noise of thunder has, in many cultures, associations with power and divinity. There is a sense in which great noise is often seen to facilitate communication between humans and the supernatural. From Western religious tradition, one thinks of the exhortation of the psalmist to "Make a Joyful noise unto The Lord, all ye lands" (Psalm 100).

Cosmological and calendrical events such as solar eclipses and new years are characteristically greeted in many cultures with the loudest clatter the technological level permits (Lévi-Strauss 1969: 287). Over the centuries, fireworks, gunshots, horns, and sirens have been added to the initial stock of drums, bells, and gongs. In the din of the modern world, we may forget how extraordinary and rare truly loud noise was to most of the previous generations on the earth. Loud noise continues to connote great power, as with electronically amplified music and roaring car engines. But it has lost its sacred character.

Our problem in dealing with the significance of noise is to cope with too many associations, not too few. Already we have three correlations of increasing generality: drums and death, percussion and transition, loud noise and supernatural power. There is little point in discussing which is the correct correlation. For instance, *all* are present in the Berawan events mentioned above. There is the great drum that resounds only for death. There are the gunshots that specifically punctuate the transition to the graveyard, and there is the continuous tumult of games and music associated with the presence of spirits of the dead. Many threads of significance are woven together in the Berawan use of noise. As Van Gennep noted, the funeral is, of all rites of passage, the one with the greatest emphasis on liminality. It is not surprising that symbols used at the funeral are often vague and indeterminate, and yet connote mystery and power. Death and liminality must, of their very natures, retain a certain elusiveness.

RITUAL ACTIONS AND DAILY ACTIVITY

Noise production is a cultural feature, yet its use in funerals achieves the same kind of universality as the emotion of grief. Percussive noise is frequently found in rituals of transition, and examples can be found in every region of the globe. But that does not imply that all societies use noise in this way or use it to a similar extent.

It follows that the observation of the quasi universality of grief and percussive noise at funerals does not exhaust those topics. The variation that occurs from one society to another, and one culture area to another, is equally demanding of explanation. As an example of this, we examine the special propensity for percussion that is found in Southeast Asia, and we draw on the recent work of Marie Jeanne Adams (1971, 1977).

Adams is concerned with repeated patterns of behavior occurring in ritual contexts that seem to parallel everyday work activities. The similarities are often striking, but Adams is careful to avoid the implication that either is derived from the other. On that score, we simply have no evidence. However derived, these recurring actions appear to lend a power and intensity to the rituals that it is difficult for the outsider to grasp.

Adams pays particular attention to pounding: a very simple technical process to be sure, but especially pervasive in Southeast Asia. Pounding actions figure prominently in the production and preparation of many foods. Breaking up the ground prior to planting is often accomplished with a heavy digging stick that relies more on momentum than sharpness for its effect. Alternatively, in irrigation agriculture particularly, buffalo are used to pound the topsoil in the newly flooded plots with their hooves. Even in slash-and-burn systems, where no soil preparation occurs as such, the seeds are planted in shallow conical holes made with a heavy dibble.

Many foods are inedible without preparation involving pounding. Most obvious in this connection is rice, which must have its husk removed before cooking. For those accustomed to agriculture based on wheat, grinding is the process that immediately comes to mind. But in Southeast Asia the grinding of rice is associated with the Chinese. Indigenous peoples prefer some kind of pounding technique usually involving a pestle and mortar. The rhythmic thump of the women pounding rice is often the first noise that one hears on approaching a village. In some societies employing sago, the woody part of the palm is separated from the nutritious part by beating.

But even foods that can be cooked just as they come from the ground are often preferred in some processed form involving homogenization by pounding. The favored way of eating many kinds of beans is to beat them into a paste. Corn, peanuts, and edible seeds are reduced to crushed powder. Fruit such as bananas is preserved by drying and then pounded into a thick paste. Fish are dried and then pulverized.

In trades, crafts, and all manner of technical processes, pounding constitutes an important step. In the making of rope and yarn, vegetable fibers are obtained by prolonged beating of the raw material to remove pulpy parts of the plant. We need hardly point out the importance of this technology for everything from fishing to house building. Pottery techniques in general spurn the wheel or hand molding, and instead employ the paddle-and-anvil method. Surprisingly, weaving also involves a good deal of beating. Heavy flat wooden wands are used to close up the weft and make the fabric tight and hard wearing. Sharing some of the features of weaving and fiber making is the production of bark cloth. In this process, beating is employed only to soften woody fibers, not to order them in strands.

Metalworking involves much beating. Without modern furnaces, iron cannot be brought to its melting point, and so must be worked by hammering the red-hot ingot. Iron for blades is produced by layering ingot on top of ingot and then beating them wafer thin. But even with metals that could be cast, like brass and silver, hammering methods of working are preferred. Decorative patterns are punched onto the finished product.

One final example. Anyone who has watched women washing clothes in Southeast Asia will have noticed the way that the women roll them into a ball, soak them in water, and then beat them on a stone. Alternatively, they swing the wet cloth over their heads and bring it down smartly on a washboard or a convenient rock. Seldom do they employ the rubbing actions that come most naturally to Westerners.

Pounding actions appear with equal frequency in ritual contexts in Southeast Asia. The Berawan again provide an example. At funerals, drums, gongs large and small, slit gongs, and rice pestles are all unambiguously pounded. At other festivals, such as weddings, the gongs are played (using different rhythms), but the big drum and the funeral games are prohibited. This lesser level of percussion is consonant with the relative unimportance and ritual simplicity of all life-crisis markers other than death. The only rites that compete with funerals in terms of duration and complexity are head-hunting festivals, and they have their own peculiar percussive practices. When new heads are brought into the house, the men break into a stamping dance quite unlike the graceful, light-footed warrior's dance seen on other occasions. Also the felicitous opportunity is taken to expel evil influence from the house in the following manner. A crowd of people, mostly women, line up at one end of the longhouse veranda armed with rice pestles, canoe paddles, or heavy sticks. Together they march down the veranda, pounding these implements on the floor. Three times they go up and down the house, supposedly driving bad spirits before them.

We cannot conclude that these pounding actions in ritual derive in any simple way from similar ones in everyday life. That this cannot be the entire cause of their occurrence has already been shown by Needham, for the worldwide use of percussion cannot be explained by localized technologies of food production. However, it is still possible that the special frequency and importance of pounding technologies in Southeast Asia augments a universal resort to percussion for making noise. Though drums and gongs may be very widely employed at funerals, there is a particular intensity to the crashing, clanging, booming noisiness of Berawan rites.

Moreover, there may be cultural differences of emphasis in the significance of noise. The reason that is given by Berawan for the restriction on the playing of tops to funerals is that the whirring noise that they make is like the speech of ghosts. Normally it would be dangerous to attract ghosts with such noises, but at funerals the generations of the dead are invited anyway. Percussion is associated in the same way with the presence of the ancestors. Drumming and gong playing cease at the moment when this intercouse is broken off and the souls of the living are summoned back to the longhouse away from the departing dead.

LIMINALITY AND THE CORPSE

We cannot leave this consideration of the general and the particular in funeral practices without considering the corpse. It is our thesis throughout this book that close attention to the symbolic attributes of the dead body provides an avenue into a culture's understanding of the nature of death. These attributes have the same kind of quasi universality and subtle variability in connotation as do color symbolism and the use of percussive noise.

Corpse symbolism is a special case of the use of the human body as a symbol. As we have mentioned, Hertz's essay on the almost universal representation of positive and negative moral qualities through the opposition of the right and left hands is one of the classic studies in body symbolism. The mourning usages involving shaving the head or letting the beard grow touch on another aspect of body symbolism. Throughout history and in most cultures, the human body has been used to represent moral and social verities. In connection with circumcision and scarification at initiation, Van Gennep writes that "the human body has been treated like a simple piece of wood which each has cut and trimmed to suit him" (1960: 72). If the human body in life provides such a reservoir of moral representations, this same body after death carries its own possibilities for symbolic expression.

The surprising thing about corpse symbolism is how widely it is used in contexts divorced from death per se. Van Gennep saw that an immense variety of rites involve a rebirth in a new status, either for the individual or the whole society. But birth in the new condition presupposes death in the former, so that all liminal conditions involve deathly, terminal representations. Victor Turner has paid great attention to the recurring symbols of liminality:

> The symbolism attached to and surrounding the liminal *persona* is complex and bizarre. Much of it is modeled on human biological processes. . . . They give an outward and visible form to an inward and conceptual process . . . The symbols . . . are drawn from the biology of death, decomposition, catabolism, and other physical processes that have a negative tinge. [Turner 1967: 98]

In Turner's view, it is the process of rotting, of dissolution of form, that provides the metaphor of a social and moral transition. Hence the prevalence of disagreeable reminders of dissolution at otherwise optimistic rites such as initiations and installations. Following Turner, one could argue that the corpse is associated with death because its decay is a metaphor of liminality. However, the direct connection between the two is so obvious as to hardly require such ingenuity. Whether death or liminality is seen as primary depends upon whether one begins with funerals or other rites of passage. It is useful to explain liminality in initiation rites as deathlike, but it is tautologous in connection with funerals. However, Turner shows us a way to pursue the symbolism of the corpse by focusing upon the process of dissolution. Though, like percussive sound, corruption is a nearly universal symbol, it varies greatly in its metaphorical significance.

ROTTING, FERMENTING, DYEING, AND DISTILLING

Adams (1977) shows that in Southeast Asia there are strong parallels between certain manufacturing processes and the whole format of mortuary rites.

Blue-black dye is the most common color used for decorating cloth in Southeast Asia. Its preparation from indigo is widely practiced, and one of the simplest methods is that employed by the Meo of Thailand (Bühler 1972). Two pits are dug side by side, but at slightly different elevations. In the higher pit, the roots and stems of the indigo plant are soaked in water and left to rot. The liquid is then drained by a bamboo connecting pipe to the lower pit. Lime is added, and after a week or so of fermentation, a sediment forms. This is the dye, recovered by draining the pit. Elsewhere in Southeast Asia, clay pots are used to hold the liquids, but the process is the same.

In the preparation of hemp for cordage, the hemp stalks are left to rot in water for some weeks, after which the useful fibers can be separated from woody or pulpy material. Fermentation is widely employed as a means of rendering toxic food edible, or of preserving perishable foods. Fish and vegetables are stored for future consumption by means of partial anaerobic rotting in tightly sealed containers. These techniques were probably even more common 100 years ago, when rice was a less available staple and root crops made up a larger part of the diet of Southeast Asians (Pelzer 1945: 6–8). Even where not strictly necessary, fermented foods are often preferred because of their astringent flavor, such as shrimp paste and fermented tea leaves for chewing.

All these techniques involve decomposition – decomposition to produce useful things like dye and hemp or tasty things like shrimp paste and pickles. But there is a formal symmetry between these techniques used to process indigo and rotting in a less utilitarian context, the secondary treatment of the dead. Both involve the three stages of preparation, decomposition, and extraction.

The Berawan of Borneo do not prepare dyes and only occasionally ferment foods. The most familiar process of this kind for them is the making of rice wine, which is consumed in large quantities at social gatherings. Rice is first washed, cooked by boiling, and sprinkled with a prepared yeast. Then it is rolled into tight balls, which are stacked in large earthenware jars. The jars are sealed and left for some days, during which time a watery liquid runs off the balls of fermenting rice and collects in the bottom. When the crowd is assembled and the party about to start, the jars are opened. The remains of the rice balls are picked out and squeezed to remove the last drops of the liquor. The rice wine is now ready for consumption, after straining to remove the sediment. One characteristic Berawan method of treatment of corpses is wholly similar. After washing and dressing, the corpse is stored in a sealed jar. Decomposition proceeds similarly, except that it is the sediment that people wish to retain this time, not the liquids. The latter are drained off by means of a bamboo tube inserted in the bottom of the jar. The bones are removed from the jar finally, and placed in a smaller container for final storage. The jars used for rice wine are identical to those used for primary storage of corpses. Often several such jars are kept in the kitchen of a family apartment, and occasionally one is seen standing upside down. If one inquires why, the answer may be: Grandmother (or grandfather) has picked out this one for herself, and does not want it used for wine.

All these processes of fermentation or rotting produce a strong smell, often a nauseating smell. Making indigo dye is infamously stinky, and many Westerners dislike the preserved foods that we mentioned because of their pungent scent. The familiarity that Southeast Asians have with such smells may indicate different attitudes to corpses. It was not our experience that the Berawan were indifferent to these smells of decomposition, but they did show great fortitude in the presence of corpses. Rotting does not have the *wholly negative* connotations for them that it does for us. This is important, for it explains a radically different set of attitudes to the decomposition of the corpses than those found in the West. It is also relevant to the now-defunct custom of endo-cannibalism, by which the products of decomposition were consumed, sometimes mixed with rice, by the close kin. In view of the above discussion, this famous ethnological chestnut can be seen in a new light.

A second important feature of the comparison is the notion of extraction. In the making of indigo, hemp, rice wine, and so on, raw materials are refined to produce valuable finished products that are of less bulk. From something perishable, inconveniently bulky, and useless in its present form, something long lasting, compact, and useful is obtained. The bones of the deceased partake of this nature, so that it is logical to take the time to recover them and store them with the other ancestors, from where they may exercise a benign influence upon their descendants.

This is the analogy. We cannot show that secondary burial rites like those found in Borneo evolved out of techniques for processing dyes. There is also no evidence that such an analogy is made in the minds of participants in such rites. No Berawan was heard to compare the making of wine to the making of ancestors. Nevertheless, the parallels are there, and they are striking. It may be that at some subconscious level, familiarity with practical techniques of distillation and fermentation makes the practice of secondary treatment of the dead more acceptable to Southeast Asians than it is to other peoples. If at some remote period, such practices were more widely distributed in the world, it may explain their persistence in some parts of Southeast Asia. These are the strongest statements that we can make.

Finally, it is worth noticing that this analogy is not inconsistent with Hertz's analysis of secondary treatment. Hertz pointed out that in these rites the fate of the corpse provides a model for the fate of the soul. Adams would only add that both are refined: the former to ossiferous relics, the latter to perfect spirit.

Universals and Culture

THE NEED FOR CASE STUDIES

In the first part of the book, we have rejected the possibility of a simple panhuman explanation of the forms of funeral rites. Although we may posit a general psychic unity of mankind, the identification of vague quasi universals does not preclude variation at levels lower than that of the whole species. In trying to understand why Berawan funerals are so noisy, we were led to examine the worldwide use of percussion, the special propensity for pounding in Southeast Asia, and items of belief peculiar to the Berawan. Great care is needed in order to sort out the nature of variation from one place to another. Hence the need for case studies. Placed in the context of a particular ideological, social, and economic system, rituals of death begin to make sense in a way that they cannot if we pursue elusive cultural universals.

Caution is doubly necessary in connection with death rites because of an odd paradox. Contrary to what one might expect, conceptions of death are not only elusive, but also highly variable. Rivers remarked many years ago:

> Death is so striking and unique an event that if one had to choose something which must have been regarded in essentially the same light by mankind at all times and in all places, I think one would be inclined to choose it in preference to any other, and yet I hope to show that the primitive conception of death . . . is different, one might say radically different, from our own.
> [Rivers 1926: 40]

Meanwhile, concepts of life, which seems so much more complex a notion, have a certain universal familiarity about them. Ethnographers the world over constantly report the same symbols occurring in rites designed to promote fertility and the preservation of life, and the museums are full of life-promoting charms and ritual equipment. Death is more intangible:

> . . . on the whole there does commonly seem to be a contrast between a relatively patent and apprehensible conception of life and a more obscure and perplexing conception of death. One reason for this readily suggests itself. We have our being in a life that we know; we are struck down into a death that we can only surmise. [Needham 1970: xxxv]

PART II

DEATH AS TRANSITION

III

SOULS, GHOSTS, AND THE HEREAFTER: A RE-EXAMINATION OF HERTZ

In common with several of the influential essays originally published in the *Année sociologique*, Hertz's "A Contribution to the Study of the Collective Representation of Death" is more complex than is immediately apparent. At first sight, it appears to follow one topic in a direct fashion. Scholars already wedded to a particular theoretical viewpoint find it easy to pick out only familiar lines of argument. But a closer study reveals several interwoven themes. This is what makes the essay useful. Each argument is worth following out; each suggests a new interpretation of one's field data. But in order to make full use of Hertz's insights, it is necessary to tease apart the distinct threads of argument.

THE THREE SIDES OF HERTZ'S ANALYSIS

The most direct way to begin is with Hertz's dramatis personae: the corpse, the soul, and the mourners. Each part of the essay is devoted to one of these three, producing a tripartite structure made explicit in the section headings. Even though he had little to say specifically about the death essay in his introduction to the English translation, Evans-Pritchard pointed out the "three sides"

61

of Hertz's arguments (see the quotation in the section on Hertz's study of secondary burial in the Introduction).

The power of Hertz's explanations lies in showing how one aspect of the death rites affects other aspects in a complete system of ritual and belief. Contrary to what Evans-Pritchard implies, the arguments differ not in which of the three actors takes center stage, but in which *pair* of actors is brought into dialogue. We may imagine the arguments as the sides of a triangle, the corners of which are the aspects of the corpse and its disposal, the soul and the dead, and the living and the mourners (see Figure 2 below).

A nice example of the three sides of Hertz's argumentation concerns the answers that he gives to the deceptively simple question: Why is the corpse feared? What is the origin of the horror that surrounds it? At first glance, the answer seems obvious enough. Surely disgust at the process of bodily decay, even before death, but especially after death, is natural. However, the strength and the character of this reaction vary widely from one culture to another. Some dispose of the corpse hurriedly, others slowly and with painstaking attention. Americans do not care to witness a death, but will readily view the corpse once suitably treated. Even within one culture, reactions may vary according to the mode of dying. In many parts of Borneo, for instance, the cadaver of a woman who dies in childbirth is the subject of special revulsion. Nor are attitudes to the process of decomposition always the same, as we saw in the concluding section of Chapter 2. For Hertz, the expression of fear is important as evidence of cognitive and sociological motivations, not as a source of motivation or an adequate explanation in itself. But he rejects at the outset any explanation of it that relies on natural disgust:

> This is not a matter of hygiene (as we understand it), nor even, exclusively, a concern to ward off foul smells: we must not attribute to these people feelings and scruples about smell which are foreign to them. [1960: 32]

Near the end of the essay, Hertz offers this explanation:

> The horror inspired by the corpse does not spring from the simple observation of the changes that occur in the body. Proof that such a simplistic explanation is inadequate lies in the fact that in one and the same society the emotion aroused by death

varies extremely in intensity according to the social status of the deceased. . . . At the death of a chief, or a man of high rank, a true panic sweeps over the group. . . . On the contrary, the death of a stranger, a slave, or a child will go almost unnoticed. [Hertz 1960: 76]

This argument is explicitly sociological, because it turns upon the social status of the deceased. The passing of an influential person, on whom many people depend for leadership or livelihood, is a momentous event and perhaps a calamity. It leaves a large rent in the fabric of society. The same is not true of the socially insignificant.

Earlier in the essay, Hertz offers a different explanation:

These tribes thus explicitly connect the dissolution of the corpse and their belief in a temporary stay of the soul on earth, together with the obligations and fears that derive from this belief. . . . This representation is linked to a well-known belief: to make an object or a living being pass from this world into the next, to free or to create the soul, it must be destroyed. . . . As the visible object vanishes it is reconstructed in the beyond, transformed to a greater or lesser degree. The same belief applies to the body of the deceased. [Hertz 1960: 46]

The corpse is feared because, until its reconstruction in the beyond is complete, part of its spiritual essence remains behind, where it menaces the living with the threat of further death.

These two explanations are not identical. The important point in the present context is that it is not necessary to choose which of the explanations is the correct one. Both have validity and utility, but they are of a different order; they simply *explain different things*. The second shows why the death of any person causes anxiety and fear. The first shows why this reaction varies in scale from one person to another. Moreover, each has a different utility in trying to understand death ritual. The former explains why some funerals are large and some small. The latter provides the formula for a particular shape that the rituals may take – in this case secondary burial. It follows that the two explanations are different in the level of their generality also: The former might be applied to grand funerals anywhere, but the latter applies only to one category of death rites. In this chapter and subsequent ones, we will pursue the implications of these two lines of argumentation.

Nor is the nature of the fear the same in each case. The horror of death is not the same as the shock of some particular death, and neither is identical with the fear of the dead. But Hertz has yet a third explanation to cover that reaction:

> Death . . . by striking the individual, has given him a new character: his body, which . . . was in the realm of the ordinary, suddenly leaves it; it can no longer be touched without danger, it is an object of horror and dread. Now we know to what degree the religious or magical properties of things are regarded as contagious by "primitives": the "impure cloud" which, according to the Olo Ngaju, surrounds the deceased, pollutes everything it touches. . . . [Hertz 1960: 37–8]

At first sight, this explanation appears the simplest, and not very different from the hygienic rationale that Hertz rejected at the outset. But *this* pollution is supernatural, not literal. It occurs even where no physical contact exists, as with the land, even the trees, owned by the deceased (1960: 38). Also there are practices that seem directly to contradict the avoidance of pollution. The widow may be obliged to rub the products of decomposition of the corpse on her own body, for instance (1960: 51). Typically, Hertz offers two explanations for this practice: that for the widow, pollution is inevitable anyway, and that by so doing she deflects the animosity of her husband's ghost.

In the Indonesian context, pollution is not fundamentally a matter of contact with, but of relationship to, the source of contagion. Nonkin may sit near the corpse, and even touch it, without incurring infection. But close kin, wherever they happen to be, are immediately struck by the "petrifying thunderbolt" when a death occurs. More distant kin and fellow residents of the longhouse are affected to a lesser extent (Hertz 1960: 39). Unlike the Hindu or Semitic case, already well described in Hertz's time, pollution is not a conspicuous feature of Indonesian religions. In fact, it is found almost exclusively in the context of death. Their evaluation of rotting differs from our own. Though they certainly do not find it an attractive process, yet it has positive connotations that it does not have for us, having to do with the release of the dead from the bonds of the flesh. Thus the pollution of death has more to do with the ghost of the dead than the corpse. Or, to be more precise, it has to do with the gradual elimination of the social person of the deceased and the effect that that has on the status and self-conception of the living. Each relationship severed by death leaves a living person that much reduced: a social and psychological amputee. Of all relatives, the widow is the most disfigured by death. Like the dead man, she must undergo a liminal phase during which her identity is readjusted. To a lesser extent, the entire community goes through a period of redefinition.

Hertz's third explanation for the fear that death engenders turns, then, upon the extinction of the social person. What appears at first sight to be a statement about the corpse is in reality an explanation that relates the soul (in the form of the memory of the dead) to the living. Meanwhile, the first explanation that we reviewed above relates the corpse and its disposal to the mourners, and the second explanation relates the fate of the soul to the body, giving us the three-sided argumentation diagramed in Figure 2.

Moreover, each type of explanation can be utilized to account for different aspects of the funeral rites. Explanation 1 shows why the scale of funerals varies, and consequently how the rites express the social order by differentiating between people of unequal status. This type of argument lends itself to extension in many directions. Hertz himself connects it with the practice of preserving relics of individuals of high esteem, and hence the origin of ancestor cults (1960: 57). In a detailed analysis of the Merina of Madagascar, Bloch (1971) shows the importance of funeral rites in organizing the society of the living. Because the tomb that an adult Merina plans to occupy plays an important part in defining the corporate group to which he or she belongs in life, it follows that the society of the dead structures the society of the living. As Bloch acknowledges, his study is primarily sociological (1971: 220). We utilize arguments of this type in Chapter 5, where we examine how the remains of important men are manipulated to serve broad societal functions or the narrow ambitions of their would-be successors.

The arguments that can be elaborated out of explanation 3 are different in character. They focus on the gradual disentanglement

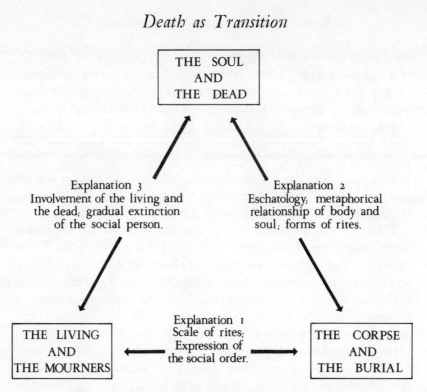

Figure 2. Schematic diagram of Hertz's arguments

of the living and the deceased. This theme is very pronounced in the funerals of the LoDagaa of West Africa, described in an important study by Goody (1962). The funerals of the LoDagaa involve several large ceremonies spread over many months. Goody shows that the effect of the rites is to dismantle the legal and emotional roles of the deceased and redistribute them among the living. The weightiest issue is the inheritance of property, which is not accomplished at once, but in stages. The LoDagaa carry the process through with unusual thoroughness. Even such nonjural and seemingly uninheritable roles as friend and lover are reallocated: "The LoDagaa are loath to extinguish any of the dead man's relationships; hence the funeral ceremonies provide institutionalized methods for the taking over of these roles by other persons. During the course of the burial service certain relationships that have been marked by satisfactory personal feelings are provisionally re-organized, and among these are . . . friend and lover" (Goody 1962: 133). This formulation is similar to Van Gennep's: The living pass through a liminal phase during which society is reintegrated without the lost member. The liminal phase has both a sociological dimension, concerned with rents in the social fabric, and a symbolic or psychological one, having to do with society's image of itself. Hertz did not fail to notice the latter: " . . . when a man dies, society loses in him much more than a unit; it is stricken in the very principle of life, in the faith it has in itself" (1960: 78). This societal crisis is most severe in the case of sacred kings, and it is the symbolic aspects of the death of kings that we take up in Chapter 6.

Explanation 2 has a unique power. It enables us to penetrate the meaning of mortuary rituals by paying attention to the details of the treatment of the corpse. In his essay, Hertz demonstrates "A kind of symmetry or parallelism between the condition of the body. . . . and the condition of the soul" (1960: 45). This relationship makes it possible to derive eschatology from the metaphorical relationship of body and soul. Consequently, such analyses have a symbolic character. Given the extraordinary variety of methods used throughout the world and at different epochs to dispose of the dead, we are provided with a rich vein of material for analysis. This approach enables us to deal with the *particular forms* of death rites, so that their specialness and individuality are not lost.

This line of argument is the most original feature of Hertz's essay, yet it has so far received very little attention. We shall follow it in subsequent chapters by keeping the corpse clearly in view.

It is an approach that can be applied to any type of funeral. Hertz chose to apply it to one particular variety of mortuary rite, that of secondary disposal. He drew much of his data from Borneo, where there were instances of the practice that were already well documented in his day. However, Hertz was obliged to rely on the accounts of travelers, in which this bizarre custom figures prominently. The Berawan of central northern Borneo still practice secondary disposal, and they provide an appropriate test of Hertz's analysis in the light of detailed field data.

Death as Transition

Berawan rites of secondary treatment Between the four Berawan communities there are many differences in the details of ritual of secondary treatment of the dead. Nevertheless, there is an overall similarity of format. Briefly, there are two major ceremonies, each lasting several days and involving many people, separated by a period of at least eight months, and sometimes as much as five years.

The first ceremony begins immediately after death occurs. The corpse is displayed on a specially built seat for a day or two. When all the close kin have seen it, it is inserted in a coffin or large jar. At the end of four to ten days, depending upon the status of the deceased, it is removed for temporary storage. This may be within the longhouse, or more frequently on a simple wooden platform in the graveyard. When the time has come to perform the second ceremony, guests are summoned from far and wide to attend. The coffin or jar is brought from its place of temporary storage to a small shed built onto the longhouse veranda. If the initial storage container is damaged, the relatives may decide to open it, clean the bones of the deceased, and store them in a new jar of smaller size. The ceremony lasts four to ten days, and every evening there is a boisterous party on the veranda adjacent to the jar or coffin. Then the bones are transferred to their final resting place. This may comprise a single massive post, often richly carved, with a niche near its head into which a small jar may be inserted. Alternatively, the remains may be stored in a large decorated wooden mausoleum raised on one or several supporting posts, and housing several coffins.

The second ceremony corresponds to what Hertz called "the great feast." Because the Berawan do not typically store corpses or skeletons below ground, the familiar anthropological term "secondary burial" does not seem appropriate to describe these rites. To avoid circumlocution, we will use the Berawan name *nulang*. Significantly, it is a close cognate of their word for bones.

What is the significance of these rituals, spread out over so long a period? The answer that the Berawan give is that the nulang

rites, and in particular the death songs sung at that ceremony, conduct the enduring spiritual component of the deceased to the land
of the dead. But an inconsistency immediately appears in this
account, because Berawan also claim that this entry into the land
of the ancestors occurs immediately at death; indeed, this is the
definition of death. In order to resolve this contradiction, it is necessary to understand how the spiritual component of human
beings is perceived.

Berawan notions of the soul, sickness, and death   The Berawan
conceive of the living human being as the conjunction of the body
(*usā*) and a spiritual component (*təlanak*). The obvious gloss for
təlanak is soul. But we must beware of the tendency to assume
that the two concepts are identical. They differ in at least two
ways. First, the Berawan soul changes its nature and manifestation
in different contexts. At healing sessions it appears as minute and
particulate, so that the shaman is able to catch it on a sword blade.
But in the death songs we find it paddling a canoe and singing
laments, in short, appearing as a homomorphic counterpart of the
deceased. Second, the Berawan soul is not considered eternal. On
the contrary, the soul of a dead person changes some time after
death into something else, and the word *təlanak* is no longer used
in connection with him or her.

What the soul changes into is called *bilǔ ləta*, a spirit of the
dead. *Bilǔ* (spirit) is a word often heard in Berawan prayers and in
casual conversation. Supernatural agencies ranging from the Crea-
tor (*Bilǔ Ngaputong; ngaputong* = to create), to omen birds
(*bilǔ aman; aman* = omen creature), to mischievous sprites
that are assumed to be behind any unusual occurrence, however
trivial, are all parts of a limitless spirit world. The spirits of the
dead inhabit a region called *lia dē lo ləta*, simply, the place of
those who are dead. Berawan refuse to speculate on where it is,
replying to enquiries with the pragmatic answer that they are
only human and cannot know. They do, however, assert that the
land of the dead is a beautiful place full of radiant spirits.

The unaging perfection of spirits contrasts with the infirmity of
humans. Some common ailments, such as skin diseases and upset
stomachs, are attributed to environmental causes without supernat-

ural implications. Others, including some serious conditions, are believed to result from violation of a taboo. But the most important category of illness stems from "soul loss." The soul wanders from the body in sleep, but should not be long absent. If it is tardy, or is ensnared by some malevolent spirit entity, then illness soon results. Curing practices center around recovery of the soul, and its restoration to the body of the patient. This is the province of the shamans, who control many techniques for the location and securing of errant souls.

If sickness is caused by the prolonged absence of the soul, what is death? The unanimous and immediate answer to this question was that if the soul continues to wander, and eventually strays so far that it enters the land of the dead, then at that moment the victim is dead. One informant told the following story to illustrate graphically his answer. Once, as a young man, he had been very seriously ill and had lost consciousness. He had dreamt that he was paddling upriver, and had turned off into a stream that he later realized was the Lamat, that is, he was following the route to the land of the dead as described in Berawan death songs. He paddled up the Lamat, and beached his canoe at the foot of a steep hill, which he climbed. On top of the hill were beautiful people dressed in fine clothes, harvesting rice that shone like gold. These people were spirits of the dead. They invited him to go with them, and together they descended the hill on the other side from the Lamat, and came to another stream. The spirits crossed over this stream, but he suddenly realized that to do so would bring him finally into the land of the dead. So he set his face away from the entrancing vision of the beautiful spirits and returned the way that he had come. Later he regained consciousness, and having passed the crisis of his illness, soon recovered.

Such is the Berawan notion of death. Physical death is usually referred to by the expression "to lose breath." But if the soul reaches the land of the dead at the moment of "losing breath," what is the ritual purpose of the rites of secondary treatment?

The journey of the soul: the death songs Despite local variations in custom, for all Berawan the climax of the nulang ceremony is the singing of special death songs. On the following morning, the bones are taken to their final resting place in the monument prepared for them. But first the soul must be provided for, and the death songs sung on that last night give it very specific instructions as to how to make the journey to the land of the dead.

The sequence from the village of Long Jegan will serve to illustrate the nature of the death songs of the last night of the nulang.

The first to be sung has an important purpose, the recovery of any souls that may be tempted to wander off with that of the dead person. But it is sung in a lighthearted and playful manner. A verse is sung for every member of the community, and the soul of someone of the opposite sex is delegated to "pull" the soul home. This is an opportunity for ribaldry and innuendo to which no one may object.

The most important of the death songs comes next, and it is sung in a formal and serious manner. The lead singer stands beside the coffin facing upriver. He takes up a large bamboo, the one that was used to bring water to wash the corpse at death, and which has been preserved near the coffin since then. Lightly but firmly, he strikes the coffin with the end of the bamboo, making a resonant noise. Simultaneously, he calls upon the soul to prepare for the journey to the land of the dead. The song instructs the soul to go to the river to wash. Having returned, the soul is told to put on fine attire, as appropriate to the sex of the dead person. Now it is told to go out of the longhouse and, without so much as glancing backward, to descend to the canoe at the river's edge.

At this point, the format of the song changes. Now successive verses consist of questions posed by the journeying soul and answers provided by the living. The soul begins, through the voice of the lead singer: *"Long iniu, lasarn?"* (What place is this, live ones?). The reply comes from the chorus: *"Long Inoun, ladiern"* (The place of the longhouse, dead one).

The soul is instructed to paddle upstream. Then it asks its whereabouts, and is told that it is at Long Marude, that is, the place where the Marude Stream joins the main river, a short distance above the longhouse. The next place arrived at is where a small nameless stream runs into the main river, and this is referred to conventionally as Long Bǝk, *bǝk* meaning a tiny watercourse. So the song proceeds upriver, mentioning all the places where named side streams join the main river, and using the rubric Long Bǝk each time an unnamed stream is passed. Each time the site of a previous Berawan longhouse is passed, the name Long Inoun is heard once again. Every three or four verses the soul is urged to paddle vigorously, making the spray fly up behind the canoe.

This recitation of place names makes up a large part of the death songs of the final evening. The journey of the soul has more cosmological significance than is at first apparent. The Berawan of Long Jegan have for several centuries been migrating away from an idyllic ancestral homeland in the Usun Apau plateau, down the river that the soul is now traveling up. Berawan stories of migration move back in time to longhouse sites ever further upriver, and to hero figures who gradually become more stupendous, until a mythical time is reached in the Usun Apau when the living and the dead lived together. At the moment when this arrangement ceased, and men became mortal, nulang was invented. It can thus be seen how fundamentally the rites of secondary treatment are, for the Berawan, woven into their idea of what it is to be human. As the soul travels upriver, it not only travels toward the dead, but also backward in time. It moves from the mundane to the sacred, via the larger-than-life heroes of a few generations ago, back past mythical ancestors that dug rivers and climbed the sky, to the creation itself. For the audience listening to, and participating in, the death songs, the songs constitute an exposition of the most fundamental concepts of Berawan religion.

Eventually, in the song, the soul arrives at the mouth of the Lamat stream, and instead of passing it by, it is instructed to enter. From the Lamat it goes into the Meta, a yet smaller watercourse. This route would bring one close to the highest point in the neighboring mountain range. In this region, the soul is told to get out of the canoe, and to search for *sirih*, the leaves used in chewing betel. At this juncture, the death song sequence of Long Jegan abruptly terminates. It is thought that while the soul is searching for *sirih* leaves it will be discovered by emissaries from the land of the dead, who will conduct it on the remaining part of the journey. The whole recital has lasted six to eight hours, and dawn is close.

But if the soul arrived in the land of the dead at the moment of "losing breath," is not this second journey at the nulang redundant? It was necessary to press informants in order to get any answer to this question. They gave blank looks, or recapitulated data that were already familiar. Finally, a senior nobleman of Long Jegan offered the following account.

The soul of a sick person wanders from the body of its owner. Prolonged absence causes serious illness, but the soul may wander far, into spirit worlds unknown to humans, without fatal results. Only if it should enter the land of the dead by some devious route will death ensue. Then the minimal connection of body and soul is severed and the lifeless body begins to decompose. The soul does not stay in the land of the dead; it continues to wander. But on returning finally to this body it discovers that decomposition has begun, and so it is unable to reenter the body. It cannot or will not reanimate the putrescent corpse. If it did so, a monster would result. But neither can the soul easily find its way back to the land of the dead, because it arrived there previously by accident and not by the direct route. Even if it can find its way there again, it will not be welcomed by the community of the dead because it has not yet become one of those beautiful spirits. So it must wander miserably in unfamiliar spirit regions, or enviously lurk in the environs of the longhouse, near the corpse. At the nulang, the dead are summoned to the festivities, and the soul is properly conducted to the land of the dead. This ensures its welcome there. In support of this account, the nobleman cited the practice of calling back the soul of the dead person on the first night of the nulang ceremony, which may last as long as ten nights. The purpose of calling it back is to ensure that it is not wandering in some distant spirit world, and thus to prevent it from, literally, missing the boat.

This rationale removed the inconsistency, but it was clear that it had been manufactured for the ethnographer's benefit. Most Berawan have simply never considered the anomaly. What is striking is the similarity that this native analysis bears to that of Hertz.

Both posit a period when the soul is homeless, miserable, and malicious. Both place a central emphasis on the decomposition of the corpse. In the native account, the soul is unable to reanimate the corpse because putrescence has already begun. To do so would be contrary to nature, and the result would be monstrous. Moreover, the fate of the soul is related to the fate of the corpse, because the former needs time to convert itself into a spirit worthy of the land of the dead, even as the latter needs time to become dry bones.

The ritual expression of Berawan eschatology Moreover, although Berawan beliefs concerning the fate of the soul may not be explicit, there are many practices that lend substance to the informant's account. In the year or more before the soul's final release at the nulang festival, there are dozens of small rituals woven into the funeral, or having to do with the mourning usages of the close kin of the deceased, that draw attention in unmistakable ways to the continuing presence of both the corpse and the hovering soul, and to their ambivalent nature, both demanding care and inspiring fear at the same time. Here we give a few examples only.

The presence of the soul near the corpse is attested to by the practice of addressing it throughout the death rites. As relatives arrive after hearing news of the death, they immediately go to the corpse. Women mourners drop to their knees before the corpse, and throw their long hair forward over the crowns of their heads so that it hides their faces. Amid tears and sobs, they produce a dramatic dirge, the main thrust of which is: Why have you abandoned those that love you? Such dirges are a vocal art form, but they are also the vehicle of intense emotion. Close female relatives may repeat the dirge daily, or even more frequently. Men express similar sentiments but they stand back dry-eyed.

A second practice with the same implications is the provision of food and tobacco for the corpse. This begins immediately after death. In the minutes after "loss of breath" has been confirmed, a complex and rapid series of rites are enacted upon the corpse. Two of these concern us here. In one, the spouse and children of the dead person lie down in turn beside the corpse and puff upon a cigarette of native manufacture. Then they sit up and offer it to the lips of the corpse. In the other rite, the corpse is carried into the kitchen and its hand is laid in the hearth. Simultaneously, a little cooked rice is pushed into its mouth. After the corpse is displayed on its special seat, a plate is hung before its face (see Plate 2). Each time the widow or widower is fed, a little of the same food is placed in the suspended plate. A cigarette is placed in the corpse's fingers. After the corpse is inserted in the coffin or jar, the plate is placed on top, and token quantities of food are placed there as before.

But the soul is not within the corpse, and this makes the body itself a source of intense danger aside from the threat of the malicious soul. During the period before the corpse is removed from the house for temporary sepulture, a constant vigil is maintained

Plate 2. Corpse of a Berawan woman displayed on a special seat. The woman seated to the right of the picture is the daughter of the deceased. She is dressed in white mourning attire. The dead woman is decked in fine clothes and surrounded by valuables. Her hands rest in a bowl containing candy and money, and she holds a cigarette in her fingers. In front of her (partly obscured by the rich hangings) is hung a small bowl into which cooked food is placed from time to time. The deceased's husband is housed in a small cubicle of mats out of the picture to the left.

over it. In the case of an adult, the spouse and at least the eldest child are near the corpse at all times. At night a large crowd collects near the coffin to talk, drink, and play games. Officially, no adult should sleep at night during funerals. In practice, it is sufficient if each family apartment sends one representative to attend the gathering. Toward morning many people are stretched out asleep on the mats around the coffin, but earlier in the night games are played and there is much joviality. Many of the death songs sung on these occasions resemble games more than somber dirges. Such levity is in accordance with one stated aim of the gathering, namely, to entertain the soul of the dead person, and make its last hours in the longhouse jolly.

The other stated aim of the vigil is to prevent harm from befalling the corpse. The noise of the crowd and the bright lights kept burning all night discourage the intrusion of evil spirits. Intense horror centers on the idea of the putrescent corpse becoming inspired by some demon. There is a particular spirit that attempts to gain control of fresh corpses, and if it should succeed a monster results of superhuman strength and nightmarish mien that is invulnerable to human weapons. On one occasion, a coffin resting on the longhouse veranda was heard to emit a mysterious knocking sound, as if there were something inside rapping on the lid. The noise may have been caused by contraction of the timbers of the longhouse in the cool of the late afternoon. But the women sitting casually nearby saw a different explanation. They fled carrying their children. Men came carrying weapons, which were waved above the coffin. Extra bands of rattan were tied around the coffin, so as to secure the lid more firmly, and magical plants intended to repel evil spirits were placed on top of it. Calm was not restored until the old shaman arrived, and declared that nothing was amiss with the corpse. Reassured, the crowd resumed its vigil.

A further instance of the care taken with new corpses is the practice of hanging mats along the open side of the veranda. These mats are lowered an hour or so before sunset, and raised again during the early hours of the morning. Sunset is a dangerous time, when many evil spirits are abroad, and the corpse is best shielded from their view. Color symbolism is also involved in this fear: Berawan say the sunset is too "busy," too full of threatening red hues.

The many privations visited upon a widow during the funeral also express the theme of the danger of the corpse and soul. She is cooped up for as many as eleven days in a tiny cell made of mats, next to the corpse. Her ordeal is considerable. She may not bathe, and must defecate through a hole in the floor, wear filthy clothes, and eat only the poorest of foods, which she "shares" with the deceased. These harsh prescriptions fit nicely with Hertz's suggestion that she partakes in the condition of the deceased. But we must be careful to observe in just what way she shares his condition. That the widow is not simply in "quarantine" so that she can not spread her "pollution" is revealed by another rule: She can sit or sleep only with her legs tucked up in a cramped position. It is hard to see how this prevents the spread of infection; on the contrary, it is explicitly designed to ensure the discomfort of the widow. She must be made to suffer not because of the *corpse*, but because of the *vengeful soul* of the deceased. Its envy of the living, caused by its own miserable state, is softened by the spectacle of the hardship visited upon those it formerly loved. Nor are these practices intended punitively, but paradoxically out of a concern for the widow's welfare. As the one closest to the deceased she is most likely to have her soul stolen to keep him company. Only by suffering can she deflect his malice. Only by sharing his condition metaphorically can she avoid sharing it literally.

The same set of collective representations reveal why the funeral, even the funeral of unimportant people within the longhouse, is an intensely communal affair. The widow, by her confinement, deflects the hostility of the vengeful soul. She thus performs a service for the entire community, and all its members have a reciprocal moral commitment to see to the workaday details of the rites. A widower is subjected to an identical restriction, and other close kin, although not physically confined, wear mourning attire, maintain a somber disposition, and spend many hours sitting silently by the corpse. Consequently, the responsibility to feed guests or construct a suitable tomb is spread among more distant kin, and the cooperation enjoined at funeral rites has a powerful integrative function. There is no more binding duty on the long-house resident than that of participation in death rites.

In the months following the funeral, the close kin, especially the widow or widower, observe many rites and restrictions. For instance, at each full moon a new widow addresses a dirge to the dead man. Kneeling alone in the moonlight, keening pitifully, she makes a dramatic figure.

All these practices lend credence to our informant's account of the nature of the deceased's existence in the months following death. The corpse and the soul are likewise the object of fear, and of solicitude. The corpse must be protected lest it become some terrible monster, and is feared for the same reason. The soul is pitied because of its discomfort, and feared because of what its discomfort might lead it to do. The double character of the funeral, half ordeal and half party, like the nature of the soul, both pitiful and dangerous, are alike consequences of the state of the corpse, which both demands attention and repels it at the same time.

The relationship of the abridged rites to nulang   The metaphorical relationship that Hertz observed has enabled us to see a remarkable consistency in Berawan rites of secondary burial. Both the overall format and the details of ritual express the same set of ideas.

However, a problem arises in connection with the abridged death rites. Not everyone receives nulang. In fact, it is a relatively rare event. The more common practice is to give the corpse the initial funeral rites, and then to store it permanently in the tomb. Hertz suggests that such abbreviated rites are the result of foreign influence (1960: 58). Miles (1965) makes a similar argument for societies of southern Borneo. The same argument is not convincing as applied to the Berawan. They claim that both a full and an abridged death ritual sequence have always been available, and the monuments in old graveyards bear out their statement. In the Berawan case, there is no evidence of devolution from an epoch when the full rites were performed for every corpse.

What concerns us here is the ritual significance of the abridged rites. The question is: Are the notions of the fate of the soul in death the same if only the abridged rites are performed? If so, how does the soul get to the land of the dead without the death songs of the nulang? If not, why are some people, including those most respected in the community, made to suffer the horrible fate of the intermediary period? In some longhouses, the songs conveying the soul to the land of the dead are sung during the initial wake. At others, they are never sung at all. In communities of the first type, do they believe that the soul can be formally introduced to the ancestors after so brief a period? Our answer is that even where the songs are sung, basic notions of the fate of the soul in death remain identical to those revealed by the extended death rites. Many practices point to this conclusion.

First, despite the removal of the corpse from the longhouse, and its entombment in a permanent death monument, the soul is still talked to and fed. The most obvious occasion on which this occurs is a rite performed during the first full moon after the rice harvest subsequent to the death. A ritual apparatus is erected in the open space in front of the longhouse adjacent to the dead person's apartment. It consists of a bamboo pole, about fifteen feet tall, with ears of the new rice arranged in geometrical patterns around its top. This rice is the share offered to the dead person, who may have lent a hand in planting it. A time of full moon is chosen so as to be sure of encountering the dead person's ghost. If the deceased was male, his widow makes a dirge much as described above.

Second, the ghost is still feared, because it is still likely to be near the longhouse, and vindictive. Mourning continues after the removal of the corpse from the house, with a slow relaxation in severity. The privations visited upon the widow or widower are relaxed two days after the removal of the corpse from the longhouse. But mourning clothes and sobriety of living are prescribed for a full year. For months she will not go into any other family apartment than her own, even the adjacent ones that house her daughters and grandchildren. She will not sing or dance during that year. Close female relatives will observe the prohibition on dancing for several months. The widow cannot remarry for at least a year.

Certainly these mourning usages are observed partly from

sorrow, but their function in placating the dead man is explicit. Any further deaths in the community are likely to be attributed to the vengeful soul. Particularly if there was some irregularity concerning the death or the funeral, an apprehensive period ensues. This period lasts about one year.

In Berawan thought, the soul of a dead person undergoes a protracted metamorphosis whether or not its corpse receives secondary treatment. If the death songs are sung too early, they serve to conduct the soul along the path to the land of the dead, but the soul still cannot gain admittance. This is why some communities dispense with them in the abridged rites.

We can now summarize Berawan eschatology and its relationship to funeral ritual. Their conception of dying is uniform from one longhouse to another, regardless of the particular ritual employed. The stability of these ideas is illustrated by the comment of a Berawan convert to Catholicism that purgatory is the place to which Christian souls went "until their bones are dry." He argued that it was a morally responsible act to convert because in purgatory God could keep an eye on the souls of the recently dead, and prevent them from bothering the living.

What is variable is the ritual expression of these beliefs. Different rites are observed in each of the four communities, and even within one longhouse at least two sequences are available, the abridged and the full. All these ceremonies embody the recognition of the slowly changing nature of the dead. But they do not embody it equally. Only in the ritual climaxing in nulang are these conceptions given full expression. That is why nulang is important out of all proportion to its frequency.

The nulang celebrates the passing of the soul into an exalted realm. In those cases where it is performed, it provides the occasion for the transit to the land of the dead. But souls for whom nulang is not performed are not denied entry into the company of their ancestors forever. It is only that that event goes unmarked by ritual. Nulang is an honor, and not a punishment, because the soul of the recipient is given a moment of consummate glory. The ritual of secondary treatment is confirmatory in nature, rather than instrumental, and it is this feature that removes the paradox of its relative infrequency.

Hertz's exclusive focus on the most elaborate rites of secondary treatment, probably a function of the sources that he used, leads him to incorrectly dismiss other kinds of rites as modern developments symptomatic of cultural impoverishment, and to arrive at a mechanistically instrumental view of the rituals. But these are minor quibbles: In general, Hertz's formulation succeeds admirably in unlocking the religious ideas that lie behind Berawan funerals.

VARIATIONS ON A THEME

Needless to say, secondary treatment of the dead is not restricted to Borneo, nor are such rites elsewhere identical to those of the Berawan. Our next objective therefore is to examine briefly some variant forms, to see if the metaphor that Hertz isolated in the core of such rites can be discerned in them also.

Before beginning, it might be useful to review the elements that we expect to find together. The metaphor is that, where secondary treatment occurs, the fate of the corpse is a model for the fate of the nonmaterial component of the person. By secondary treatment, we mean the regular and socially sanctioned removal of the relics of some or all deceased persons from a place of temporary storage to a permanent resting place. "Temporary" storage means a period of a few months or years, but not a few days. At least two things follow in terms of ideology. First, that dying is a slow process of transition from one spiritual state to another. Second, the process of spiritual change is disagreeable, in the same way that the decomposition of the corpse is disagreeable. In addition to these minimal items, other beliefs that may be found include: an emphasis on decomposition in symbols or statements referring to the recently dead; a fear of the recently dead; a fear that corpses may be horrifically reanimated; an assumption that the malice of the recently dead will gradually wane, being replaced by the benign influence of the long dead, and also that the recently dead somehow hover near human habitation, whereas the long dead are removed and anonymous.

Other instances of secondary treatment from Indonesia: Ma'anyan, Toradja, and Balinese   Hertz principally bases his analysis on the peoples of southeast Borneo, whom he refers to collectively as the Olo Ngaju. This name means nothing more than "people from upriver," and disguises the fact that there is considerable cultural variation within the area of southern Borneo that has come to be designated by the term. However, in this he simply followed the usage of those who provided his sources (Braches 1882; Grabowsky 1884, 1889; Hardeland 1858; and others). More recent work has been done by Schärer (1963) and Hudson (1966). We draw on Hudson's detailed account of the funeral rites of one particular ethnic group in the area, the Ma'anyan.

Ma'anyan mortuary practices involve temporary storage of the corpse in a coffin, which is buried in the graveyard. Instead of having a rite of secondary treatment for one person at a time, as in the Berawan case, corpses are allowed to accumulate over a matter of years and then all of them receive these rites together. This community festival of the dead lasts over a week and attracts large crowds. At its climax, all the accumulated coffins that are sufficiently old are stacked on a grating and burned in relays of a dozen or so. After each firing, the ashes containing fragments of bone are collected. Later they are stored in a large raised wooden container in the graveyard, together with relics from former festivals (Hudson 1966: 361–98).

The nonmaterial component of a living person is called *amirue*. After death, it is no longer referred to by that name, but is called *adiau*. No ordinary shaman can aid or manipulate the adiau; instead, another ritual specialist must care for it. It is her job (they are always women) to guide the adiau to the land of the dead, and protect it on its journey by means of long ritual chants. These chants terminate on the day the coffin is burned, and simultaneously the adiau arrives at the land of the dead, and reverts to being amirue.

The land of the dead is regarded as a pleasant place, although notions about it are vague compared to the elaborate seven-layer heavens described to Schärer by the Ngaju of the Katingan River (Schärer 1963: 157–8). Mourning usages are similar to those of the Berawan, with gradually decreasing severity after interment of the corpse. Of themselves, these usages are not evidence of a fear of the recently dead, because some kind of mourning is well nigh universal. It is the emphasis on deprivation that is indicative here. In particular, one close relative, often the mother of the deceased, is kept locked up in a room for seven days with only a very poor diet of water and cold cassava (Hudson 1966: 371). This is reminiscent of the privations visited upon the widow in Berawan funerals. Also, food is taken regularly to the grave for as long as three years, unless secondary treatment occurs first.

Among the Ma'anyan, the intermediary period is even more clearly marked than among the Berawan, and the transition is similarly conceived. This is not surprising, given that the rites of the Ma'anyan and their neighbors were the ones that originally prompted Hertz's analysis. In addition, it is interesting to note how different are the Ma'anyan rites from those of the Berawan, although they express very similar ideas. The scheduling of cremation is particularly instructive: It provides a final sterilization *after* bacterial decomposition is completed. Were it not for the notion that the corpse is associated with a transition of the soul, it would surely make more sense to cremate the corpse immediately after death, as is done in India.

In addition to southern Borneo, Hertz also made use of data from Celebes, but important material on the mortuary rites found there appeared shortly after his essay was completed. In 1912, Adriani and Kruyt published a three-volume account of the Bare'e-speaking Toradja of central Celebes. Their account is rich in detail but poorly organized, so that a more recent reanalysis of their data on Toradja religion is welcome (Downs 1956). Downs is careful to indicate the variation found among Toradja communities, and below we summarize general features only.

Corpses are stored after death in a rough hut, built some distance from the village. A slave is designated to stay with the corpse to mop it clean of liquids of decay and to protect it from being stolen by witches. Mourning usages are similar to those of the Berawan, particularly with regard to the widow, who is walled up in mats, deprived of good food, and forbidden to stretch out her legs. Every few years, a mass second funeral takes place for all the accumulated skeletons, but the ceremony may happen more frequently if epidemics break out, or if plagues of mice attack the rice crop. These disasters are attributed to the unquiet dead. At the second funeral, the bones are brought from their rough huts to the village wrapped in a cloth. The slave that kept the death watch is thereafter freed, but is shunned by other people. Sometimes the bundles of bones are made into small effigies of the deceased by the addition of a mask. When the ceremony is completed, the bone bundles are inserted in a small wooden box and stored finally in a cave together with their kin (Downs 1956: 78-91).

Meanwhile, the fate of the nonmaterial component of the deceased is that it has changed from *tanoana* to *angga* immediately upon death. The angga of the recently dead are greatly feared. They persistently return from the underworld in all manner of fearful guises, and their presence can be detected by smells of decomposition or low grumbling sounds. Their touch burns the skin, their breath causes dizziness, and they frequently frighten people at night. Constant small rites are performed to try to get them to return to the underworld. At the second funeral, a shaman summons the angga from the underworld or wherever they may be and instructs them in a chant to wash and dress themselves preparatory to going on their last journey to the underworld. This they accomplish by climbing through a hole in the ground off to the west, and dropping into the upper branches of a *pinang* tree whose roots grow in the underworld. Safely arrived in the underworld, they are reunited with their dead relatives, at the same time that their bones are inserted in the cave with those of their ancestors.

As to the nature of the underworld, there are inconsistencies in Adriani and Kruyt's account. Some references report that the underworld is somber, but that the dead are content there anyway. Others say that on the completion of the rites of secondary treatment, the dead are allowed to leave the underworld and proceed to a joyful existence in the upperworld. The confusion may originate with Adriani and Kruyt, but not necessarily so. As we have seen, inconsistencies of this kind often go unremarked by their propounders. After the dead are settled into their final worlds, they join the company of the "revered ancestors" and are thought to exercise a benign influence. In particular, distinguished ancestors are vaguely conceived as guardian spirits of the community (Downs 1956: 31-2).

Toradja mortuary rites exhibit all the features listed above, and incorporate the symbolism of the decaying corpse even more specifically than Berawan or Ma'anyan practices. The Ma'anyan are satisfied to allow the corpse to rot in the graveyard, removed from people, until they are ready for secondary treatment. The Berawan usually follow the same course of action, although they occasionally keep the remains within the longhouse in a sealed container with a drain tube. But the Toradja provide for the corpse to be watched over during the entire process of decay. The slave must sleep in the hut, and minister to the corpse, which is laid out directly on the floor. The task is important as well as repulsive, for the corpse must not be allowed to fall into the hands of witches. It possesses the dual nature that was so much a feature of Berawan funerals.

Hertz makes only passing reference to funeral rites on the island of Bali, which was only brought under Dutch control in 1906–8, just as the death essay was being written.

Balinese mortuary practices involve secondary treatment, by cremation, for those who can afford it. Others receive simple burial only. All mortuary sequences follow a similar ritual pattern, but those of noblemen are on a far grander scale, with all manner of artistic and ritual refinements. Corpses are generally buried without great show of emotion, in a simple earth grave and without a coffin. The cadavers of priests and very prestigious individuals are not buried, but retained within the compound of the house on a special platform (Wirz 1928: 13, 20). The corpses of rulers are laid out in a pavilion erected for the purpose within the palace grounds, and attended by a slave who collects the products of decomposition for burial. This slave earns his freedom by this duty, but is shunned by other people in a manner reminiscent of Toradja practices (Covarrubias 1937: 386). After a minimum of forty-two days, preparations may begin for the cremation. This is a briefer intermediary period than those prescribed among the Berawan, Ma'anyan, or Toradja, but few people can afford to proceed immediately, and even the rich have elaborate preparations to make, so that long delays are the rule. Moreover, the minimal period is specifically to allow the corruption of the corpse to be completed (Wirz 1928: 17).

When preparations for a mass cremation ceremony are completed, the graves of commoners are dug up and the earth is raked over for pieces of bone. No great effort is made to collect all the bones, and it is possible to proceed even if *no* bones are found. The bones that are found are laid out in roughly their correct relationship to one another, and a crude effigy is built around them with herbs and flowers. Later this is packed into a bundle. Next the essence of the deceased is ritually captured in another small effigy. After a noisy all-night gathering, both the effigy containing the bones and that containing the spiritual component are loaded into a tall elaborately decorated tower, and rushed to the cremation ground by the sea. Many diversions are taken to confuse the departing dead, and there is much jostling, including mock battles for the control of the remains. Arriving at the cremation grounds, the effigies are taken down, loaded into coffins shaped to represent various animals according to the caste of the deceased, and burned. Later the ashes are strewn upon the sea (Wirz 1928: 51–105; Hooykaas 1973: 22–3).

It has often been remarked that the culture of Bali is an amalgam of indigenous and imported Hindu elements (Boon 1977: 18–19). In the death rituals, the Indic element is shown by the casualness with which the corpse is treated: Bits of bone are pulled haphazardly out of the grave, and remains are poked about and jokingly urged to burn rapidly. This is in accordance with Hindu dogma that the body is but a container of the soul, and of little significance. However, Indonesian elements are also conspicuous. Balinese cremation resembles Ma'anyan rather than Indian practices in one important particular: It must occur *after* corruption of the corpse. Also, the efforts made to confuse the skeleton in its final journey suggest fear of the returning spirit. A similar polar-

ity occurs in beliefs about the afterlife. The Hindu-derived doctrines speak of progression through an elaborate hierarchy of
heavens and reincarnations, but this is the stuff of the priestly
caste. Popular belief is dominated by a concern to settle the ghosts
of the recently dead, who lead a restless existence. They roam
around the graveyards and are irritable because of not having
reached their final stage. They require constant small offerings
(Hooykaas 1973: 22). Swellengrebel (1969: 203) remarks that the
recently dead are demonic and are entitled to sustenance and
offerings by way of exorcism. But a completely different attitude
applies to the purified dead, who are venerated in household and
clan temples. Consequently, the close relatives are anxious to see
their dead cremated, even in modest style, as soon as possible. In
the courtly, Hindu-dominated rituals of Bali, the symbolic identification that Hertz pointed out can still be discerned.

Application of Hertz where secondary treatment is not found
Having examined four cases – the Berawan, Ma'anyan, Toradja,
and Balinese – where secondary treatment is found, we may
seem to have defined a universal Indonesian conception of
dying. But this is not so. For example, let us look briefly at the
eschatology of the Iban of Borneo. (The locations of ethnic
groups discussed in this chapter are shown in Figure 3.) The Iban
are neighbors of the Berawan to the south, and share many cultural features, such as longhouse residence. But they are far more
numerous, and, what is most significant from our point of view,
they do not practice secondary treatment of the dead.

Nor do they share Berawan ideas about death: Their eschatology is radically different. Iban funerals are extremely rapid. The
corpse is hurried out of the house soon after death, certainly on
the same day. The men carrying the corpse to the graveyard stop
at some convenient point along the way and prepare a rough
coffin from a log cut from a softwood tree. The corpse is stuffed
inside, and the coffin is tied up with rattan. Arriving at the graveyard, the coffin is buried in a shallow grave. Various grave goods
are left and a marker may be set up, and then the funeral party
returns rapidly to the longhouse. The corpse is not tampered with

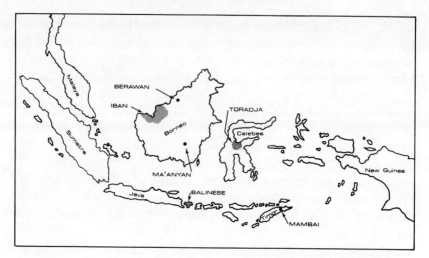

Figure 3. Indonesia and Borneo, showing the locations of ethnic groups discussed in the text.

again, and the graveyard is full of old bones dug from their shallow graves by wild pigs and other animals (Gomes 1911: 134–42; Jensen 1974: 93–4).

This disregard for the corpse and its fate is in striking contrast to the attitudes of the Berawan. Moreover, the Iban concept of dying is very different. Gomes (1911: 134) describes how the living and the dead are conceived of as engaged in a struggle for the dying person. The relatives cry "Pulai!" at the near-corpse ("come back"), and consider that the spirits of the dead are close at hand, pulling their new companion away from the living. This is very different to the Berawan spirits of the dead, who, far from coming to capture the newly dead, are unwilling to receive them into their company. This proximity of the dead explains the haste with which the Iban wish to have done with the corpse once death is pronounced.

The Iban ceremony that formally introduces the newly dead person to the spirits of the dead occurs on the *third day* after burial. A bundle of offerings is prepared, dedicated to the dead, and thrown out of the longhouse. Sometimes a song is sung recounting how this food is taken to the country of the dead by a bird. When the offerings are presented to the dead, they are pleased and warmly welcome their new member. Thereafter, the ghost of the dead person is not expected to trouble people (Gomes 1911: 139–41).

In some Iban communities, but by no means in all, another festival of the dead occurs, *gawai hantu*. There are many varieties of Iban *gawai: gawai batu*, the festival of the whetstones; *gawai benih*, the festival of the seeds; *gawai kenyalong*, the hornbill festival; and others. The festival of the dead is not different in format to these other gawai (Jensen 1974: 198), and they do not mark a change in status of those who died since the last celebration. They are an attempt to gain the supernatural aide of famous warrior ancestors regardless of when those ancestors died (Gomes 1911: 195–6; Perham 1896: 208–9).

The Iban case demonstrates that even within Indonesia ideas of the fate of the soul are found that are radically different from those expressed in Berawan, Toradja, and Balinese funerals. This would not have surprised Hertz, who warned against the overextension of his analysis: "We must beware of attributing to the various representations a generality and an explanatory value which they do not have" (Hertz 1960: 48). As we have already emphasized, not all the arguments that Hertz advances in his essay are of the same level of generality. The Iban funeral does not undermine his analysis of secondary burial rites; it simply provides a *negative case*, or control.

However, there are cases that present a more serious challenge for Hertz. In the Lesser Sunda Islands of eastern Indonesia, death rites are found that incorporate many of the ritual and symbolic elements that derive from the metaphor of corporeal dissolution, but do not involve secondary treatment of the corpse as defined in the previous section. Examples of this kind are described by Fox from Roti (1973, 1977) and Hicks from the Tetum of Timor (1976). We draw on material from the Mambai of Timor, recently described by Traube (1977).

First, the rites. At death, a corpse is immediately removed to the cult house of its agnatic descent group, where it is laid out on a mat. The corpse is dressed in ritually appropriate clothes, but is not put into a coffin. It is allowed to remain there for several days while all close kin are summoned. When the stench of the corpse can no longer be tolerated by the mourners, it is rolled into its mat and buried in the dancing ground at the center of the village. Because the dancing ground is not large, the bones of previous burials are often turned up in digging a fresh grave, and no great respect is accorded to these relics. In a ritually unimportant village, corpses may be buried just outside its perimeter. After burial, the corpse is not intentionally disturbed again. However, there is a festival or series of festivals that follow many years later that is concerned with the dead. This festival is called *maeta*, which means simply "death" or "the dead" (Traube 1977: 354–423).

At death, the nonmaterial component of the living person (*samakan*) becomes *maet samakan* (*maet* = dead person), and is conceived of as making a journey to the mountain of the dead to the west of the Mambai country. A vertical pole is erected beside the corpse, so that the soul may exit through the roof rather than using the door. The afterlife is considered to be much like the life of the living, but less burdened with troubles. The journeys of the dead are accompanied by elaborate ritual chants that name the places on the route.

The format of the festival of the dead is a repetition of the funeral, using a number of props to represent the already rotted corpse. The festival is held at irregular intervals to honor all those who have died since the previous one. It begins with a mimed reenactment of the death of an individual, who is represented by a pestle and mortar. After the inevitability of death is announced by divination, the implements are dressed in the cloths and ornaments used for a corpse. The kin are then summoned, as at a funeral. For the interment, the dead are represented by the betel nut bags that they used in life and which have been kept hanging in the cult house. It is these bags that are buried in the dancing ground, in a metaphorical second burial. Sacrifices and other prestations are made to the dead, who are thereby rendered wealthy and favorably disposed to the living. In the closing ritual of the festival, the dead are sent to their final home in the sea, and the festival is also called "to send away the dead." If this final rite is not performed, the dead remain upon the mountain, and may be enriched by yet another festival at a later date.

The journey of the dead to the sea is vaguely associated with their transition from the recently dead to the long dead. But the association is not important, and it lies on the hazy edges of Mambai dogma. Some people think that all the dead, recent and long dead, attend important rituals and influence the affairs of humans. Others consider that only the recent dead have this role. Nor is the afterlife in the sea clearly conceived, except as a reservoir from which they may be reborn into the living.

Sensu stricto, the Mambai festival of the dead is not an instance of Hertz's "great feast," either in the rites that are performed or in what those rites are believed to accomplish. They can therefore be seen as simply a negative case like the Iban. No secondary treatment of bones occurs. No fundamental transformation of the soul is accomplished that is geared to the fate of the corpse. The soul is not regarded as vindictive and in a miserable state during the putrescence of its vacated body. There is no horror of reanimated corpses, nor pronounced fear of the dead. In theory, the festival of the dead may occur immediately after death, and frequently it does not happen for twenty years.

However, these distinctions have to be drawn with great exactitude. From a slightly wider perspective, it is the *similarities* that are noticeable between this festival and rites of secondary treatment found elsewhere. The schedule of events is very similar to the Ma'anyan case: Invariably, at least a year goes by before the festival is made for any particular dead person, and then all those that have accumulated in the interim are dealt with jointly. Moreover, there is a transition of the soul accomplished at the festival, though in a rather weaker form from that found in Berawan rites: In the latter, the soul moves from near and dangerous to far and benign; in the former, it proceeds from relatively far away and generally helpful, to very far away and irrelevant (except as a supply of souls). Among the Mambai, the ghosts of the recently dead are not routinely dreaded, yet they cause alarm if they are seen, and if their mortuary rites are too long delayed, they may cause sickness.

But most of all, it is the constant reiteration in ritual language of the motif of the decaying corpse that is so strongly reminiscent of Hertz. The significance of this motif relates directly to fundamental ideas of Mambai religion and cosmology. These ideas are expressed in the most sacred and esoteric of their myths, which only the most knowledgeable ritual specialists know in its entirety. It is a creation myth. Impregnated by Father Heaven, Earth Mother gives birth to the mountains, the trees, and the first people. Having instructed her children about mortuary rituals, she dies. But her body docs not entirely decompose. An outer layer forms the "black earth," but beneath this topsoil formed out of her own body the Mother remains whole and pure, her white milk undiminished by death and decay. From this milk plants draw life, and in turn men and animals feed upon the plants (Traube 1977: 51–61).

The debt that humans owe to the Mother for the gift of life is the underlying motivation behind Mambai death rituals. That debt must be paid back with their bodies, which return to black earth again. Failure to return the debt would throw the entire cosmos out of kilter; plants would not grow to nourish humans, and children would not be born.

We have seen that attitudes to death and the decomposition of corpses are not universally the same. For the Berawan, with their fluttering spirits, corruption is an ugly necessity: Only through it can the soul be released from the appalling bonds of the flesh. But for the Mambai, the same process takes on a positive, life-renewing quality in and of itself. Where the Borneans, as Hertz showed, equate the fate of the soul with the fate of the corpse, the Mambai make an even stronger association. For them, disposal of the corpse affects the fate of the whole world of living things. The power of Hertz's approach remains plain. It explains why the Berawan recover the bones of the deceased, and also why the Mambai sit by and watch for as long as they can tolerate it, while the corpses of their kin rot away.

IV

DEATH RITUALS AND LIFE VALUES: RITES OF PASSAGE RECONSIDERED

LIFE THEMES IN DEATH

Death is a transition. But it is only the last in a long chain of transitions. The moment of death is related not only to the process of afterlife, but also to the process of living, aging, and producing progeny. Death relates to life: to the recent life of the deceased, and to the life he or she has procreated and now leaves behind. There is an eternity of sorts on either side of the line that divides the quick from the dead. Life continues generation after generation, and in many societies it is this continuity that is focused upon and enhanced during the rituals surrounding a death. The continuity of the living is a more palpable reality than the continuity of the dead. Consequently, it is common for life values of sexuality and fertility to dominate the symbolism of funerals.

We can carry our comparison of the variety of funerals to the westward limits of the Malayo-Polynesian culture area: to the island of Madagascar (see Figure 4). The forebears of the Malagasy inhabitants of the island sailed their outrigger canoes from Borneo and Indonesia thousands of miles across the Indian Ocean more than a millennium ago. Over the centuries in Madagascar,

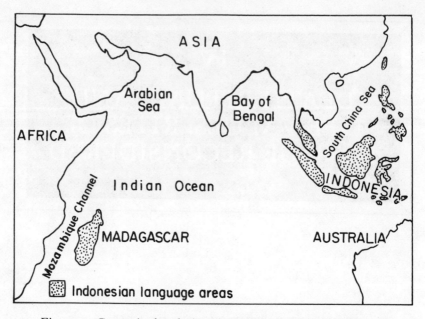

Figure 4. Countries bordering the Indian Ocean, showing the
distribution of speakers of Indonesian languages

these Indonesians mixed with peoples of Arab and African descent
to form the unique Malagasy culture and language. Even after
centuries of mixing and blending, and after long isolation from the
East, the Indonesian and Bornean elements still dominate Malagasy culture. The linguistic evidence suggests that the Malagasy
are most closely related to the Ma'anyan of Borneo (Dahl 1951).

The cultural variety within Madagascar is almost as great as
that that we have seen among societies of the Indonesian area.
The variety of funeral rites and tomb design is also very great;
some peoples construct large showy tombs, whereas other groups
dispose of their dead in secret and camouflaged caves. Yet, despite
the variation among the eighteen ethnic groups that comprise the
Malagasy people, the ritual of exhumation and reburial is of great
importance in almost all regions of the island. For instance, the
Merina people open the family tomb every few years, bring out
the skeletons, rewrap them in new cloths, add the newly exhumed

relics of those who have died since the last general tomb opening, and then replace all the relics and close the tomb. As the dominant ethnic group, the Merina have moved away from their homeland near the capital city and spread throughout the island. For these general exhumation ceremonies, kin from all regions converge on their ancestral hamlet as an expression of family solidarity and to arrange practical matters such as endogamous marriages (Bloch 1971). Among the Sakalava of the western region, only the relics of royalty receive this sort of periodic attention. The royal ancestors belong, in one sense, to everyone. Commoners do not exhume and rebury their own dead, but rather they attend the annual ritual treatment of the "national ancestors." Among the Bara people of the South, the focus of this chapter, each person is buried individually shortly after death and then later exhumed and placed in the family tomb. Details of secondary treatment of the dead are not available for all the Malagasy peoples, and so it is difficult to chart all the variations with accuracy. But it is clear that secondary treatment of the skeletal remains is an important custom that is called upon to give expression to various social and political values among the different ethnic groups.

These funeral rituals are the most important cultural institutions in traditional Malagasy societies. The expenditures of time and resources for death rituals and the maintenance of tombs are considerable, especially in light of the often meager economic base. The conspicuous burial of the dead is the central activity in Malagasy systems of religion, economics, and social prestige. Even a casual visitor to Madagascar quickly becomes aware of the large role burial customs play in the lives of the people. In many parts of the island, tombs, whose elaborate and solid construction far exceeds the care given to the houses of the living, dominate the landscape. During the cool season, one finds the roads full of people traveling to their family reburial ceremonies. Even in the taxicab on the way from the international airport, the visitor reads on the official list of cab fares that the rental rate for exhumations is negotiable.

Let us contemplate for a moment the implications of this centrality of death in Malagasy culture, for most of us belong to a society in which death is kept on the periphery of our experience. In order to begin to understand the death rituals of the Malagasy, or of many of the other peoples considered in this study, it is necessary to see that the social and cultural context of funerals is utterly different from that in our society. Death rituals, especially the seasonal reburials, are, in much of Madagascar, as normal and as pervasive as is Christmas or the Fourth of July in the United States. The Malagasy funeral-related institutions are both private and public affairs of religious as well as social significance, and they are a great expense to individual families and a stimulus to the general economy. These activities are closely associated with positive and central familial, social, and political structures, and this connection deprives them of that sense of abnormality and near indecency that seems to hover around funerals in most Western societies.

There is in most Malagasy funerals the sort of emphasis on life and vitality that Wilson described for the Nyakyusa, and which he suggested may be a universal aspect of death rituals. Certainly the themes of rebirth, love, and sexuality as symbols transcending death have been explored by countless poets and dramatists. If people feel the need to confront death with an emphasis on life, then, nonetheless, the theme will be uniquely implemented in societies that put death and the dead at the center of their social and moral system.

In our society, both sexuality and death belong somewhat outside the normative and public values pertaining to the family and the community. Hence love and death, sex and death, rebirth and death provide symbols whose great power is partly derived from the fact that they oppose everyday institutions. The relationships are very different in Madagascar, where death and funeral customs pertain to the ancestral order that is at the heart of the normative social system. Furthermore, this ancestral system directly requires the birth of new generations, and the ancestors themselves are seen as the most important agents encouraging virility and fertility. Funerals, social order, fertility, and all that these entail are naturally and positively related in Madagascar. The combination of themes of death and sexuality contains little of the antisocial power that these themes evoke in our cultural tradition.

Death Rituals and Life Values

PROBLEMS WITH HERTZ'S
AND VAN GENNEP'S APPROACHES

Both Hertz and Van Gennep were familiar with the funeral customs of Madagascar and both made important use of this Malagasy data in their studies (Hertz 1960: 47–8; Van Gennep 1960: 148–9). Van Gennep in particular was a leading authority on the religion of Madagascar and was the author of a major monograph on the topic (1904). Although the examples he cites in *The Rites of Passage* have a worldwide distribution, the elaboration of his theory is strongly influenced by his long familiarity with Malagasy ethnography.

There are, however, problems in the application of the theories of Van Gennep and Hertz to the ritual data of Madagascar. Both viewed such rituals as a symbolic representation of the ambiguous ("liminal") state of the deceased while in passage from life toward some fixed eternal condition. But, in spite of the widespread custom of secondary treatment of the dead in Madagascar, the emphasis on beliefs about the afterworld present in our Indonesian examples is lacking in Madagascar. There are few concepts of a journey of the soul, or of a land of the dead off somewhere in the distance. The dead reside in the tomb. This is not to say that eschatological concepts are entirely lacking. It is just that they are not important enough, explicit enough, or central enough to the culture to provide a basis for such elaborate rites of burial and reburial. Bloch (1971) has wisely noted this difficulty in his study of the secondary burial rituals of the Merina. He asked about the world of the dead and received scant information.

Hertz identified a metaphorical relationship between corpse and soul that makes sense of the rituals, large and small, of death in Borneo. The same is not true in Madagascar. There, a different significance is placed on the separation of bone and flesh that is celebrated in the rites of secondary treatment. In view of the discussion of cultural universals in Chapter 2, it comes as no surprise that there are symbolic uses of the corpse that achieve considerable generality without becoming universal even within a single culture area. How these differential symbolic elaborations arose is a matter for speculation. Meanwhile, it is interesting to note that

97

there are echoes of Malagasy notions about death in Bornean funerals, just as eschatological ideas are not entirely absent in Madagascar.

Ven Gennep's notion that a funeral ritual can be seen as a transition that begins with the separation of the deceased from life and ends with his or her incorporation into the world of the dead is merely a vague truism unless it is positively related to the values of the particular culture. The continued relevance of Van Gennep's notion is not due to the tripartite analytical scheme (separation, liminality, reincorporation) itself, but to the creative way it can be combined with cultural values to grasp the conceptual vitality of each ritual. In following this theoretical approach, it is necessary not merely to apply an old formula to new rituals, but in a sense to create anew the *rites de passage* in a dynamic relationship among the logic of the schema (transitions need beginnings and ends), biological facts (corpses rot), and culturally specific symbolizations.

The most striking aspect of Malagasy funerals is the bawdy and drunken revelry enjoined upon the guests. Malagasy participants state that these lively events are necessary because the deceased is in transition. He or she is isolated and lonely and needs to be amused and entertained. But such an explanation is obviously incomplete. It fails to tell us why these particular forms of entertainment are seen as the appropriate amusement for the spirit of a recently departed relative. Why drunkenness, sexual liaisons, and bawdy songs? Why not respectful hymns of praise or a decorous show of family morality and solidarity? To answer this and provide an analysis of the specific symbolic content of Malagasy funerals, one must look away from beliefs about ghosts and the hereafter and examine basic values and concepts about the nature and meaning of life.

BARA LIFE VALUES: ORDER AND VITALITY

We focus the rest of this chapter on one ethnic group of Madagascar, the Bara, sedentary pastoralists of the island's southern plains. Only by looking at one situation in some detail can we evaluate the several analytical aspects that have been discussed so far in this book. In a single case, we can view the complex interplay of the expression of emotion, ritual action, specific beliefs, the universal rite of passage schema, and the phoenix theme of rebirth with those basic values and categories that are pervasively important to Bara social life. The Bara, of course, cannot stand as a substitute for any other society either within or outside Madagascar. But they can stand as a demonstration of how people of one culture face squarely the fact of death.

A difficulty in the analysis of Bara funerals stems from the fact that although the rite of passage approach stresses the ambiguous and transitory aspect of dying, important Bara values stress that it is life that is transitory and dying that is tragically unambiguous. In terms of the Bara phenomenology of the person, life is maintained by a tenuously balanced combination of what can be referred to as "order" and "vitality." As a biological being, a person is formed when the fertile blood of the mother's womb is ordered and arranged by the sperm of the father during sexual intercourse. To be socially and economically successful, an individual must balance out his or her relationships with his mother's and father's families. A person's life is seen as a journey leading gradually from mother's womb to father's tomb. Bara kin groups, if they are to maintain themselves, must balance their members' desire for agnatic solidarity against the need to maintain affinal alliances. Dying, tombs, ancestors, father, and social order are explicitly associated by the Bara. Keeping this in mind, we seek to explain Bara funeral behavior with the hypothesis that they view death as an overdose of order upsetting the life-sustaining balance, and that much of the funeral behavior is an attempt to redress the imbalance through a symbolic increase in vitality.

By formalizing these Bara notions of order and vitality into a table of oppositions and extensions, it is possible to begin to understand how such conceptions articulate with the ritual behavior.

Order	Vitality
male	female
father	mother
semen	blood

Order	Vitality
bone	flesh
sterility	fecundity
dying	birth
tomb	womb

However, oppositions include relationships of many different natures.

> Consider the pairs black and white, and odd and even. . . . The first pair admits intermediates (grey and other colors), but the second pair does not. It is not the case that all colors are either black or white, but every whole number is either odd or even.
> [Lloyd 1966: 87]

Additionally, some terms admit only one opposition, whereas others may be opposed to several terms. "Male" can only be opposed to "female"; but "father" can be as easily opposed to "son" or "mother's brother" as to "mother," depending upon the context. By examining the above list of opposed pairs in terms of the varying natures of the oppositions, it is possible to begin to see in what ways the notion of death as a transition relates specifically to Bara culture.

As one moves down the above columns, the relationships of opposition become more and more extreme. The upper pairs are each complementary, with the two poles combining to produce viable existence (male/female, father/mother, semen/blood, bone/flesh). But for the other three pairs, this complementarity is replaced by a profound antagonism. In fact, this antagonism is so pronounced as to be almost inexpressible, for as the one column progresses toward the maximal order of the tomb, the other column progresses toward maximal vitality and chaos. We have used the terms "fecundity," "birth," and "womb" merely to indicate the sorts of attributes the Bara view in opposition to death. But actually, the opposite of pure order cannot be expressed in an orderly fashion. In reconsideration of the above table of symbolic oppositions and extensions, it is clear that there are two different relationships of opposition represented, one complementary and one antagonistic. The pair flesh/bone partakes of both these forms of opposition. Bone and flesh are complementary in the human body but become antagonistic when breath has ceased. The two columns presented above can be elaborated to express the change in the nature of the symbolic opposition that accompanies dying.

The corpse clearly occupies a "liminal" state between that conjunction of bone and flesh that is considered "life" and that separation of these substances that is considered "death." And, as Hertz and Van Gennep explained long ago, this understanding of the liminal nature of the corpse does much to explain the rites of burial, exhumation, and reburial that mark Malagasy, Bornean, and Indonesian funeral customs. But the sexual aspects of these funeral rituals relate more to the mortal consequences of this liminality than to the liminality per se. This consequence is that the dead, sterile order of bone is taking dominion over the ebbing vitality of the decomposing flesh. Reality has moved from a state of mediated equilibrium between order and vitality to a state of pure, fatal order. This extreme aspect of order cannot be mediated, but can only be opposed by the most extreme aspects of vitality. The sex and sex-related activities of the funeral nights are symbolic ammunition in the open warfare between the extreme ends of the polar continuum of the human condition (see Figure 5).

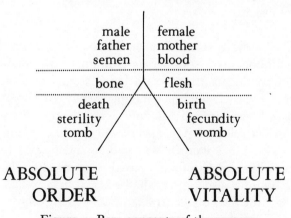

ORDER / VITALITY

male father semen	female mother blood
bone	flesh
death sterility tomb	birth fecundity womb

ABSOLUTE ORDER   ABSOLUTE VITALITY

Figure 5. Bara concepts of the person

Death as Transition

THE BARA FUNERAL SEQUENCE—
BURIAL, GATHERING, REBURIAL

Let us bring this abstract interpretation down to earth and see how this opposition between the male orderliness of death and the female vitality of life is worked out in the activities of the funeral-goers. The Bara perform a series of three ceremonies in the process of providing final disposition for each person. There are (1) the burial, which takes place in the first few days after death; (2) the gathering, which is a great feast celebrated after the harvest following the death; and (3) the exhumation and reburial after the corpse has completely dried and the flesh rotted away. This is the sequence for the deceased, but the living experience these rituals somewhat differently. Death and burial are often shocking events that disrupt the normal flow of village activity. But the gathering and reburial events are experienced as an annual season of festivities during which families go first up to this gathering, and then, perhaps the following week, over to that gathering; or to a nearby reburial celebration. It is partly in this sense that we suggested that funeral ritual in Madagascar is somewhat like Christmas to Western Christians. It is a seasonal event which is highly social and jolly, but also very serious and important. We will consider these rites in order – burial, gathering, reburial – and, in so doing, we can observe the relevance of Van Gennep's and Hertz's insights.

Burial The radical separation at death of the "male" and "female" components of the person is dramatically established in the first few moments after breath has ceased. The death is not immediately acknowledged or announced, but the preparation of the body and houses are quickly and silently begun. A male and a female house are selected. The corpse will rest in the female house for three days. Here women will gather and keep a long vigil punctuated with periods of loud ritual weeping. For this reason, the female house is also called "the house of many tears." In the "male house," the men of the stricken family will receive male visitors from whom they accept stylized expressions of condolence. The formality in the "male house" is striking with regard both to seating patterns and verbal exchanges. Here also the men will keep a vigil and organize the logistics of burial. At first, while these two houses are being cleared and arranged, all are enjoined to silence and weeping is forbidden. The most important task is the preparation of the body. The eyelids and jaw are closed. The limbs are straightened and the body is placed on its back. The jaw and limbs may be tied in place until the postmortem stiffening sets in. Quickly, after the last breath, while the body is still warm and soft, the personality is divided in two, as it were. The male aspect, deriving from the soon-to-be-joined ancestors, is represented in one house from which the burial is directed. Yet the corpse remains with the living, with the women, for a little longer.

The rigid separation of males and females is broken during the nighttime festivities. Girls must leave the "house of many tears" to sing and dance out in the courtyard where the young men come out to watch and gradually join in. Rum and food are served, a musician is hired, and these funeral nights generate an orgy of sorts. These festivities exhibit a very close, almost licentious relationship between males and females that is most unlike the normal cross-sex behavior patterns. All in all, the burial is a ritual of extremes. The sexes are almost absolutely separated by day and enjoined to an obscene, boisterous togetherness by night. There is also the extreme contrast in sound: Funeral activities are separated from the preceding normality by total silence at the time of death, which is then followed by loud wailing, singing, shouting, and gun shooting.

On the third day, the men enter the "house of many tears," put the body in a coffin, and take it outdoors over the tearful protests of the women. The coffin is covered with a cloth, which must be new and in an unsewn, unfinished state. At this point the coffin is carried around and around the "house of many tears" while unmortared, fertile rice is sprinkled in its wake. Several gunshots may be fired and the procession heads toward the burial mountain several miles away. The funeral procession stretches out over the countryside with the youths and young girls quickly leading the way with the coffin, followed at a distance by adult men, then women and children, and finally the family cattle herded at the rear. The youths with the coffin pull farther and farther in advance, running all the way, carrying the coffin in relays. Only those youths who have had sexual experience can take part in this episode, which is essentially a sexual contest between the girls and the boys for possession of the corpse.

The procession halts and regroups at a prearranged place about halfway to the mountain. At this point, the cattle are brought up and stampeded around and around the coffin while the young men vie with one another in the somewhat risky sport of cattle wrestling, which consists of leaping up onto the hump of one of the members of the stampeding herd and holding on as long as possible. When this is over, the young men and girls go on with the coffin to the burial cave, accompanied by two or three older men to perform proper burial. The remainder of the people sit and wait several hours for the party's return and make minor preparations for the final celebration.

At the tomb, an elder acting as "owner of the death" approaches, sprinkles rum on the entrance, and announces the presence of the mourners to the ancestors. The rocks are all taken away from the entrance and the principal workers and sometimes everyone present are served rum. The coffin is slid head first into the small opening of the tomb-cave. Most of the assistants feel safer entering the tomb feet first, in contrast to the corpse. After the coffin is properly placed inside, the assistants come out and the entrance is carefully closed and covered with large rocks. The elder then addresses the ancestors within:

> Here is your grandchild.
> Born here. Do not push him
> away, even from here.

Then the elder picks up a green branch and raps the entrance to the tomb several times, addressing the newly deceased:

> There you are, brother.
> If someone has bewitched you,
> then look for this tree.
> If it is God [Gods] who has taken you,
> who can command God, brother?

But if it is merely a person
who has bewitched you,
Then you take him, you bewitch him.

People say that the branch is like the new corpse, cut off but still wet. Before they become dry the witch too will die.

Gathering The gathering is the biggest, most important, and most elaborate event in Bara social life. Whereas at the burial ceremony there may be 50 to 100 people, as many as 500 people may attend a gathering. Whole families walk ten, twenty, or thirty miles and then move into the village for several days. A hundred liters of rum is considered very adequate for a burial ceremony, but at a gathering there are often 500 liters. Ten or twelve cattle are slaughtered, providing abundant beef for all. The gathering is essentially a conspicuous display of wealth. The rum is paraded before the people to be counted, admired, and anticipated, likewise the cattle. And even the girls, dressed in their finest clothes, are paraded single file before the crowd. All expenditures are announced to the public: the fee for the dance specialists, the amounts of money given to the wrestlers and cattle riders, the number of slaughtered cattle, and most important, the amount of rum. Normally, the Bara are quite modest about their material success, and they never boast of or even admit to the size of their herds or the success of their harvests. But a gathering is not a time for modesty.

Although these activities are largely a grand extension of the earlier burial ceremony, the gathering does not exhibit the extreme polarities that characterize the burial. In particular, the relations between the sexes are more normal. There is a women's hut and a men's hut as at the burial, but now women and men often enter the opposite hut for a variety of reasons. The young men and girls dance together at night, form liaisons, and couple discreetly; but their public demeanor is somewhat reserved. The bawdy songs and sexual taunts are notably absent. Also, the paradox of extreme grief and great celebration is diminished with the passage of time. Death and burial are sudden, unplanned-for, shocking events. Gatherings, on the other hand, are prepared, organized celebrations that occur each year at the same season. So, in spite of the huge consumption of resources and its association with the activities surrounding death, the gathering partakes of a regularity and normality that clearly distinguish it from the burial ceremony.

There is, however, a dark side to the gathering, which is due to the great danger of witchcraft. A witch causes illness or death by deftly slipping a minute amount of evil medicine into rum or food while serving it to the victim. Rum is considered to be especially dangerous in this regard, and I have seen Bara order that a liter bottle of valuable rum be poured out because its cork seemed to have been disturbed. Also witchcraft medicine is transferred from one person to another by being placed on the genitals before sexual intercourse. In cases of adultery, incest, and witchcraft, the victim suffers from a similar malady: a grotesque and fatal swelling of the stomach. It is no wonder, given this analogy between witchcraft, sexual excess, and gluttony, that a ceremony at which hundreds of people eat, drink rum, and copulate should generate a degree of inquietude regarding witches. Additionally, it is the dry season; the "wet branch" and the corpse are drying out fast. If the man was killed by witchcraft, time is running out for the responsible party. A gathering, then, is particularly dangerous, both because it is a perfect opportunity for witches in general, and because it is seen as the logical time for specific witchcraft attacks in retaliation for the death that has already occurred.

In summary, the gathering is characterized by multiple but related dangers. The standard entertainments of wrestling, cattle riding, and specialized dancing are all believed to be extremely dangerous to the practitioners, who must carry protective charms and observe numerous taboos. The risks of witchcraft, sex, incest, and adultery have already been explained. Rum is considered extremely dangerous, not only as a vehicle for witchcraft, but also because of its power of intoxication. I have seen gatherings that ended in large-scale fighting or individual hatchet attacks. Often, all the spears, clubs, walking sticks, and rifles, which Bara men always carry to these affairs, are collected and placed in a large pile some distance away before the rum is served. The occasion is beset by what the Western observer would classify as both natural and supernatural dangers. But the Bara do not seem to make such a distinction. They are concerned with the danger of unrestrained, excessive, and destructive vitality, whether it comes as a hatchet attack or a witchcraft attack.

Reburial   At the first burial ceremony, the deceased is placed in an individual coffin and put in the family tomb or in some other temporary location. After the flesh has decayed, the body is exhumed and the bones are cleaned and then put in the final resting place in the tomb. This reburial ceremony, which like the gathering takes place during the dry season following the harvest, is referred to by several names and euphemisms such as "doing the corpse," "dropping the tree or branch," and "moving the dried-out one." This activity lasts one day only and although there is usually rum, beef, music, and dancing, it is a smaller affair than the gathering. But it is ritually more important than the gathering. Although reburial can be delayed for many years, it is an absolute obligation of the descendants toward the deceased.

Inside the tomb are numerous large, decorated, communal caskets, each containing the dried bones of perhaps ten persons. The number of caskets varies, but the tomb of a well-established family may contain between ten and fifteen of these caskets. To the north are grouped the caskets containing the bones of all the male ancestors. Each skeleton is placed in its rightful position with that of its father. At the south, by the door, are grouped the caskets holding the bones of the female agnates. The bones of a woman are grouped with those of her sister, father's sister, and brother's daughter. Also in the female casket are the bones of young children of female agnates. These skeletons properly belong to the tomb of the father, but are given to their mother's family as an affinal prestation. Women are always buried in the tomb of the father, never with the husband. This common custom, "dividing the children," is the only way a woman can be buried with immediate kin. Otherwise a woman is cut off in death from her father (with whom she shares a common tomb but not a common casket), mother, husband, and children. The male caskets embody a lineal order of grandfather, son, and grandson; the female caskets are like collection boxes for the skeletal residue of this agnatic system.

If a corpse is to be moved from another location to the official tomb, then the "strong birds" leave early in the morning to exhume the body. The composition of the group of "strong birds" is very much like that at the burial, but now there are more senior male relatives of the deceased. At the opening of the temporary tomb (usually another cave), the "strong birds" take care to announce themselves, sprinkle a little rum on the rocks, and then drink the remainder. The old coffin is pulled out and opened and then the bones are scraped clean, rubbed with cow grease, and placed in a new cloth. All signs of grief are forbidden during these preparations, just as they are forbidden during the preparations immediately following death. The return down the mountain is also much like the burial procession, with everyone running and the boys carrying the remains in relays. They do not return to the village, but join the rest of the people already gathered at a pre-arranged location out on the savannah. There is one last wailing scene with both male and female kin joining in, and then the "strong birds" pick up the remains, perhaps a new casket, as well as clothing for the deceased, and start on the merry run up to the final tomb.

The tomb is opened with the usual rum sprinkling and drinking; the remains and other objects are taken inside and arranged. At reburial, new clothing is placed near the corpse to replace the now rotted unfinished cloth that he or she was originally buried in. The clothes are his or her "best," and often include Western items such as long trousers, shoes, used military uniforms, and even an occasional umbrella. One additional item brought to the tomb is a pair of horns from a newly slaughtered ox to be placed with those from previous reburials. At some tombs, there are as many as 100 pairs of ox horns placed in front of the wall opposite where the male caskets are grouped. When these arrangements are completed, the "strong birds" rejoin the group down in the savannah for a celebration with more beef and rum.

Bara reburial rites are much like the burial and gathering ceremonies. But in spite of the similarity of the feasting, drinking, dancing, running, and general merrymaking, there are important differences. The reburial activities take place entirely by day and entirely out of the village. There is little of the extreme polarity and paradox of the original burial, and little of the dangerous element so conspicuous at the gathering. Bawdy songs, professional dance troupes, wrestling matches, and cattle-riding contests would all be out of place at a reburial. Not surprisingly, the reburial signals a return to normality, one important aspect of which is that the deceased's spouse is finally free to remarry.

SYMBOLIC GENERATION OF "VITALITY"

The full funeral sequence is long and complex. Let us now focus our attention on the symbolism of one brief phase leading up to the initial burial. Dying, to the Bara, involves an imbalance in the components of human being. As we have indicated, the extreme and fatal dominion of "male" order must be countered by a radical increase of "female" vitality. Vitality is represented in songs, dances, and contests that express the interrelated themes of sex, birth, life, disorder, incest, danger, war, and fertility.

Songs These powerful themes are most explicitly presented in the lyrics of the girls' songs that continue throughout the pre-burial nighttime festivities. New songs come into fashion every year and the most popular songs of even recent years are rarely heard. Like popular music in much of the world, new songs rapidly replace old, but the themes remain the same from year to year. The most popular funeral song of 1970 was a clever and rousing piece of ribald double entendre.

> Now hide it
> Now hide it, boys
> Now hide it because there is a death
> Together let us copulate
> Together let us copulate, boys
> Now hide it
> Now hide it because there is a death

"brroo" flies the quail
To perch at the head of the *sely* tree
The eye wants to sleep?
The eye wants to copulate

"Brroo" flies the quail
To perch on a bump of a *sakoa* tree
The eye wants to copulate
The eye wants to ejaculate

"Brroo" flies the quail
To perch at the head of the mud
Hide it!
Hide it boys!
Now hide it because there is a death
Together let us copulate
Together let us copulate
Whether big
Whether little
Now hide it!

The onomatopoeic "brroo" of the quail is an expression commonly used to refer to ejaculation in sexual intercourse. The word for quail is also the word for belly. The word for eye also refers generally to any center, hole, circle, or vortex, in this case, the vagina. The vagina is also suggested by the word for mud, which refers generally to any wet slime or slipperiness. And the quail, according to the Bara, is quite incapable of perching either at the head or on the knob of a tree. There is the suggestive image of the quivering quail looking for the appropriate place to hide. First it tries the head of a tree, then a lower knob of a tree, and finally settles into the stickiness below. The comparison between these Bara songs and the long funeral travelogues of the Berawan elders discussed in the previous chapter is interesting. Playful sexual themes are also present in the Berawan song cycle, but they play a subordinate role to the songs pertaining to the land of the dead. By contrast, the sexual theme dominates all the funeral singing of the Bara.

Another popular funeral song takes up a serious related theme as the girls sing a lament on the difficulties of childbirth. This

song, like all these funeral songs, is sung at funerals and at no
other time.

> O bright red
> O I am hurting now
> O bright red
> I am hurting from this birth
> O bright red
> My breasts have fallen heavily
> O I hurt, mother
> Massage my stomach
> Make it easier

Energy When referring to participation in these preburial vigils,
the Bara say they are going to await *faha*. The word "faha" is difficult to translate, but its various usages and connotations include:
nourishment, ration, a live prestation to a visitor, rifle cartridge,
the winding of a clock, elasticity, rebound, resiliency, and energy.
Bara most commonly use the word in referring to a thin cow
(lacks faha) and as a name for those curing ceremonies that aim to
strengthen one who has been weakened by illness. In general, faha
signifies vitality, but the emphasis is on a potential, stored-up vitality rather than on the dissipation of energy in activity.

Here again there are parallels with Berawan practices. At Berawan funerals, there is an emphasis on lively, even tumultuous,
socializing and play. In Chapter 2 we described several energetic
games in connection with the making of noise. Horseplay among
young people is common at funerals, and is encouraged by the
older folk. Frequently this involves an element of flirtation, as
when a teenage girl attempts to rub pot black on the face of a
young man. Often such ambushes result in chases up and down
the longhouse, and melees involving dozens of people. During this
skylarking more body contact between the sexes is allowed than
would normally be tolerated, and young people think of funerals
as an opportunity to initiate new sexual liaisons. Although themes
of vitality play a less conspicuous part in Berawan than in Bara
funerals, yet Berawan do express the sentiment that displays of
exuberance are proper in order to offset the presence of death.

Death as Transition

The sleepy and the comatose are fair game for all manner of practical jokes.

Dance The concept of storing up vitality is perhaps evident in the mode of dancing associated with Bara funeral activities. The meaning of a dance style is less explicit than that of the lyrics of a song and perhaps less amenable to analysis. However, there is a definite contrast in style between funeral dancing and all other Bara dancing. In addition to the three funeral ceremonies, Bara also dance at circumcision and spirit-possession ceremonies. On these occasions, the dancing is wild and unrestrained, with dancers individually showing off their skills. At funerals, the girls dance in a slow, tight circle in front of the "house of many tears." One by one, the boys join so that there are often two or three circles, one inside another. The dancers in the innermost circle move very slowly forward in a tense double-time while those in the larger outer ring come down hard on the beat. Often one or two pre-adolescent boys dance at a languid half-rhythm very quickly around the outside of the other circles. Each succeeding circle (from outside) is tighter, faster rhythmed, and slower moving. The dance gives the appearance of the winding up of a human clock spring. It is this dancing combined with the girls running (while singing) around and around the hut containing the body that are seen by the Bara as the epitome of faha, vitality.

Cattle Cattle play important roles in Bara funeral events in two ways. First, there is the little cattle wrestling at the burial and gathering ceremonies. This sport of stampeding the herd around and around resembles a bovine version of the funeral dances (see Plate 3). When describing the event, Bara boys always emphasize the snorting, panting, and bucking of the cattle as signs of intense vitality. This sport is practiced at only one other occasion and that is at the sowing of the rice fields when the trampling hooves perform a plowlike function. The association of cattle with the fertility of the earth is also clear in a number of Bara legends. In one such tale, the cow states:

When I die do not bury me in a tomb but your stomachs shall
be my tomb. My head you shall not eat. Bury it in the earth.

Plate 3. Cattle wrestling at a Bara funeral.

After one week corn sprouts and rice, manioc, and sweet pota-
toes. And the herd too shall give you life. And this is why you
must offer up the first Fruits in thanksgiving. [Faublée 1947:
381]

Another legend recounts how God was once about to give all the
animals a potion of life so that death would be eradicated. The
cow accidentally drank the entire supply and because there was
no more to be had God advised the other animals to kill the cow
during times of danger and eat of its flesh, which contains the
force of life. This relates to the second role of cattle in the funeral
events, namely the slaughter of numerous cattle to provide for the
feasting. The killing of the cattle is done differently at funeral
events than at all other ceremonies. Whereas in other ceremonies
cattle are carefully sacrificed to facilitate communication with the
ancestors, at funerals cattle are slaughtered en masse so that the
living can protect themselves by absorbing the force of life inherent in beef.

Chaos: incest and war   An important aspect of the representation of vitality is the idea that it is chaotic, as opposed to the order of the ancestor cult. In one of the songs, the girls call upon the boys to act crazy, unrestrained, and shameless during the funeral fete. It is in this regard that rum takes on special significance. Rum is served not merely because intoxication is pleasant, but because disorderly conduct is essential.

The most important mode of generating a sense of disorder is through incest. For the neighboring Betsileo funerals, Father Dubois describes what he considers "the moment of horrors," when everyone copulates incognito with a total disregard for incest regulations (1938: 666). The Bara do not tolerate unexpiated incestuous intercourse, not even at funerals; but the songs, dances, and bawdy remarks exchanged among kin at a funeral would at any other time require the sacrifice of a cow in expiation. An actual attempt at intercourse with a relative at a funeral celebration constitutes a wrong and must be expiated. But the attitude of the Bara toward such incest is that it is an inevitable part of the funeral fetes and the offender should pay the penalty (one cow, bony) with good humor. The incestuous behavior of the participants in the burial and the gathering celebrations is in opposition to the fundamental Bara principle of moral and social order.

The dance troupes are also viewed as possessing dangerous and asocial qualities. They are hired for virtually every gathering and occasionally for a burial if the family can afford it, but they are prohibited from singing or dancing at any other function. Should such performers sing to a sick person, it is said that the patient will die. At the gathering celebration, the dancers perform only during daylight to stimulate and amuse the guests. At night, with the occasional exception of early in the first evening, it is considered far too dangerous to have them performing. They may not enter the village before the start of the gathering celebration and must be out of the village before the final closing ceremony. They dress outrageously. The men wear their hair in long braids entwined with coins and bells. They are explicitly dressed in the symbols of warriorhood, and no dancer ever dances without his elaborate spear. The dancing is wild and sexual, with particularly energetic dances being done to entice even more money from members of the audience. The dancers do not merely have low status, but are seen as being, in a sense, outside the system of social and moral order.

RESOLUTION: INTERCOURSE AND REBIRTH

During the time following death, extreme vitality is generated through the various excesses of the funeral celebration in an effort to counterbalance the extreme order of death. But this unstable situation cannot persist, and the funeral activities become directed toward effecting a return to normalcy. Because the instability of the situation derives from the antagonism between the bone and the flesh of the corpse, the resolution depends upon removing the corpse from the world of the living. For as long as the corpse in which bone (order) is taking dominion over flesh (vitality) remains, then the life-giving balance of order and vitality is impossible. In another Bara legend, a man with ten cows asks the king for advice because his cows are barren. The king says this is because the man did not bury his father, who died when he was young. The man then holds a funeral, builds a tomb, kills cattle and buries his father. Soon there are many new calves and his wife also gives birth.

The actual burial takes the form of a double metaphor of sexual intercourse and birth. First, the competition between order and vitality is intensified during the removal of the corpse from the village to the tomb on the mountain. This funeral procession resembles a "burial by capture" as the men enter (for the first time) the "house of many tears" and take away the coffin over the tearful protests of the women. The young men then run, carrying the coffin in relays, toward the mountain of the ancestors. A group of young girls, often with their hair and clothes disheveled, run and catch up to the coffin bearers to distract and detain them from their task. Often the girls intervene physically to stop the journey to the tomb and there ensues a tug-of-war over the coffin as the girls try to pull it back to the village. When this fails, the girls may run ahead and line up across the boys' path. The boys charge, using the coffin as a battering ram to penetrate this female barrier and continue toward the tomb.

This sexual symbolism is continued at the tomb itself as the coffin is poked head first into the small hole at the mouth of the cave. But the symbolism shifts as attention focuses on the arrival of the deceased among his ancestors. The dominant theme becomes that of birth, with the deceased entering the world of the ancestors head first like a fetus. When asked to comment on the meaning of burial, the Bara invariably use the metaphor of birth. This theme is evident as well in the song cited earlier and in the tomb-side address to the ancestors: "Here is your grandchild, born here. Do not push him away, even from here." Just as one must be born into the world of the living, so must one also be born out of it and into the world of the dead.

Bara burial is indeed concerned with the transition of the deceased from the world of the living to the realm of the dead, just as Van Gennep and Hertz would maintain. But the Bara recognize only one mode of transition that is adequate for changing the state of being for a human: sexual intercourse and birth. Not unexpectedly, the process of being born into the world of the dead is the inverse of the process of entering the world of the living. Biological conception begins with the chaotic fecundity of the mother's womb and menstrual blood, to which must be added the ordering power of the father's semen. Order is added to fertile vitality. Entering the tomb, however, is quite the reverse. The cessation of life and breath in the deceased has created a situation of sterile order, to which must be added a massive dose of vitality to accomplish the difficult birth into the world of the ancestors. Vitality is added to sterile order. It is not enough merely to bury someone, merely to dispose of the body. The survivors must bring about the successful conception and rebirth of their deceased kin into the world of the ancestors. This process, like the conception and birth of an infant, is a difficult and risky endeavor for both the deceased and his or her survivors. Should this transition fail, the consequence is nothing short of catastrophic infertility, with the deceased remaining like a dead fetus in the womb of his or her survivors' world.

Death Rituals and Life Values

During the burial ritual itself, then, the deceased, the living, and even the cosmos go through a period of transition: beginning with the separation from normalcy (the silence at the moment of death) and ending with a reintegration (rebirth at burial). This almost universal sequential ordering of a rite of passage is expressed through a uniquely Bara configuration of values relating to the two modes of structural opposition between flesh and bone. Because the notions of flesh and bone are closely associated with ideas of male and female, father's line and mother's line, ancestors and affines, and the ultimate human problem of reconciling unchanging order with the disruption of necessary renewal, the corpse is a powerful symbol relating the fate of the individual to the ongoing moral order of society. The imbalance of the male and female components of the corpse threatens the balance of the same components of the Bara social and moral universe. And it is only through the symbolic manipulation of these essentially sexual components that the corpse with its inherent imbalance can be removed.

But this burial rite of passage is not the end of Bara mortuary customs. Two ceremonies remain. For a situation as complex as death, there is not just one transition to be made but several. Each of the three Bara funeral ceremonies concentrates on a transition of a different sort. The burial is largely concerned with the transition of the corpse. The gathering is distinguished from the other ceremonies by the concern shown toward the reordering of social relationships that have been altered by the loss of a kinsman. This is manifest in the witchcraft fears and accusations that are largely concerned with the settling of social scores, especially with regard to the death of the person in whose honor the gathering is held. The affair closes with the granting of new names to the deceased and to some of the living, which is followed by a short speech stating that it is time to leave off yearning for the departed.

The reburial focuses explicitly on the transition of the remains from the individual coffin to the final resting place in the communal coffin containing the ordered bones of agnatic kin. The ritual itself is a miniature and subdued replication of the original burial. The exhumation is marked by the same mandatory silence and prohibition of weeping that mark the moment of death itself. There is a festive procession between the temporary burial place and the family tomb, ending with the placement of the bones in their proper place and the closing of the tomb. Separation, transition, incorporation. It is a rite of passage concerned with arranging the ambiguities that death creates in the organization of the ancestors. The proper relationship between the two worlds of the ancestors and the living is also reestablished.

Additionally, one can view the whole funeral sequence as a single rite of passage, seeing the original burial as a rite of separation, the gathering as a period of liminality, and the reburial as the ceremony of reintegration. It is a question of how wide a perspective one takes. There are transitions within transitions within transitions. For the Bara, all of life is ultimately a transition and only a perspective wide enough to include birth allows an understanding of death.

The deepest Bara value is vividly expressed in one of their legends about the origin of death. God gave the first man and woman a choice between two kinds of death. They could die like the moon, being reborn over and over. Or they could die like the tree, which puts forth new seeds, and, although dying itself, lives on through its progeny. It was a difficult decision, but the first man and woman chose to have children even at the cost of their own deaths. And which of us, asks the storyteller, would not make the same choice today?

PART III

THE ROYAL CORPSE
AND THE BODY POLITIC

V

THE DEAD KING

There is a paradox about death. On the one hand, it is the great leveler, badge of our common mortality. As Hamlet reflects:

> Alexander died, Alexander was buried, Alexander returneth
> to dust; the dust is earth; of earth we make loam;
> and why of that loam whereto he was
> converted might they not stop a beer barrel?
> Imperious Caesar, dead and turned to clay,
> Might stop a hole to keep the wind away.
> O, that that earth which kept the world in awe
> should patch a wall t'expel the winter's flaw!
>
> *(Hamlet, Act V, scene i)*

Yet, earlier in the play, the worldly Rosencrantz conveys a very different sentiment:

> The cess of majesty
> Dies not alone, but like a gulf doth draw
> What's near it with it; or 'tis like a massy wheel
> Fixed on the summit of the highest mount,
> To whose huge spokes ten thousand lesser things
> Are mortised and adjoined which when it falls,
> Each small annexment, petty consequence,

> Attends the boisterous ruin. Never alone
> Did the king sigh, but with a general groan.
>
> *(Hamlet, Act III, scene iii)*

It is to this latter theme that we attend in the third part of this book. We examine the funeral rites of great men in societies large and small: the Dinka "masters of the spear" and the pharaohs of Egypt; the chiefs of Borneo and the monarchs of Renaissance France. For present purposes, we stretch the word "king" to embrace them all.

In some of the stricter sects of Islam a conscious effort is made to stress the "leveling" aspect of death. So, for instance, the kings of Saudi Arabia are buried with spartan simplicity, their only monuments being rough piles of stones. They are the exception. More frequently, the death of a king sets off a tremor of ritual activity that climaxes in a display of national pomp unrivaled even by the coronation of a successor.

Royal death rites are special because they are part of a political drama in which many people have a stake. Especially in kingdoms in which the state was personified by the monarch, the king's funeral was an event that reverberated with far-reaching political and even cosmological implications. Royal deaths often set in motion powerful ritual representations of unifying values designed to offset a blow that leaves society "stricken in the very principle of its life," to use Hertz's phrase. Moreover, for the citizens, the king-as-hero encounters a death that is the archetype of the end of Everyman. In almost all situations, one finds that the remains of the dead king have great symbolic, and hence political, importance.

Even in modern bureaucratic systems, the funerals of heads of state are often grand and highly politicized events, and their corpses subject to national cults. Consider Lenin in his glass coffin in Red Square. He has probably been seen by more people than any other leader in history. In his will, he asked to be buried simply, in accordance with his egalitarian principles. But he was overruled; his successors still needed him. Later, the corpse of Stalin came and then disappeared, according to political expediency. Another example concerns a counterestablishment figure, whose remains wandered about homelessly, in contrast to the solid permanence of Lenin. They were those of Eva Perón, wife of the Argentinian dictator. During her husband's period in power, she gained a saintly reputation among the working classes. After her death and his fall, her relics were shunted about two continents to serve as a rallying point for the Peronista faithful.

In this chapter, we look at royal funerals to see how they express and influence the social order. We focus on the corpse, seeing how it is manipulated to serve the ends of the living.

ROYAL FUNERALS IN THE INDIC STATES OF SOUTHEAST ASIA

Royal rituals were extremely important in the numerous Indic states that rose and fell in Southeast Asia after the fourth century A.D. In several respects, these polities contradict our notion of the state. They did not so much possess territory as a center. Frequently, the names of the kingdoms were those of the capital city, which was conceived of as the pivot of a mandala, or set of concentric circles. At the very center lay the royal palace; outside that the city; then the royal realm; and beyond that lesser tributary polities in idealized patterns of eight, sixteen, or even thirty-two units. This conceptual plan rendered the kingdom as a miniature reproduction of the cosmos. At the center, the palace represented Mount Meru, the pillar of the universe, and the king and his nobles the divine hierarchy.

We would be wrong to assume that these sublime associations translated into a totalitarian state. On the contrary, each tributary unit was based upon its own smaller-scale reproduction of the cosmic plan, and each operated with considerable autonomy within its own borders. As one traveled farther from the center, the authority of the king decreased, until one entered the periphery of some neighboring state. Moreover, these semiautonomous tributary units maintained pretensions of their own, and were capable of becoming independent centers that, in time, might compete with their one-time suzerain or even absorb it. For these reasons, S. J. Tambiah, whose recent study we draw on, describes these polities as "pulsating" (Tambiah 1976: 102–9, 112–13).

The king was not only unable to administer his realm in any real sense, he was also hard pressed to extract agricultural produce from it with which to support his center. Even in relatively strong polities, the majority of the surplus extracted from the peasant producers was retained at successive local levels to support the courts of nobles. Though the gross amount collected was large, only a trickle arrived at the capital. The best the king could hope for was a large force of peasants for brief periods only, enough to attempt a prestige building project or a rapid military campaign. Nor could the peasants be too heavily exploited, because they would then be tempted to shift their allegiance to some other lord, or even another state. The only secure royal income was from the monopolistic control of trade (Tambiah 1976: 129).

It is within this framework of cosmic pretension and chronic competition that royal funerary rites in Southeast Asia must be seen. We examine them in two kingdoms that survived more or less intact into the twentieth century, and that have been the subject of recent studies.

Thailand: the enshrinement of royal relics Over the several centuries of its existence, the Thai kingdom experienced variable fortunes. It engaged in constant warfare, not for land, which was plentiful, but for population. Whole villages were detached from neighboring states and resettled within the royal orbit. More debilitating were the frequent wars over succession. Because the Thai kings had many wives and concubines, as a device for establishing kinship links with influential families throughout their realms, there was always a good supply of claimants to the throne. From the foundation of Ayutthaya, succession passed through younger brothers of the legal heir, uncles, half-brothers by royal concubines, minor members of the royal family, and downright usurpers (Smith 1967). It is here that mortuary rites become significant. This account comes from Quaritch Wales (1931), and mainly concerns nineteenth-century Thailand, although the rites have also been employed in this century.

After death is pronounced, the king's corpse is washed, dressed in fine clothes, and displayed briefly on a bier. Then it is folded with the knees drawn up under the chin and inserted in a large golden urn. The urn is stored on a catafalque in a special hall of the palace for a minimum of 100 days, and usually much longer. Food is regularly placed before the king's urn. At the funeral of King Rama VI in 1925, the food was prepared by the king's own chef and served at his habitual mealtimes. The liquids of decomposition of the corpse are collected in a vase (also made of gold) below the urn (Wales 1931: 137–48).

These details strikingly recall Bornean practices described in Chapter 3. But secondary processing shows greater technical elaboration, involving cremation, the collection of bone fragments, and the storage of these relics in a shrine. Soon after the death of the king, work begins on the erection of the "funeral pyre," which is an imposing structure with a series of concentric terraces from which emerge four tall columns supporting a conical spire (see Plate 4). These columns are fashioned from massive teak trunks that were in past times as much as 250 feet in length and 12 feet in circumference. The cone atop the building represents the sacred mountain of Meru. The pyre proper is prepared on the top terrace, under the spire. The whole is magnificently carved and gilded (Wales 1931: 145).

After a suitable period has elapsed and preparations are complete, the urn containing the remains of the deceased king is brought to the pyre amid much pomp. In a special pavilion adjacent to the pyre, the bones are removed from the urn, washed with scented water, anointed with perfumes by the new king, wrapped in a white cloth, and placed in a sandalwood box that in turn is placed atop the pyre. At sundown the fire is lit, and carefully controlled all night to provide for complete combustion without the main structure catching fire. Spices are burnt in the fire to make a pleasant aroma.

In the morning, the fire is extinguished and the new king and members of the royal family search through the ashes for fragments of bone. Some fragments are given to the children of the dead monarch to be worn in gold lockets. The remaining relics are placed in a golden container and carried in state to the palace, where they comprise the focus of a royal cult. The ashes of the

Plate 4. Funeral pyre of King Rama VI. The pyre proper was
lit at the top of the staircase, under the roofed structure
(from Wales 1931: 145).

funeral pyre are stored in a monastery favored by the dead king
(Wales 1931: 144–54).

Wales includes his discussion of cremation rites under the section of his book dealing with "Ceremonies of Installation." He
explains this paradox in terms of the similarities between the coronation of a Thai king and his funeral, so that the cremation can be
seen as a "Spiritual Coronation" (1931: 162). The scale of the
mortuary rites is actually greater than that of the coronation.

Prior to insertion in the urn, the newly deceased king's body is
dressed in embroidered silks, diamond-studded baldricks, gold
shoes and epaulets, heavy gold bracelets and anklets, and a
golden mask. The new king then places the late king's personal
crown upon the head of the corpse, to which all present make
obeisance. These accoutrements are richer than any worn by the
king in life. They are retained in the urn during primary storage,
and only removed immediately before cremation.

The procession of the urn to the pyre is stately. Excluding its
contemporary military units, the funeral procession of King Rama
VI in 1926 comprised:

troops
THE ROYAL FUNERAL PARTY
two three-tailed flags
160 red drums of victory
20 silver drums of victory
20 gold drums of victory
headmen of the pipe and war drum
20 blowers of the foreign bugles
28 blowers of the Siamese bugles
4 blowers of conch shells
2 seven tiered umbrellas, 6 five tiered, and four sunshades
3 sword bearers
a bearer of the priest's fan
royal car with a prince reading the scriptures
4 sword bearers
a royal umbrella, sunshade and fan
8 representatives of Indra with lances
8 representatives of Brahma with lances

civilian guards
umbrella bearers
6 sword bearers
THE GREAT FUNERAL CAR, bearing the urn, and drawn by
200 soldiers and six royal horses
a royal umbrella, sunshade and fan
16 representatives of Indra and Brahma bearing
silver and gold ornamental trees
2 seven tiered umbrellas, 10 five tiered and
8 sunshades
2 palace officials with personal effects
4 sword bearers
32 pages
4 chargers with grooms
KING PRAJADHIPOK'S PARTY
8 royal lictors
the Monkey Standard and the Garuda Standard
THE KING, walking
royal umbrella
10 aides-de-camp
princes of the royal household
representatives of foreign states
high government officials
military units with bands

This procession was similar to that for the coronation of King
Prajadhipok some time before, and more splendid (Wales 1931:
108, 148–9). Both processions were loud with drums, bugles, and
military bands.

Until recent times, during royal funerals the fields surrounding
the pyre were alive with stalls providing free food and drink for
commoners, stands for the sale of fireworks, and theatrical entertainments and sideshows of many kinds. It is clear that the cremation of kings is popularly regarded as a time for jubilation.

The ideology behind the similarity of funerals and coronations
is compatible with both the Brahminic and Buddhist traditions
represented in the Thai court. It conceives not of a single corona-

tion, but of a series of ascending grades of anointment spread over the lifetime of the monarch – a periodical renewal of the divinity of the monarch. Wales mentions several of these (1931: 121–5), and for one of the most exalted a representation of the sacred mountain is prepared not unlike the one fashioned for the funeral pyre. The anointment of the king's bones with scented water and spices just before cremation is simply the last and most important in a series of anointments.

The political significance of these sumptuous rites was profound. First, and most important, they served to refocus attention on the center. Given the parameters reviewed above, it was crucial, even for a resilient and enduring state like that of the Thais, that the prestige of the royal court be maintained. Any tarnish on its claim to be the most sublime representation of the cosmos immediately translated into a diminished orbit of influence. Second, the mortuary rites not only provided a major opportunity, if not *the* major opportunity, for ritual display, they also occurred at a dangerous moment of transition. Even when struggles for the succession did not break out, or were rapidly stifled by a few deft assassinations, a certain period of vulnerability was inevitable. The format of the death rites provided an opportunity to combat this vulnerability, because of the way that the rites of succession were nested within them. Because the cremation of the old king must await the drying of his bones, the coronation of the new king preceded it. At the final rites, the new king was present for all to see. Paradoxically, the funeral could be used to express the continuity of kingship, and this is no doubt the reason why even usurpers found it expedient to give sumptuous cremations for their predecessors.

Third, the secondary treatment of the corpse resulted in the production of royal relics that reinforced the centripetal tendencies of the kingdom. Stored in the palace, they formed a kind of charismatic stockpile, distilled from the genius of ancient kings. The eighteenth-century king Boromakot seized the throne from a better-qualified heir by a daring military stroke, climaxing in a brisk fight for control of the palace. After the palace fell, the legal heir was slowly abandoned by his allies. As he moved away from the palace, his claim became steadily less credible, until he finally suffered the fate of unsuccessful competitors for the crown (Wood 1926: 231–3, 238–41).

Bali: royal cremations as public theater On the island of Bali, much the same dynamic can be seen in funerary rites, if anything in even more pronounced form, as Clifford Geertz has shown (1974a). He describes the several small states of nineteenth-century Bali, not as a neat set of well-demarcated realms, but as a highly complex web of dissimilar political ties thickening here and there into nodes of varying size, the centers of states and client nobles. Within the same village, there were peasants that owed allegiance to different lords through the intermediary of a host of seneschals. But the role of the lord was limited anyway. He played no part in the organization of agricultural production, or even in the administration of law in the village. The peasant was neither a tenant nor a serf. The duties that he owed to his lord were those having to do with support of the center – participation in ritual and, secondarily, war. Although the threat of war was always present, other tools were preferred, such as cajolery, bluff, and alliance, because the prize was prestige, not territory. Geertz characterizes the role of the peasant, not as a subject, but as a stagehand or *claquer* in an endless pageant (1974a: 18–28).

Mortuary rites figured largely in that pageant. In Chapter 2, we described the sequence of Balinese mortuary rites. For those of modest means, they involve primary interment in a simple grave, with the possibility of final cremation when funds become available or when an opportunity occurs to join the cremation ceremony of a kinsman or patron, perhaps many years later. For priests and nobles, burial is not appropriate. Their corpses are stored within the courtyard of the house or palace for at least forty-two days – the conventional time required for putrefaction to be completed. When the necessary resources have been assembled, the bones are lustrated a final time, carried to the cremation ground, and burnt. An identical religious significance informs every cremation, regardless of whether the individual participates as principal or client, and irrespective of the cost of the proceedings. However, the scale, elaboration, and drama of the rites vary widely. In the present context, it is only the most grandiose that concern us.

The cremation of an important man is an event that attracts people from all over the island, and nowadays even from overseas. The tower (*bade*) in which the bones are transported to the cremation ground amid milling crowds is a favorite topic of Balinese painters. The tower itself is a representation of the cosmos. Around its base, demons swirl in carved relief. In the middle, the world of men is represented by a little "house" in which the bones of the deceased are placed, and at the top are realms of the gods, symbolized in tiers of conical Meru roofs. The number of these roofs indicates the level of heaven to which the soul of the deceased aspires: the single one of the commoner, three or five for the lesser gentry, seven or nine for a lord, and eleven for a king of one of the major realms. Preceding the bade tower come orchestras, dancers, bearers of the animal-shaped coffin in which the bones are to be burnt (a different variety for each class), carriers of sandalwood, heirloom weapons, regalia, and trays of offerings. Then there are women carrying holy water, doll-like effigies of the dead, and offerings to the lords of hell. Next, the high priest on his lotus chair, chanting mantras, and connected by a long cloth to the close relatives of the deceased and the bade tower. Behind the tower come the palanquins of the wives of the dead king, who formerly might choose to sacrifice themselves in the flames of his pyre. Finally, a long trail of the towers of lower-class people who have awaited this opportunity to disinter their dead for their final rites (Wirz 1928: 86–99; Plate 5).

The height of the bade tower, the fineness of its decoration, the number of people required to carry it, the number of attendants and towers of the commoners (often hundreds of them, with dozens of corpses to a tower) – all express the status of the deceased. But, as Geertz makes clear (1974a: 7–8, 56–7), more than counting and measuring are involved. The ceremony is also assessed in terms of its impact as drama. The principal actors must preserve a perfect serenity while an explosive burst of chaotic energy swirls around them. There are mock battles to delay the loading and unloading of the bones of the king, spinning of the tower to confuse bad spirits, scrambling for coins in the mud

Plate 5. Tall bade towers stand beside the cremation ground in
an elite Balinese funeral. Later they will be torn apart by the
crowd. The ashes of the funeral pyre are strewn upon the sea
(from Covarrubias 1937, with the permission of
Alfred A. Knopf, Inc.).

along the route, and plundering of the tower at the cremation site
after the bones have been removed, all amid the clangor of war
music.

Cremation is the largest and most expensive of royal rituals.
According to Geertz (1974a: 55), it is the rite most thoroughly
dedicated to the aggressive assertion of status, a "headlong attack
in a war of prestige" that pervades much of Balinese culture.
Goris (1955: 126) compares it with a potlatch.

In Bali, numerous political units were engaged in constant
rivalry to maintain their autonomy and extend their influence.
What they competed for was not land but allegiance. The carefully staged cremations of kings were a principal weapon by
which their successors maintained or advanced their standing.

The Dead King

THE BERAWAN OF BORNEO:
CHIEFLY LEGITIMIZATION
THROUGH DEATH MONUMENTS

The Berawan of Borneo comprise neither a populous centralized state like the Thais, nor a complex of highly stratified and competing realms like the Balinese. By comparison, Berawan society is small in scale, relatively egalitarian, and composed of just four autonomous ritual and political units – the separate longhouse communities. Nevertheless, extended death rites play an even more important part in its ongoing political process than in that of the Thai and Balinese states, because they affect the survival of the entire community.

In Chapter 3 we saw that, among the Berawan, secondary treatment is not extended to every corpse, and that an abridged ritual sequence is more common. The question raised there was the ideological rationale, or meaning, of the two types of funeral. We argued that they both reflect an identical eschatology. Now we take up a different question: Given the ritual equivalence of the two sequences, why are some individuals picked out for special attention? Complex considerations of prestige are involved. Though political and religious specialization and differences of wealth do not exist among the Berawan to anything like the degree that they are found among the Thais and Balinese, yet there *are* differences of rank among the Berawan, and only those of superior rank merit nulang. Only they can muster the necessary resources and support: rice to feed the large crowd of guests, to prepare rice wine for them to drink, and to feed the specialists working on the tomb; the social standing to attract the guests in the first place; and the solid support of the community so that its members are willing to fish, hunt, work on the tomb, and prepare food endlessly, in order to make the event a success reflecting credit on all concerned.

However, a problem arises in specifying the conditions making for nobility. Claims to high rank rest upon relationships to the great men of the past, whose names are frequently heard in prayers and whose spirits are thought of as protecting the community.

Almost invariably, these great men are titled Penghulu ("chief")
or Orang Kaya ("rich man"). The former is now employed by
the Malaysian government to designate men selected to act as
official chiefs. Previously, the British colonial administration used
it, and the regime of Rajah Brooke before that. Before 1882, the
Sultan of Brunei used both titles to honor upriver potentates who
earned his favor. These two titles have been in use by the Berawan for more than a century and serve to denote undying reputation. But some individuals achieved the same level of immortality
without outside recognition. The famous rebel chief, Aban Jau,
caused much trouble to authorities on the coast, and was never a
candidate for honorific titles. Undismayed, he styled himself
Rajah Ulu (king of the interior). His name still glitters in the
genealogies of several important Berawan.

But these genealogical claims alone cannot explain differences in
rank. In a small, largely endogamous community that recognizes
all consanguineous links as equally valid without discrimination of
sex or birth order, there is hardly a single person that cannot
dredge up *some* link to a great man, even if sometimes obscure and
of dubious validity, to back up a claim of high rank.

Part of the answer lies in residence. In each longhouse, one
family apartment is designated as that of the chiefly family, the
former residence of the last outstandingly prestigious man of the
community. Because a new longhouse may well have been built in
the interim, it is obviously not the physical structure that is
referred to. Residential social units have an existence over time
that outlasts the individual members, and indeed they are the only
corporate groups of Berawan society of which this is true, apart
from the longhouse community itself. They are, for example, the
groups in which land rights are ultimately vested. A prestigious
man will attempt to ensure the continued high rank of his residential unit by keeping the cleverest of his sons at home and import-
ing a wife for him, *contra* the almost universal Berawan practice
of uxorilocality. Such marriages require the payment of brideprice
and in themselves confer status. Lacking sons, or able sons, the
prestigious man will try to import a husband of known ability for
his daughter. After the demise of the great man, the favored son,
or the husband selected for the favored daughter, becomes head of

the household. Such a household is often larger than other households in the community, having perhaps retained both sons and daughters and their spouses. When a new longhouse is constructed, the group may choose as a matter of convenience to split into several apartments in the new structure, but the one containing the chosen heir will be designated as the continuing residential group of the prestigious dead man, from which the others are offshoots. In this way, a chiefly apartment may persist over a period of time and through a succession of longhouses.

From this it will be seen that factors of noble birth are interwoven with personal achievement to create the individual of high rank. To maintain the advantage of high birth, the aspiring young man needs to demonstrate adeptness at cajoling or bullying the fellow members of his community; in short, he needs his own charisma. Berawan nobles are neither born nor created, but both.

High rank is a prerequisite of extended mortuary rites. But there is no simple equation in this. A high-ranking person is also more likely to have on hand the stocks of rice necessary to proceed with a large-scale funeral immediately within a framework of abridged death rites. Far from connoting inferior status, such a procedure makes plain the wealth of the family, and may be preferred if death occurs soon after the harvest and if a suitable tomb is already available to house the deceased. If death occurs at an inconvenient moment or rice stocks are low, a nulang festival will be planned for a later date. One thing, however, makes selection of the extended sequence absolutely necessary, and that is the decision to build a new death edifice.

Berawan mausoleums vary considerably in style. Some are single massive posts up to forty feet tall and four in diameter, with a small niche in the top to accommodate one small jar. Others have chambers varying in capacity from one to forty coffins or jars, supported six to thirty feet above the ground on one, two, four, five, six, or nine posts, or sitting on the ground, or even underground. The aboveground styles are frequently elaborately decorated with fine incised carving in floral, abstract, and anthropomorphic designs, filigree buttresses and ridgepoles, all highlighted in red, white, and black. Often they are decorated with expensive brassware or pottery. Invariably they are carved out of

Plate 6. Finely carved Berawan mausoleum, with five supporting posts. It stands over thirty feet tall. Originally, it was painted with bold curlicue designs, which have now weathered.

dense hardwoods (see Plate 6). Their construction requires a considerable effort on the part of a community with a simple, shifting agricultural system and little specialization.

Such tombs are to be found in the graveyards adjacent to every longhouse site occupied for any length of time. If one searches them out, as the anthropologist is wont to do, one finds them for the most part in twos and threes near the riverbank, spaced at irregular distances going upriver. This spacing is a consequence of Berawan migration over a prolonged period out of the hilly center of northern Borneo westward down major rivers toward the coast.

As the ancestors of the Berawan moved slowly downriver, they set aside a place for the building of tombs adjacent to each successive location. The wood from which the tombs were built is remarkably durable, and each former graveyard where their remains can be detected indicates a previous longhouse. Longhouses themselves tend to become dilapidated after twenty or thirty years, and then there is a strong tendency for people to spend more time at their farms, or even to fragment into smaller daughter longhouses consisting of a few households whose farms happen to be close together. These centrifugal forces are frequently exacerbated by factional quarrels and, if leadership is weak, the community can easily fall apart. In the last century when warfare was endemic in central northern Borneo, this situation was highly dangerous. A large war party could destroy a scattered population, whereas they would find a properly defended longhouse discouragingly formidable because of its greater manpower, solid construction, and elevation on massive piles – a veritable fortress, in fact.

Only when a new leader of exceptional ability appears can such incipient fission be reversed and the entire community cajoled into unified action. Because disunity was, in the last century, a matter of danger, so a supply of charismatic leaders able to overcome the egalitarian quarrelsomeness of individual Berawan was vital.

That this need was real is demonstrated by the fate of other small ethnic groups living in the Lower Baram in the nineteenth century, when large war parties swept downriver in search of plunder and slaves. The chaos that they caused is recorded in the journals of anxious European observers. These warlike expeditions originated from the relatively numerous Kayan and Kenyah folk who were newly arrived in the Baram watershed. In this situation, several of the small downriver groups moved farther toward the coast and put themselves under the protection of coastal Muslim peoples. Today these groups are assimilated into Malay culture. The Berawan gathered together in large fortified houses. At one point, the ancestors of three of the four present-day Berawan communities all lived together, along with some allied groups, in one heavily defended site. The remaining Berawan community was in a less-vulnerable location away from the major routes of travel of the war parties, but even so found it advisable to share a longhouse with another small non-Berawan group. The Tring – longtime rivals of the Berawan – neither fled toward the coast, nor allied themselves with other groups, nor even settled their own factional disputes. Instead, they relied on the infamous fierceness of their warriors. By the turn of the century, they were virtually extinct. A small remnant now lives absorbed into one of the Berawan villages.

What emerges is a model of the life cycle of the longhouse, related to the career of the great man associated with it. Construction or reconstruction begins as he first succeeds in commanding allegiance, and proceeds as he reaches his prime. During his vigor, the community is active and unified. After his death the house declines, matching its ruin to his.

It is within this historical process that the construction of mausoleums must be understood. The longhouse is itself a monument to the authority of its leaders. But the construction of a new longhouse may take many years. Each household bears primary responsibility for its own apartment, and some are slower to build than others. Moreover, it is the community as a unit that is emphasized. What the new leader requires to cement his position is a demonstration of community solidarity behind him personally.

The building of mausoleums provides an opportunity for such a demonstration. Funerals have an important integrative function. The obligation to assist in the funeral of a fellow community member is the most basic duty of longhouse residence. To fail to do so consistently is to break the link with the community. It is therefore a particularly appropriate theme to emphasize when unity is being consolidated. Even for a poor person, every household will try to provide a little assistance and will send a representative to keep the vigil each night that the corpse is in the house. For members of the most important family, more vigorous participation is prompted as a matter of pride, in view of the numerous visitors summoned from neighboring houses. The emergent leader must channel and build upon these sentiments.

However, it would be unthinkable to prepare a mausoleum for someone not yet dead. Even the slightest preparation for death is proscribed among the Berawan. On the other hand, the emergent leader can hardly wait to aggrandize himself until after he dies. The solution is simple, and it explains a feature of the mausoleums that confused the ethnographer for some time. All mausoleums are known by the person for whom they were prepared, and paradoxically these people often turn out to be nobodies. Further investigation reveals their special merit: They were relatives of emergent leaders (affines or consanguines, but residents of the same apartment) who *happened to die* at the right moment. In honoring them with a mausoleum the leader ennobles himself.

If the longhouse life cycle runs its course, the great man may himself occupy a humble grave, because the community is left disunited by his passing. The exceptions are cases where the important man shares the tomb he originally built for another, or where he succeeded in begetting, adopting, or recruiting a young man capable of commanding respect in a similar fashion. In this regard, the building of mausoleums is also important because it ennobles the heir as it establishes the legatee.

There are many reasons, ideological, symbolic, and social, why mortuary rites are central to Berawan religion and society. But it is not hard to see why they are utilized by leaders in order to make a statement about their own positions. Weddings and other rites of passage also provide an opportunity for community cooperation and conspicuous consumption. The Kenyah, close neighbors of the Berawan, employ name-giving ceremonies as their most important ritual of prestige. But the Kenyah have a more rigid system of prescribed rank than the Berawan, including endogamous class strata. For them it is possible to specify the status of a child in a way that it is not for the Berawan. They are accordingly less concerned with death rites. They do not practice secondary treatment.

The Berawan have no naming ceremonies comparable to Kenyah ones. They do appreciate the status implications of grand weddings. But when all the rice wine has been drunk, and the guests have shakily made their way home, what is there to keep a wedding in mind, to preserve it against the envious denigrations of rivals? The Berawan require something more concrete, and it is mortuary rites that provide it. Mausoleums are always built on the riverbank so that passersby can admire them and wonder at the power of their architects.

At the outset, we noted that only people of high rank can command the support required to conduct a nulang or build a mausoleum. But we found it hard to define what rank is. We can now offer that definition by turning the original statement on its head. Berawan rank is, in part, the product of personal abilities: That person who can fuse the community together in coordinated action, that person *is* an aristocrat.

In this century, the role of the charismatic leader in Berawan society has changed. In the 1890s the Baram watershed, in which they live, was slowly brought under the control of the Sarawak government. The endemic and genocidal warfare that had raged throughout the area during the nineteenth century was checked, and then eradicated. As confidence in the new order grew, so also did trade. That there had for many centuries been a trickle of luxury goods into the interior is demonstrated by the fine old brasswear, beads, and Chinese pottery that can still be found there. But now the volume of this trade increased greatly.

Under these circumstances, the functions of leadership changed. Many of the old skills were still called for, however, revolving around the ability to cajole or bully people into corporate action, such as the collection of jungle produce, and expeditions to the coast to trade it for prestige goods. The military function of the longhouse declined, albeit warily, and the new type of leader may have been less prone to quixotic violence than his warlike forebears. But the necessity for community solidarity persisted, and indeed persists today in the need to protect land rights against encroachment.

In the new formula of power, legitimation through the construction of mortuary edifices still had an important part to play. In fact, a certain vying for elegance is noticeable. The tombs grow more lofty, delicate, and numerous. The Berawan themselves look back upon the period from about 1900 to the arrival of the Japanese in 1941 as a golden age, a time of serenity and cultural florescence. They reminisce about the fabulous bridewealth paid by important men and the scale of ritual events. They compare it favorably with the tempestuous times before, when the disruption of headhunters made it hard to accumulate a surplus, and with the uncertainty of the modern era. The apogee of tomb construction reached in the 1920s and 1930s bears out their recollections.

In the rites of secondary treatment, the bones of distinguished Berawan are recovered and stored in tall tombs that cast a shadow down the generations. As the jungle creepers engulf and finally topple these structures, so their architects gradually fade from view. Monumentalization amplifies the equation that Hertz made between the fate of the body and the fate of the soul. The corpse, by association with its container, is made enduring and larger than life in order that its owner's name may be the same.

PYRAMID BUILDING IN THE CONTEXT OF EARLY EGYPT

The Berawan are not unique in the energies that they devote to the building of death edifices. On the contrary, there is hardly a region of the world that lacks examples of similar tendencies to monumentalism, and in each case we may be sure that the dynamics of power and legitimacy are somehow involved in their construction. But one example stands out above all others. For the title of *most* enduring and *most* imposing of death monuments there can be only one candidate: the Pyramids of Giza. It is indeed a far cry from the wooden tomb posts of Borneo to the artificial mountains of Egypt. They are separated by vast stretches of time and space. Nevertheless, useful insights may be gained by comparing one with the other.

Statistics hardly serve to express just how stupendous the Pyramids of Giza are. To say that they contain well over 20 million tons of stone makes little impression upon the mind. They are still, 5,000 years after they were finished, far and away the biggest stone structures ever built. The cathedrals of Florence and Milan, Saint Peter's in Rome, and Saint Paul's Cathedral in London could all be grouped inside the base of the Great Pyramid of Khufu with room to spare.

Ever since Napoleon's Egyptian adventure thrust them into Western consciousness, the pyramids have inspired awe and bafflement. Who built them? When? How? Why? Such monumental mysteries have attracted serious scholars and crackpots with equal frequency over the last century and a half. The who and the when have been established. The question of how remains puzzling, although several interesting contributions have recently been made (Tellefsen 1975; Mendelssohn 1974).

But, for originality of theorizing, the most stimulating question has always been: Why? For what purpose were the pyramids built? It is self-evident that the construction of the pyramids cost their builders a vast effort. Their purpose must surely have been correspondingly important, their significance correspondingly timeless. It is the staggering size of the pyramids that makes all mundane explanations appear trivial, and prompts some observers to see a Grander Design in them.

The originator of the theory of Divine Inspiration was a retired book publisher named John Taylor, who, in 1859, wrote the first of many books entitled *The Great Pyramid*. This fascination with the Great Pyramid and the folklore that it has spawned constitute a subject worthy of study in its own right. But it is not the subject that concerns us here. Divine prophecy aside, what other functions have been suggested for the pyramids? They cannot have been stellar observatories, for we know that Egyptian astronomy was not advanced, and that the stellar alignments found in the pyramids are few and simple. Despite a current fad attributing to the right-rectangular cone the ability to sharpen razor blades and reduce hypertension, there is no evidence to support the idea that the Pyramids of Giza were built with such functions in mind. Rather, it will be necessary to return to those purposes, rooted in the social and political circumstances of the Archaic Period of ancient Egypt, that at first sight appear so ephemeral compared to the great mass of the structures themselves.

In accordance with the findings of archaeology, we conclude that the pyramids are what they appear to be: tombs. Further, that the social factors that account for their construction are not entirely different from those that produce elaborate mausoleums in central Borneo.

An immediate difficulty appears with this notion. Of the ten major pyramids begun or completed during the height of the Pyramid Age, beginning with Zoser's and ending with Menkaure's, none contains irrefutable proof that a pharaoh was ever entombed in it. In fact, what evidence there is points in the opposite direction. Though the pattern varies from pyramid to pyramid, each one contains a number of passages, sometimes within the structure, and sometimes hewn out of the live rock below. Each tunnel system contains an inner chamber, heavily defended from intruders by sliding stone portcullises. In four cases these inner chambers contain massive, finely worked stone sarcophagi, which are, however, empty. Possibly the royal corpses were stolen by the grave-robbers that are known to have entered the chambers in antiquity. Five other pyramids have no sarcophagi in them at all. Can it be that the robbers removed the heavy and essentially useless objects? How could they have got them out down the tiny corridors? (Evidently they were inserted during construction.) But the most difficult case is presented by the Step Pyramid of Sekhemket, the chamber of which was found intact. Inside was the expected sarcophagus, its opening still sealed with the original cement. Frustratingly for its excited discoverers, it turned out to be completely empty (Edwards 1946: 83).

How is it possible that the pharaohs built themselves such impressive tombs and then failed to use them? The answer must be sought in the social, technical, and stylistic developments that led up to the Pyramid Age, and particularly in the burial edifices of the earliest pharaohs. In this context, the corpseless tomb is a recurring phenomenon.

For many years, the place of entombment of the pharaohs of the First and Second dynasties (the Archaic Period) has been controversial. The problem is not a lack of identifiable sites, but a plethora of them. In the opening years of this century Petrie, whose name figures so prominently in Egyptian archaeology, made a painstaking excavation at the plundered site of Abydos. He was able to identify there the tombs of eight pharaohs of the First Dynasty and two of the Second Dynasty, together with other royal graves. However, later, in the mid thirties, Emery excavated at Sakkara a series of tombs that turned out to be associated with the same roster of monarchs. Emery argued that the Sakkara tombs were the real ones, but despite the fact that they are larger and more impressive, the majority of experts now feel that it was the Abydos site that actually housed the royal corpses (Hoffman, in press). For our purposes, it is enough to know that these kings each built two large tombs, provisioned them elaborately with food, luxury products, and valuables of all kinds, and surrounded them with the subsidiary graves of their courtiers or officials. We can only conclude that one of each king's tombs was designed from the outset to remain empty.

Why these ancient kings should have constructed dummy tombs is a question that leads us away from the hard data of archaeology. Despite several brilliant studies, of which those of Breasted (1912), Frankfort (1948), and Wilson (1951) are the best known, many features of ancient Egyptian religion remain unclear.

Our uncertainty is most pronounced concerning the Archaic Period, from which no written records survive. The religious rationale that was used to justify the two tombs of the kings of the first dynasties is a matter for speculation. What is beyond doubt is the location of the two royal cemeteries. Abydos is in Upper Egypt, not far from some of the most ancient settlement sites in the area; Sakkara is in Lower Egypt, not far from the first capital of the unified country, Memphis. We have good archaeological data to show that predynastic Egypt had developed in two cohesive but distinct culture areas: the Nile Delta region, and the striplike floodplain of the Nile, that is, Lower and Upper Egypt, respectively. We know that the two regions were brought under unified rule sometime around 3100 B.C. by a king of Upper Egypt. It is likely that the dual tombs of the earliest pharaohs made a political statement in addition to any ritual justification they may have had.

This interpretation is rendered more likely by the many symbols of duality surrounding the institution of the pharaoh, several of them explicitly representing Upper and Lower Egypt. A common artistic motif is the lily of Upper Egypt intertwined or alternated with the papyrus of Lower Egypt. Often the gods Horus and Seth, themselves associated with the two regions, are shown in the act of binding the two plants together. Given the importance of mortuary ritual, an expression of the same duality in tomb structures is not surprising.

With the model of the Sakkara tombs before them, the pharaohs of the Pyramid Age may well have planned massive mausoleums that they did not intend to occupy. But why *so* massive? Again, an examination of the archaeological record reduces the singularity of the pyramids by revealing them as the climax of a long process of evolution.

Around 3000 B.C., Egypt suffered decreasing annual rainfall. This brought on an ecological crisis, the effects of which are only now being worked out by archaeologists (Butzer 1976; Hoffman, in press). One effect seems to have been an increase in status differentiation, due perhaps to competition for reduced areas of productive land and intensification of irrigation. The changes were particularly pronounced in Upper Egypt. The increasing stratification of society is reflected in a steady elaboration of grave furnishings and architecture.

In 1894, before his Abydos dig, Petrie explored an extensive necropolis at Naqada that had evidently been in use for a prolonged period in predynastic times. It contained over 2,000 graves. The oldest, as dated by the seriation techniques pioneered by Petrie, consisted of shallow oval pits crudely roofed over and marked by small mounds. The body lay in a flexed position, and, even at this early date, was surrounded by a variety of grave goods. Later tombs consist of vaults lined with mud-brick masonry, are more carefully roofed, and presumably had larger mounds. Gradually, additional chambers were added to the main vault, and despite the depredations of grave robbers, who seem to have plied their trade from earliest times, it is clear that these chambers were filled with provisions and luxury goods of several kinds. Finally, at Naqada there are traces of a mysterious early step pyramid. Several features mark it out as an early experiment: its small size, crude use of the new medium of stone, and the inaccessibility of the simple vault in the rock below it. No tunnel led out of it, so that once the first course of the superstructure had been laid reentry was impossible. Significantly, the chamber was empty. It is not known whether its owner was a protodynastic or archaic potentate (Edwards 1947: 89).

The line of development begun at Naqada was continued at Abydos and Sakkara. Both sites contain a great number of tombs, often arranged in groups. The central edifice of such groups typically consists of many chambers, of which the central ones are usually subterranean. Their appearance above ground is of a low, rectangular building, as is suggested by the Arabic word used to describe them: *mastaba*, meaning a bench. The walls were often vividly painted, and decorated with recessed paneling in the same way as palaces of the era, a resemblance marred only by the lack of internal connecting doors between the tomb chambers. Our greatest area of ignorance concerns the original superstructure of the mastabas. Reisner (1936) believed that later tombs ascended in two or three steps to a summit much higher than now visible. Later commentators disagree, but the pyramid motif is presaged in other ways. The earlier tombs have a rectangular mound of sand cased in bricks directly above the burial vault, a feature, Edwards suggests (1947: 43), harking back to the mounds of sand atop predynastic graves (see Figure 6). Later tombs have a stepped central mound of larger proportions (see Figure 7).

Although what now remains of these Archaic Period royal graves is less impressive than the monuments of the succeeding Pyramid Age, we should not underestimate the concentration of wealth and labor that their construction represents. Hoffman (in press) suggests that they constituted such a drain on luxury goods

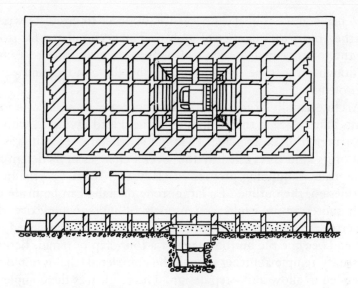

Figure 6. A First-Dynasty mastaba (after Edwards 1947: 44)

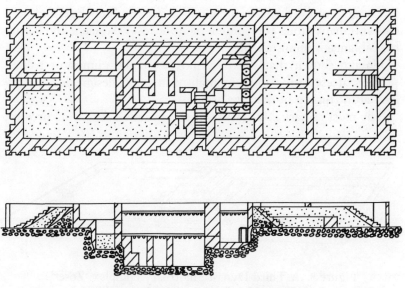

Figure 7. A Second-Dynasty mastaba (after Emery 1961: 83)

as to make grave robbery a necessity, in order to circulate wealth. Further, the great quantity of grain and oil accumulated for stocking the tomb provided a kind of national reserve fund that could be drawn on in time of shortage during the construction of the mausoleum.

Architecturally, the largest single increase in scale of monuments takes place at the beginning of the Third Dynasty, with the construction of Zoser's Step Pyramid at Sakkara. That it was the first of its kind is revealed by the several changes in its design that were made as building progressed (Edwards 1947: 53–78). In the first design, the outline of a large stone mastaba can be made out, with subterranean vaults and tunnels of more complexity than hitherto seen. In a first extention, the mastaba was lengthened, and one end became the bottom stage of a four-step pyramid. Before a mortuary temple abutting it could be completed, the pyramid was extended to allow a six-step design. The result was the complex of buildings shown in Figure 8, in which the pyramid overshadows the original mastaba. During the Third Dynasty, several more step pyramids were begun, presaging the final developments in the Fourth Dynasty. The features of the Pyramids of Giza are too well known to need description here (see Figure 9). The Great Pyramid is more than twice as tall as Zoser's Step Pyramid, and contains many times the volume of stone. Nevertheless, the family resemblance is unmistakable.

Having shown that the pyramids were the climax of a long process of escalating monumentalism in tomb design, let us now look at the timing of this escalation.

The most remarkable feature of the Pyramid Age is its brevity.

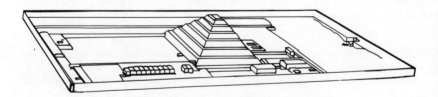

Figure 8. A Third-Dynasty mortuary complex: Zoser's
Step Pyramid (after Mendelssohn 1974: 41)

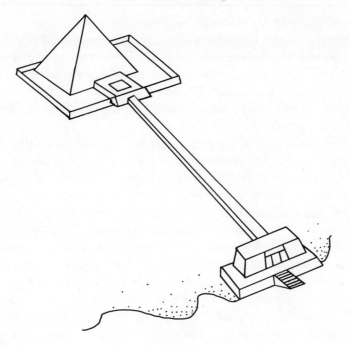

Figure 9. The classic pyramid complex of the Fourth Dynasty
(after Mendelssohn 1974: 46)

At first sight, one might imagine that a pyramid was erected every
few centuries as an expression of hubris on the part of particularly successful pharaohs. In fact, the five largest pyramids were
all built within the space of one century. Shepseskaf, last pharaoh
of the Fourth Dynasty, contented himself with a mastaba of
Archaic Period type. Thereafter, pyramids were sometimes constructed, but they were invariably of inferior size and workman-
ship. Mud brick was substituted for limestone, and all that is left
of them today are shapeless mounds. Between Shepseskaf and the
legendary Menes, who first imposed his rule on a unified Egypt, lie
little more than 500 years. It was during those centuries that the
Egyptian state was welded together from the diverse traditions of
predynastic times.

As Wilson has pointed out (1951: 44), we do not know if
Menes was an actual historical figure or only a later composition
of legend. We do not know if his "conquest" of Lower Egypt

was effected at one blow or over several generations, nor if it involved a painful imposition of rule over a subjugated population or a popular movement toward unity. We *do* know that warfare was common at the time, that rivalries existed between different regions, and that the earliest representations of pharaoh figures, such as the palette of Narmer, show him wielding a club over the heads of captives.

We also know that on two occasions *after* the establishment of the state, during the episodes known as the first and second intermediate periods, centralized rule collapsed. For the first dynasties of pharaohs, these centrifugal forces must have been all the greater because a unified cultural tradition was lacking. They had to create that tradition and to place the institution of pharaoh at the center of it. What they needed were corporate projects that focused upon the person of the leader; the construction of mortuary edifices provided the opportunity for the pharaohs just as it did for aspiring Berawan aristocrats in nineteenth-century Borneo.

This is not an evolutionist argument. We do not imply that the Egyptian sequence of political evolution was in process of being repeated in Borneo at the moment when Europeans arrived; nor that institutions found recently in Borneo are "survivals" of what was once practiced in Egypt. We employ the Berawan data only to suggest interpretations, the evidence for which must come from Egypt alone.

Like the mausoleums of Borneo, the important design feature of the pyramids was visibility. It was a matter of secondary interest who, if anyone, was entombed in them. The Berawan require a corpse before they can begin construction, so they honor their obscure relatives. The pharaohs evidently preferred simply to leave their mausoleums empty. Snofru, the greatest of all pyramid builders, actually constructed *three* (the Red and Bent pyramids and the ruined Meidum pyramid), a fact that Gardiner finds "unpalatable" because he cannot see why anyone would need three tombs (1961: 78).

Throughout the history of Egypt, the scale of royal mortuary ritual provides an index of the authority of central government. But in the first four dynasties it is particularly crucial. Wilson (1951: 44) characterizes the First and Second dynasties as a time of consolidation. Mortuary architecture reflects this in the elaboration of the mastaba form, a style of tomb carried over from predynastic times. Even so, the construction and provisioning of dual edifices (at Sakkara and Abydos) represents a considerable concentration of national effort. If we assume that labor-intensive phases of the construction went on during the off-season of the agricultural cycle, then the effort involved was largely one of coordination and organization, a task appropriate to nation building. In the Third and Fourth dynasties, according to Wilson, "The new state was stable and secure enough to express itself in a distinctively new and 'Egyptian' way" (1951: 44). In tomb construction, this new expression took the form of experimentation with, and perfection of, techniques for building in stone. Add to this a dramatic increase in scale, which in Zoser's Step Pyramid occurred in several jumps, and a need is apparent for yet further organization with emphasis on a range of new technical skills. The Fourth Dynasty began with Snofru and his three pyramids. His successor, Khufu, built the Great Pyramid. Djedefre built at some distance from Giza, and it is not known if he ever completed his pyramid. Khafre and Menkaure returned to Khufu's site, and added theirs to make up the trio visible today. This concluded the Pyramid Age.

As to the religious innovations that accompanied the social changes implied by the construction of the pyramids, our information is once again incomplete. The end result, the cult of the god-king, is well known from the texts that begin to appear in the Pyramid Age. Its elaborate symbology is described in Wilson (1946: 71–86). But as Wilson remarks elsewhere, how the rulers of the First Dynasty were perceived by their subjects is not known. Aldred (1961: 157–8) sees the divine kingship as an ancient culture trait having its roots in the rainmakers of prehistoric tribal society, but this is guesswork. It seems more likely that the pharaoh as reincarnation of Horus was an ideological innovation. Hoffman (in press) describes the change as follows: "Above all the concept of divine kingship, the principle that held later dynastic civilization together, was still evolving from its simpler prehistoric antecedents into the ceremonial absolutism of the Pyramid Age."

The mortuary edifices of the early pharaohs were the symbol and proof of royal authority. Though it would be absurd to suggest that they constituted the sole concern of rulers still in the process of building a complex state, they were a very large concern. The evidence for that stands in the desert to this day. Moreover, their fabrication must have called into being an organizational apparatus and a corporate awareness that made other state ventures possible, and further pyramid building unnecessary. As the pharaohs built the pyramids, so did the pyramids build Pharaonic civilization. And that, finally, is a purpose consonant with their vast bulk.

VI

THE IMMORTAL KINGSHIP

Western social thought has emphasized the importance of reason, law, and force in the evolution and maintenance of political institutions. Anthropologists, although not denying the role of these practical elements, focus on the crucial role of ritual symbols for political integration. One anthropologist in particular, A. M. Hocart, stands out for his insistence on the primacy of the ritualized aspects of kingship in the development of early states (Needham 1970). Beginning with the striking suggestion that "the first kings must have been dead kings" (Hocart 1954), he went on in later works to outline the proposition that "modern" bureaucratic government actually began in a ritual organization and only later took on the administrative function (Hocart 1970). In Hocart's view, "government" formed around a ritual specialist involved in the propitiation of, as often as not, the ghosts of important men, and the evolution of the state is merely the unintentional by-product of the ritual attempt to secure life and well-being from supernatural powers.

We are not here concerned with the issue of the evolution of the state in the history of humankind. Regardless of the origins of kingship, the symbolism surrounding the dead king remains crucial in many political structures. In the preceding chapter, we viewed several instances in which the treatment of the royal

153

remains figures prominently in the drama of royal succession and dynastic expansion. In this chapter, we look specifically at societies in which the person of the king, alive and dead, represents the prosperity and perpetuity of the political order. In this situation, the death of the king undermines the integrative symbol of political stability and makes all too palpable the danger of an outbreak of political violence. The decay of the royal corpse is often seen as participating in or even contributing to this dangerous situation. In many societies, the conception and representation of the "body politic" is intertwined in various ways with the body of the individual who is king, chief, or elder. The king's person is such a natural symbol of the authority and perpetuity of the political order that it becomes a problematic symbol once the man dies and his body begins to rot. Royal death presents a major symbolical problem: Given the intimate relation between abstract concepts and the physical properties of the item through which they are expressed, what happens when the very symbol of permanence and high authority begins to sink rapidly into putrescence?

We shall explore a number of solutions to this issue, some cases that are prominent in anthropological theories of political symbolism, and other cases that speak more directly to the long development of the Western ideology of the state and its representations. One solution to the problem of the decaying symbol is to replace it with a more stable representation. In this regard, royal effigies allow a grand ritual representation of the immortal kingship and the body politic. Another "solution" is to have no royal corpse at all. Through traditions of ritual regicide and royal burial alive, the corpse just disappears and is separated neatly from the task of representing the immortal kingship. Sensational as it may sound, the topic of ritualized royal murder is of solid importance to the anthropological study of political symbolism.

THE DIVINE KINGSHIP OF THE SHILLUK
OF THE SUDAN

Perhaps the most famous case of divine kingship is that of the Shilluk. In Shilluk ideology, the person of the king represents the fertility and well-being of his entire nation, and for this reason no decay of his body can be tolerated. For if the king dies, so does the land. Indeed, so direct is the connection between the king's well-being and that of the nation that not only is death a problem, but so are age, sickness, and especially decreased sexual potency.

None of those physical weaknesses, which the average man tolerates for long years before his eventual death, can be accepted in the king. The symbol of Shilluk unity and perpetuity can neither decay nor weaken. At the first evidence of lessening powers, the king is secretly suffocated and his body walled up in a mud hut. One moment, the king is strong and physically perfect. The next moment, he and his remains have vanished. Such are the customs of regicide that were reported for the Shilluk.

The royal customs of this small nation along the Upper Nile River became celebrated in anthropology (and beyond) through the writings of Sir James Frazer. Frazer devoted his life to the examination of two issues concerning death. One of his works asserted (through several volumes) that beliefs about death and the afterlife are the universal source of all primitive religion. The other, his magnum opus, *The Golden Bough* (1963), is a result of his decades-long quest for the meaning of ritual regicide.

Frazer was interested in collecting reports of the ritual murder of priest-kings because of the light such material shed on the early eras of our own civilization. Rituals, myths, and histories suggested that such cults were widespread in the pre-Classical Mediterranean world. Frazer, unable to obtain any but shadowy evidence fot the existence of these customs in Europe, searched the world for parallel customs that would confirm the reality of such barbarous cults at one stage in human history. Additionally, he wished to explain the dynamics of such customs. Frazer explained such rites as due to erroneous and superstitious beliefs about the magical powers of various kinds of "priest-kings."

Appropriately, as the Frazer Memorial Lecture, Evans-Pritchard's (1948) reanalysis of the "Divine Kingship of the Shilluk" emphasizes the political context, viewing customs of ritual regicide as a "problem in social structure," rather than of religion and magic. Even though the Shilluk king "reigns, but does not rule," even though he has almost no administrative, judicial, or military hegemony or authority, this figure, nonetheless, is the center of a political system. The beliefs in regicide and rituals of installation are best viewed as representing and contributing to the unity of the 100 or so separate Shilluk settlements that are strung out along the West Bank of the Nile.

For this type of analysis, we must locate and describe the Shilluk more specifically, for if their kingship is to be seen as a functioning part of the social structure, then this structure must be understood. In many respects, the social structure of the Shilluk is like that of their celebrated neighbors, the Nuer. They are patrilineal and their lineages are dispersed, so that each settlement contains homesteads of several lineages. As among the Nuer, certain lineages are politically associated with certain territories, so that everywhere there is a dominant lineage and several others that are locally subordinate. What makes the Shilluk different from the Nuer is that all the Shilluk settlements compose a common polity united in the kingship. This difference is crucial, however, for if the Nuer are the ultimate example of political structure and process in an uncentralized, anarchic situation, then the Shilluk are an example of what must minimally be added to create a state. That minimal addition is a symbolic kingship the nature of which is represented most clearly in the rituals surrounding the death and installation of the incumbents of the office.

The king sends his many wives, once they are pregnant, away from the royal capital to bear their children in their natal villages. Their sons, princes and potential successors, are raised by the village chief — often the brother or father of the prince's mother. Potential heirs, sons of the present king, are numerous, and each is allied and resident with an important commoner village chief who is a leader of his mother's family. Additionally, there are in most villages members of the royal lineage who are not contenders for the throne: the sons of those princes who did not become king. There are also various other groups affected by royal succession, such as the commoner clients of past kings. All in all, this kingship and its rule of succession have produced throughout the land a social hierarchy of royal house, nobility, and commoners. The king may come from a specific settlement, but he represents all the Shilluk. Furthermore, almost every settlement in the realm is

closely allied to the current king and to a potential heir, and therefore has a stake in the maintenance of the kingship. Nonetheless,
the kingship of the Shilluk is a rather tenuous institution in the
face of the divisive and competitive nature of the segmentary
system upon which it rests.

The kingship is a symbol of the Shilluk people. The king is
called *reth*, but it is not he who is said to reign, but Nyikang, the
immortal culture hero of the Shilluk, the founder of the kingdom
centuries ago. Nyikang, according to tradition, continues to reign
through all his successors, who are mere receptacles of the one and
only kingship – Nyikang. Nyikang, being immortal, is an abiding
institution "which binds past and present and future generations"
(Evans-Pritchard 1948: 200).

Nyikang, then, does not die, but the kings through whom he
rules do. On the death of a king, his corpse is walled up for some
months in a hut. Later, his bones are buried back in his natal settlement, but the burial, exhumation, and reburial are family and
clan affairs carried out in privacy, bordering on secrecy. Once the
king is dead, he ceases to be a symbol of national unity. His body,
upon whose physical condition the nation depended while he
lived, is assiduously absent after death.

The king is dead, but what has become of the kingship? The
answer is that the spirit of Nyikang is represented by an effigy
that is kept in a shrine during each king's reign, only to be reanimated, so to speak, during each interregnum to participate in the
installation of the next king.

The choosing and installation of a new king is an affair of the
whole nation. The new king is chosen by the leading commoner
chiefs of both northern and southern Shillukland. Consequently,
the successor must have wide support. Because the effigy of Nyikang is kept in the North, it "leads" a long march upriver to the
capital, picking up "warriors" and followers along the way at
each settlement. Meanwhile, the king-elect joins a similar "army"
from southern Shillukland and leads a march downriver. The two
armies meet outside the capital and engage in a mock battle in
which the army of Nyikang is victorious, defeating the army of
the South and capturing the king-elect. Later, at the installation
ceremonies, the spirit of Nyikang leaves the effigy and enters the

body of the new king, as in a spirit possession. The effigy is carted back to its shrine to await the return of the spirit of Nyikang at the death of the new incumbent.

The political unity of the Shilluk nation is primarily a ritual and dramatic tour de force that focuses on the physical representation of the "body politic" in the perfect person of the king and in the unchanging effigy. In the representation of Nyikang, signs of decay and change are eliminated. The difficult problem of the royal corpse is solved by replacing it with an effigy. Evans-Pritchard suggests that, given the crucial importance of the symbol of kingship in a polity where the king had no real power and the government no administration, the symbol must be especially compelling. It is in this context that he wishes to explain the reports of regicide in the case of a failing monarch.

Evans-Pritchard emphasizes that it is the frightening idea of regicide that strengthens the kingship by its insistence on the extreme purity and potency of the monarch. There is power and utility in the *idea* of regicide whether or not kings are ever actually murdered. Furthermore, given the logic of belief, the idea of regicide could also serve to strengthen the position of a failing incumbent. Whatever strengthens the kingship is likely to strengthen the king. For if a weak incumbent has not yet been killed by those whose duty it is or by those who stand to gain by his death, then he must indeed still be the embodiment of the immortal Nyikang.

I have failed to find convincing evidence that any Shilluk king was put to death . . . although some of the kings must have qualified long before they died . . . and I am persuaded that the story of kings being walled up in a hut is a confusion arising from the usual walling up of the remains of a dead king, the bones being buried after decomposition of the flesh. In the absence of other than traditional evidence of royal executions in Shilluk history and in view of the contradictory accounts cited I conclude that the ceremonial putting to death of kings is probably a fiction. It possibly arises from the dual personality of the king, who is both himself and Nyikang, both an individual and an institution, which accounts also for the linguistic convention that a king does not die but disappears just as Nyikang is said not to have died but to have disappeared. [Evans-Pritchard 1948: 202]

Evans-Pritchard discusses the issue in terms that have a familiar ring to Western ears. Notions of the dual personality of the king (public-corporate vs. private-individual), of kings that "reign but do not rule," and of the problem of legitimate succession all relate as much to Western constitutional thought as they do to the concerns of a Nilotic kingdom. This problem of the immortal kingship and mortal kings is an old one in Europe. Frazer seems unaware of the way his chosen problem and illustrations resonate with important English concerns. Evans-Pritchard's approach is different. He does not merely render the strange plausible to an English reader but he systematically relates the Shilluk customs to political concerns that are familiar and acceptable to his readers. It is as if the Shilluk do not really kill the king, but the belief is essentially a fictitious device to keep the Shilluk monarchy functioning. It is representative of Evans-Pritchard's view of anthropology as a process of cultural translation to define the analytical parameters in terms of institutional arrangements in the West. In this case, the "political" aspect of the Shilluk material is related to the English institution of the king as a "corporation sole."

The problems of the political symbolism of the Shilluk kingship are so strikingly parallel to the problems of the traditional English and French political systems that one is prompted to look back at European doctrines of kingship. For the devices of corporeal symbolism and funeral ritual were substantial factors in the development of the ideology of the modern state during the Renaissance.

BODY POLITIC AND BODY NATURAL

To examine this issue, we turn to the studies of historians, especially the now classic study by Ernst Kantorowicz, *The King's Two Bodies* (1957), and the related study by his student, Ralph Giesey, *The Royal Funeral Ceremony in Renaissance France* (1960). These studies trace the secularization of various medieval theological notions as the English and French political systems evolved into modern states. Subtle theological formulations pertaining to the duality of Christ and to the Holy Trinity were expropriated to create a "Christology" of European kingship. In England, generations of lawyers found it necessary to develop a complex legal fiction that the king had not one but two bodies. In France, the ambiguity about the dual nature of the king as political symbol was "resolved" not through law but through *pompes funèbres*.

Let us examine the English version first, for it is the more general case, the French ritual being a specialized derivation from English custom.

In England, the issue was expressed in a "legal" idiom rather than a ritual idiom. Kantorowicz offers as evidence the reports from a number of Tudor court cases regarding the status of transactions of deceased kings. Over and over, the jurists argue that the king has two bodies and this fact makes all his legal dealings different from those of normal men:

> For the king has in him two Bodies, *viz.* a Body natural and a Body politic. His Body natural (if it be considered in itself) is a Body mortal, subject to all Infirmities that come by Nature or Accident, to the Imbecility of Infancy or old Age, and to the like Defects that happen to the natural Bodies of other People. But his Body politic is a Body that cannot be seen or handled, consisting of Policy and Government, and constituted for the Direction of the People, and the Management of the public weal, and this Body is utterly void of Infancy, and old Age, and other natural Defects and Imbecilities, which the Body natural is subject to, and for this Cause, what the King does in his Body politic, cannot be invalidated or frustrated by any Disability in his natural Body. [Quoted in Kantorowicz 1957: 7.]

One point about this English concept contrasts markedly with Shilluk notions; that is the dominance of the body politic over the body natural of the king. Whereas the senility of the body natural of the Shilluk *Reth* threatens the well-being of the kingdom, the imbecility or old age of an English monarch do not. Again Kantorowicz can offer us the jurists' reports:

> His Body politic, which is annexed to his Body natural, takes away the imbecility of his Body natural, and draws the Body

natural, which is the lesser, and all the Effects thereof to itself, which is the greater. [Quoted in Kantorowicz 1957:10.]

The mysticism of the English formulation is striking in contrast to the Shilluk view. It seems quite reasonable and pragmatic that the aging or weakening of the human incumbent of the throne should weaken the kingship and endanger the polity. The Shilluk kingship at any moment is only as strong as the current king. However, the English view postulates an invisible body and attributes to it magical powers that remove mortal weakness from the king. The Western concept of the state, in the form that it took in late medieval and early Renaissance England, stressed the dominance of the abstraction (the state) over the individuals who composed the society, and even over that sole individual who represented the state in his person.

The nature of this English fiction of the king's two bodies, with the clear dominance of the body politic, avoids the Shilluk problem of the decay of the symbol of state either before or after the king's death. Royal death did create interesting problems for the jurists, however. For, during life, the two capacities of the king were distinct and separate, and yet at the same time formed a unity in which the political capacity dominated. This is a tricky intellectual position in itself, but it becomes even more complex when, at the death of a monarch, the two bodies simply separate (see Plate 7).

> . . . and this Body [politic] is not subject to passions as the other is, nor to Death, for as to this Body the King never dies, and his natural Death is not called in our Law . . . the Death of the King, but the Demise of the King, not signifying by the word (Demise) that the Body politic of the King is dead, but that there is a Separation of the two Bodies, and that the Body politic is transferred and conveyed over from the Body natural now dead, or now removed from the Dignity royal, to another Body natural. [Quoted in Kantorowicz 1957: 13.]

But even after death, the dominance of the political capacity has its effects on the individual who was king. Not only does the *kingship* live on through successive kings, but also the individual king receives a legal immortality of sorts. For, as Plowden reports,

Plate 7. This fifteenth-century tomb of the Earl of Arundel
graphically contrasts the grandeur of office with the frailty of
flesh, an idea elaborated into the doctrine of the king's "two
bodies" (from Kantorowicz 1957: Fig. 28,
with the permission of the Warburg Institute).

legal contracts made with King Henry VIII continue because "he
as King never dies." According to the ideology, the kingship separates and moves on (to Edward VI). Henry Tudor is dead, but
Henry VIII lives on (Kantorowicz 1957: 14).

Yet the Tudor jurists argued that every subject is sworn to the
king in the king's *natural* person rather than in his political capacity. This is because the political capacity, being an abstraction, has
no soul in the specifically Christian sense and therefore cannot
swear or be sworn to in holy oath. Furthermore, treason is also
against the king's body natural, for the body politic, being immortal, cannot be threatened or killed. Regicide, then, in the English
context bears a striking resemblance in its conceived effects to the
supposed regicide among the Shilluk. Indeed, the dogmas of the
royal jurists of the Tudor period provided the rationale for the

killing of Charles I in the English revolution of the mid-seventeenth century. Parliament summoned, in the name and by the authority of Charles I, king body politic, the armies that were to fight the same Charles I, king body natural. They succeeded in executing the king's body natural without doing serious harm to the king's body politic in Parliament (Kantorowicz 1957: 22).

The treatment of the royal corpse in medieval and Renaissance England reflects the logical gymnastics of the concept of the two bodies in a simple fashion. For it became the practice, beginning with the funeral of Henry II in 1189 (Giesey 1960: 80) for the corpse of the deceased king to be publicly displayed during the funeral procession. The practice of evisceration allowed the reasonable preservation of the corpse for a few days. The heart and entrails of an English king usually received separate burial from the remainder of the corpse. Some monarchs generously had their remains distributed among three locales. Given the English notion of the separation of the king's two bodies at this "demise," the display of the corpse served a practical and quasi-legal purpose. For all that was needed to validate (at least in a preliminary fashion) the authority of the new king was the obvious evidence that the body natural of the preceding king had come to its natural end. Again, we face the issue of the causal relation between beliefs and ritual action, and we note that the style of burial ritual developed gradually over the centuries, as did the legal concept of the two bodies. It seems, however, that as usual, ritual custom led the way, with the rationale following later.

The death of Edward II in 1327 provided unusual circumstances that called for a practical innovation that would become important. Edward II was deposed in favor of his son. When he died shortly afterward while under arrest, there were suspicions of foul play. Also, Edward III was far away and the funeral had to be delayed until the royal son could return and make a public show of filial piety. When the funeral procession took place, months later, a wooden effigy was substituted for the corpse-on-display. Whether this was done to cover possible evidence of murder or simply to allow Edward III to be present at a compensatorily grand funeral for the father he deposed, or for both reasons, is not certain (Giesey 1960: 81). But the innovation of the effigy did permit the staging of increasingly protracted and grand tributes to deceased English monarchs.

The use of effigies was adopted intermittently for a century and a half. The reasons for each use of, or failure to use, the effigy relate to practical political considerations, such as we discussed in the previous chapter. Although the first effigy was arranged for a deposed king, it was done by his son. Funeral effigies and the pomp they permitted seem not to have been provided for the several deposed or murdered English monarchs of the unstable fifteenth century: The funerals of Richard II, Henry VI, Edward V, and Richard III displayed neither corpse nor effigy. On the other hand, Edward III, Henry IV, Henry V, and Edward IV died naturally and were provided with effigies at their funerals (Giesey 1960: 80–5). Likewise, effigies were used for all the royal funerals during the dynastically stable Tudor era and for the funeral of the first Stuart king, James I. For his ill-fated son, Charles I, the concept of the king's two bodies had fatal implications.

One can never separate fully the pragmatic from the symbolic in ritual. But it is necessary to identify the meaning that the effigy held for those who used it. To what extent did the English royal effigy represent the immortal kingship and nation as the Shilluk effigy represented the timeless unity of Nyikang? Originally, it was the natural body of the deceased that was displayed, while the invisible body politic had shifted to the successor. The introduction of the effigy seems to have gradually brought about a subtle shift in meaning. For the effigy in royal garb was now visible in contrast to the invisible corpse in the casket. Kantorowicz (1957: 421) suggests that the funeral became a ritual inversion of the normal doctrine of the king's two bodies. For now the hitherto invisible body politic is made visible, and it is the body natural that can no longer be seen. Death may eventually separate the two bodies, but until burial they are not so much separated as inverted in their relationship.

However, the use of the royal effigy in England never completely loses its pragmatic aspect as substitute for the corpse (Giesey 1960: 85). There may be inversions of sorts, but the effigy remains with the casket, always proximally associated with the particular deceased monarch whose likeness it bears. It never represents the kingship or the total body politic of England. At most, it represents the perpetual royal dignity of the previous king. It relates to the jurists' explanation that King Henry VIII lives on after the death of Henry Tudor, separate from the kingship that passes to his son. Depending upon the times and circumstances of his assumption of royal authority, a successor may omit the tribute to the royal dignity of the dead king.

LE ROI EST MORT! VIVE LE ROI!

In French royal funerals, the effigy was not used until Henry V of England died in France in 1422. He was also heir presumptive of France according to the treaty that he had recently signed with Charles VI of France. Consequently, his funeral effigy was prominently displayed across France as his procession moved to Paris and finally to England. Within weeks, Charles VI also died, leaving the succession to the French throne in dispute between the young Henry VI and the Dauphin of France. The English regent for young Henry VI quickly arranged the funeral for the French king, including and English-style funeral effigy. This custom of royal funeral effigies was then continued for every French monarch until the death of Louis XIII and accession of Louis XIV. Whereas in England the practice of the effigy remained sporadic and its use and meaning peripheral to the funeral ceremony, in France the effigy quickly developed into the central symbol in an elaborate ritual allegory of the state.

The style of Renaissance French royal funerals relates to constitutional concepts and political institutions that differed markedly from English parliamentary traditions. The sovereignty of France became fused with a strong dynastic principle and the government of France moved steadily toward absolutism. The English legal fiction of the radical distinction between the king's two bodies did not apply to Continental political theory. In the context of the funeral, France was powerfully represented within the effigy of a particular monarch who was father (or brother) to the new king. Giesey suggests that it is no accident that the French custom of royal effigies died out with the accession of the "Sun King" and the establishment of Bourbon absolutism. Once the absolutism of Louis XIV's modern monarchic state had been achieved, the medieval and Renaissance notions expressed in the ritual of the effigy were no longer appropriate (Giesey 1960: 190–2). The state had come to be symbolized by the person of the *living* king and by the continuity of his family. Louis XIV's "L'état c'est moi" was no boastful invention, but the recognition of a state of affairs that had been slowly established and had been expressed through the elaboration of the royal funeral effigy.

It is interesting to consider some of the later implications of the French royal funeral symbolism and to compare the meaning of regicide in France with regicide in England. As we mentioned above, the radical English distinction between the king and the king's body politic permitted the execution of Charles I while the king's body politic continued. The consequences of the eighteenth-century execution of Louis XVI were different. The killing of the king ended the monarchy and permanently altered the structure of European society and political thought (Kantorowicz 1957: 23).

This is not to attribute to ritual any necessary priority in the chain of social and political causality. Royal customs, such as the use of the funeral effigy, often begin in response to chance circumstances and practical considerations. But once performed, any part of a royal funeral ritual sets a precedent that is repeated at the next kingly death. Once present in the ritual, such an element accumulates meanings the way a ship accumulates barnacles. Over the centuries, practical precedents become powerful symbolic configurations that constrain and inspire the course of later political events.

In many respects, the meaning of the royal effigy in France was similar to the meaning of the Shilluk effigy in that it came to stand for the perpetuity of the kingship, or the French nation. Over the years, in France, the effigy and the corpse of the deceased monarch became spatially separated and ideologically juxtaposed in the complex funeral ritual. The ritual became expressive of great dyadic tension: the triumph of death versus the triumph over death, church ritual versus state ritual, grief versus joy, all revolving around the body of the mortal king and the effigy of the immortal royal dignity.

Following the death of the Renaissance French king, the heir to the throne stays discreetly out of the public eye during the long funeral arrangements and ceremonies. During this time, all the pomp of royalty remains focused on the deceased monarch. Nonetheless, the heir to the throne actually rules the land. From his seclusion, he issues edicts in his own name as king, and most importantly directs the complex preparations for his predecessor's funeral. The government of France continues in spite of the "mutation" of the reigning monarch.

The period immediately following the royal death is one devoted to the preparation of the body and effigy for the grand ceremonies to follow. The heart and entrails are removed and each encoffined separately. The three coffins (corpse, heart, entrails) are then the objects of almost continuous high and low masses, night vigils, and services for the dead performed by members of the religious orders. After about a week, the heart and entrails receive their final service and are put in a permanent resting place.

Meanwhile, the craftsmen are working to produce the effigy of the deceased king:

> The Effigy was made with painstaking care to represent the king as closely as possible. . . . The trunk, arms and legs of the effigy were made of osier, and were completely covered by the vestments in which the effigy was dressed. The head and hands, however, were exposed, and it was to these that Clouet devoted most of his time. A model of potter's clay was made first, then a mold of plaster, and the final product of wax; the hair of the head and beard were attached with putty, and the whole visage very realistically painted. Two pairs of hands were made; one pair joined, as the effigy appeared on the bed of honor, the other pair separate to hold the sceptre and the hand of justice, as the effigy appeared in the procession in Paris.

> The effigy was dressed in the following manner: a shirt of Dutch linen; a waistcoat of crimson satin; a blue satin tunic, with fleurs-de-lis, which extended to the elbow; the legs stockinged with fine linen interwoven with gold; the feet covered

by red satin slippers; over all, a sleeveless royal mantle of purple, lined with white satin and sewn with fleurs-de-lis and having a collar of ermine; around the neck hung the collar of the Grand Order; on the head, over a small brownish-red bonnet, the imperial crown, studded with jewels. On the other side of the effigy, on pillows, lay the sceptre and the hand of justice. In short, the king in effigy appeared in the fullest majesty, in the robes he wore otherwise only at his coronation and at a *lit de justice*. [Giesey 1960: 4–5]

When all the preparations are ready, the focus of the ceremony shifts away from the encoffined body and centers upon the lifelike representation of the deceased monarch. The great hall of the palace is lavishly decorated with tapestries in joyous blue velvet and gold cloth. At the front of the hall, high on his "bed of justice" or "bed of state," sits the lifelike effigy. Along the walls and throughout the hall, now called the "hall of honor," are benches and seats for the bishops, cardinals, and nobles who attend the twice-daily ritual of the setting of the royal dinner table.

And in this state the effigy remained for eleven days. And it is to be understood and known that during the time the body was in the chamber next to the great hall, as well as while the effigy was in that hall, the forms and fashions of service were observed and kept just as was customary during the lifetime of the king: the table being set by the officers of the commissary; the service carried by the gentlemen servants, the bread-carrier, the cup-bearer and the carver, with the usher marching before them and followed by the officers of the cupboard, who spread the table with the reverences and samplings that were customarily made. After the bread was broken and prepared, the meat and other courses were brought in by an usher, steward, bread-carrier, pages of the chamber, squire of the cuisine and garde-vaiselle. The napkin was presented by said steward to the most dignified person present, to wipe the hands of the Seigneur. The table was blessed by a Cardinal; the basins of water for washing the hands presented at the chair of the Seigneur, as if he had been living, and seated in it. The three courses of the meal were carried out with the same forms, ceremonies and samplings as they were wont to be during the life of the Seigneur, without forgetting those of the wine, with the presentation of the cup at the places and hours that the Seigneur had been accustomed to drink, two times at each of his meals. [Du Chastel, quoted in Giesey 1960: 5.]

Then the mood suddenly changes. Overnight, all the blue and gold tapestries are removed and replaced with black mourning cloth. The "bed of state" and the effigy are replaced with the coffin under a large black canopy. All the attendants, who had been dressed in their finest robes, now are clothed in black mourning cloaks. The hall is no longer called the "hall of honor," but is henceforth referred to as the "hall of grief." It is in this "hall of grief" that the new king might make his only appearance during the funeral ceremonies. Seven weeks after the death of Francis I in 1547, his son and heir, Henry II, came to asperse the body of his father:

> Even to call this ceremonial "official" is misleading. Henry II came not as *Roi de France*, but as *fils de Francois* . . . Henry could not have appeared while the effigy was on display, else there would have occurred the simultaneous exposure to view of two kings of France – an impossible situation. So Henry waited until the effigy had been removed and the *salle d'honneur* converted into a *salle de deuil*. But to play the role of mourner was no less difficult for a king of France than to confront his predecessor's effigy. . . . So, when Henry II came to asperse his father's body, his great royal mourning cloak was purple in color, a darkening, as it were, of the royal scarlet, but not a blackening of it. . . . And when he left . . . Henry symbolically terminated his quasi-mourning by giving away the cloak. . . . [Giesey 1960: 7]

Let us consider the overall structure of the ceremonies. Not surprisingly, the funeral falls into three stages. First, there are the "receptions" in the palace, which we have just described. Second, there is the procession into Paris to Notre Dame Cathedral and then out toward Saint-Denis. Finally, there is the burial at Saint-Denis, the royal necropolis. And again as we shall see, Van Gennep's tripartite schema of "separation, liminality, reincorporation" is extremely illuminating. What could be a more poignant representation of separation than those last grand royal sessions and royal banquets with everything assiduously as it had been during Francis' life, and then sharply reversed to portray a black and lugubrious mourning tableau? The parallels to the simple funeral from Madagascar are striking. For there, too, we have the symbolic pretense that the deceased is still with us while he remains in the women's house, the house of life, until suddenly the men come and wrench him away.

The procession through Paris is also reminiscent of the ambiguously joyful and irreverent funeral processions in Madagascar and elsewhere. Often the royal French funeral procession degenerated into "difference, combustions, and debates" as various participant groups forcefully disputed what they felt to be their ancient privileges regarding the order and rank of marching. The most important of these rights belonged to the presidents of Parlement. It was their privilege to carry the corners of the pall placed under the lifelike effigy and to wear red robes rather than black. This symbolized the perpetuity of French justice.

The procession itself can be divided into three parts. In the front is the chariot carrying the coffin accompanied by the "pieces of honor" such as the king's helmet, gloves, and shield. This section of the procession has the characteristics of a funeral for a knight, a member of a sacred order. In the rear, representatives of the royal family march in deep mourning. There one sees the characteristics of a private funeral for a kinsman (except for the assiduous absence of the son and heir). But in the center of the procession all around the effigy there is no sign of a funeral. The effigy is the king alive making his joyful and triumphant entry into Paris. Dressed in all the rich insignia of office and with its features artfully resembling the personal features of the deceased, the effigy cannot be distinguished from the real king by observers more than a few feet away.

Finally, the procession arrives at the church of Saint-Denis, the royal necropolis outside Paris. The church is draped in black. The effigy is for the first and only time placed directly on top of the coffin, where it remains throughout the final night of the ceremony. Giesey writes of Francis I's funeral:

An awe-inspiring and ghostly sight it must have been: in the center of the choir lay the effigy of the just-deceased King of France, shining in the light of a thousand candles which cast a soft glow roundabout on the figures of the host of his predecessors – sculptured in stone atop their tombs. Francis, too, was soon to be another of the *gisants* of Saint-Denis; but while his body was not yet entombed, and his effigy still displayed, the sovereign power inhered in him still. . . . [Giesey 1960: 15]

The two-month-long ceremonial concludes with the ensepulchering of the coffin and the pronouncement of the rebirth of the sovereignty of the French king. Although later in England and France, the famous pronouncement "The king is dead! Long live the king!" became associated with the moment of death, during the Renaissance it was not uttered until the moment of burial many weeks after death.

The effigy is removed from the coffin, never to be seen again. The coffin is lowered into the vault and then all the royal insignia are placed upon it by the heralds-at-arms, the Captains of the Swiss Guard, the One Hundred Archers, the Scots Guard, the One Hundred Gentlemen, and the knightly orders. They place there the spurs, the gloves, the helmet, the shield, the coat of arms, the pennon, the crown, the *main de justice*, and the scepter. For the burial of Francis I:

> . . . the Admiral d'Annebaut, acting as Grand Master, came to the edge of the grave, carrying the Banner of France. Too ill even to stand steadily, the venerable admiral had to sit on a chair at the edge of the vault as he dipped the flag till its tip touched the coffin. The symbols of sovereignty of France, which for weeks had adorned alternately the coffin and the effigy, followed Francis I even down into his grave. But only for a moment could they rest there, for the sovereign power is immortal, and must ever rise anew.
>
> "Le Roy est mort!" cried Normandy three times, and the crowd moaned and wept. The admiral was so choked with tears he could not utter "Vive le Roy" as it was his office to do; Normandy came to the rescue by himself uttering the cry of the new sovereign: Vive le roy, vive Henri deuxième du nom par la grace de Dieu roy de France, a qui Dieu doint bonne vie.

With this cry, the banner and sword and baton were raised on high, and the various ensigns and coats of arms on the barrier around the grave recovered by the knights and heralds. The objects within the grave were not recovered until after the party had left, however, for the symbols of sovereignty belonging to the person of the king – the crown, sceptre, hand of justice, and the knightly pieces of honor – were not to be seen again until the coronation of Henry II at Reims. [Giesey 1960: 16–17]

The ritual takes, as we have mentioned, the classic tripartite form of a rite of passage. We have noted the parallels between this royal ritual in France and the simpler funeral rituals described in earlier chapters. These parallels are particularly striking regarding the final vigil and burial at Saint-Denis, where the French royal ancestors are the objects of cults not unlike the various ancestor cults of Madagascar, Africa, Borneo, and Indonesia.

We wish also to stress a parallel between the symbolic structure of the Malagasy and royal French funerals, and that is the importance of the dyadic aspect and the strategic shifts in the quality of those oppositions. The royal funeral stresses a radical separation and opposition between the two aspects of the king's person. Here, of course, it is not male bone and female flesh, but royal dignity versus personal mortality. At the beginning of the ceremonies, the symbolic opposition is most intense, with the coffin and effigy alternating their appearances, never appearing at the same place or at the same time. During the procession through Paris, both the coffin and the effigy are present, although spatially and symbolically separated. In the last church services at the church of Saint-Denis, the effigy is placed on top of the coffin. And finally the burial recreates the complementarity of the two aspects of the king's person through the proclamation of Henry II as king of France.

In summary, the funeral has a three-part diachronic structure that relates to the sociological/political issue of succession. And this rite of passage progression is animated by a synchronic opposition between the immortal dignity of the kingship and the mortal remains of the king; an opposition that is radical at first, ambiguous during the procession, and resolved at burial.

The Immortal Kingship

How complex and powerful is the symbolism surrounding the representation of kingship in the face of a royal death! When one realizes the extent to which the ritual symbolism is constructed upon what might be termed fictions (the English king has two bodies, a wax effigy rules France, the Shilluk king is possessed by the spirit of Nyikang), then the unimaginative realism of Frazer's "doctrine of survivals" becomes all the more obvious. Both the French and English Renaissance funeral rituals have their archaic qualities, and, as Giesey (1961: 190) points out, are, in their symbols and concepts, essentially medieval survivals in a later age. Nonetheless, these rituals continued to play a dynamic and ever-changing role in the development of Western constitutional thought and in political affairs and intrigues. Archaic royal funeral practices are best explained as vital aspects of changing political systems; Kantorowicz, Giesey, and Evans-Pritchard have done this admirably for the English, French, and Shilluk. In each case, the ritual material is related to cultural ideas of the permanence of kingship and the political-moral order; to institutional structures of society; to changing historical circumstances; and to the expressly political maneuverings of people competing for power and prestige.

In addition to these political questions, there is the paradoxical nature of symbolism itself. By definition, any symbol must be both itself and something other. The cognitive qualities of both the "signifier" and that which is "signified" feed back upon one another, simultaneously constraining and creating meaning. And always with any symbolic representation, there is a large measure of ambiguity, of as yet inchoate potential meaning, which, in a political context, provides the material for self-interested innovation and change.

Frazer placed his shocking subject matter, murder, in the wrong analytical context and provided a narrow, titillative, and self-serving explanation. The idea of regicide is an inevitable part of the idea of royal death and succession. It was Frazer's simplistic view that every representation of the idea of regicide had once been the

173

custom. Evans-Pritchard's view, as we have seen, reverses the analysis, stressing (as does Wittgenstein 1971) the power of the idea itself and suggesting that the belief is even more effective in strengthening the polity when the deed is not actually done. This approach stresses the similarities between the Shilluk kingship and our own cultural institutions. By stressing the symbolic over the homicidal, Evans-Pritchard removes the imputation of savagery and primitiveness that Frazer had put to all such customs.

Regicide is a symbol, part of a complex set of symbols, pertaining to the death of the king and the perpetuity of kingship. But as Beattie (1966: 570–1) has pointed out, "Symbolism is no less symbolic (and no more pseudo- or proto-"scientific") when, as it often is, it is translated into action." Charles I and Louis XVI are cases in point. They certainly were executed, and executed largely because of their symbolic position as king. In European history, such alteration of the symbol of royal death (i.e., regicide) generally aims to change or destroy the political status quo. Regicide in Europe, in spite of the rationalizations of those responsible, always carries the immoral tinge of rebellion. The original interest to Westerners of the Shilluk custom was that regicide is routinely put into the context of positive morality. That which is familiar in European custom, but rare and frightening, was reported to be common among the Shilluk and morally proper.

Frazer had no real evidence to show that the Shilluk often killed their kings, and Evans-Pritchard had no real evidence to show that they did not. For the research that Frazer drew on was a survey rather than intensive field observation, and Evans-Pritchard admittedly never visited the Shilluk. We are fortunate, however, that in recent years two anthropologists have done major research on the neighbors to the Shilluk, the Dinka, whose similar customs had also been cited in various editions of Frazer's *Golden Bough*. These recent studies address themselves to this issue of the positive morality of controlling the time, place, and means of death for the politico-religious leaders of the Dinka.

In negatively stressing the differences between our society and primitive peoples, Frazer focused on regicide and similar customs. Evans-Pritchard, in his emphasis on the *similarities* between the Shilluk institutions and our own, reacted to the Frazerian prejudice. This led him to deny the actual existence of regicide. In both analyses, there remains the implication that such customs would indicate a certain primitiveness. The two ethnographers of the Dinka, Francis Deng and Godfrey Lienhardt, are sensitive to the sensationalist aspects of such customs, and both are at pains to represent Dinka values clearly and accurately. Yet both reports lead to the conclusion that Dinka politico-religious leaders often ended their careers by being voluntarily buried alive.

DINKA BURIAL ALIVE

The Dinka are a large ethnic group in the southern Sudan who today number almost 2 million. In contrast to their Shilluk neighbors, the Dinka have never been united into a single polity, and consequently their political traditions vary considerably from one region to another. In most Dinka tribes, leadership is diffusely shared among religious leaders known as "masters of the spear." The northernmost Dinka tribe, the Ngok, is the only group to have developed a centralized chieftaincy similar to that of the Shilluk.

Deng's study is particularly interesting on this topic, for the anthropologist is himself a Dinka, the son of the late paramount chief of the Ngok Dinka:

> The principles and practices applicable to the death of a Chief are different from those applicable to an ordinary person. I have already pointed out the importance of the Chief to the spiritual and physical welfare of his society and how traditionally he was not supposed to wait until he was actually dead before burial, but would request that he be buried alive at the brink of death. This is a debated point among anthropologists. Some believe it was merely mythological and not real. Real or mythological, the Dinka believe that the custom pertained [sic] until it was prohibited by the British. My greatgrandfather was allegedly buried this way. According to the story he remarked: "Watch my eyes" as the grave was being filled in. Since the grave of a Chief is constructed in such a way as to leave a dirt-free space for his underground shelter, the possibility is not so absurd as it might

sound. It is said that my grandfather, too, would have been buried alive had not government agents seen to it that this did not happen. [Deng 1972: 132]

Nor was Deng's father, Chief Deng Majok, buried alive, for he died in a Cairo hospital in 1969. At that time, the Ngok Dinka were caught in the midst of the long and brutal civil war between northern and southern Sudan. Deng Majok was chief from 1945 on; he was by all accounts a man of considerable vision and talent, who managed to mediate successfully between tradition and modernity, between Arabic north and African south. Ngok Dinka have told one of the authors that when his body arrived back home, many people were disappointed that he was already dead and hence could not be buried alive. We cannot interpret this to mean that, had he returned alive, this would have been allowed by the authorities or desired by the chief and his family. But such statements show the continued strength and immediacy of the belief.

Deng writes movingly of the events surrounding the death of his father:

The death of Deng Majok in August, 1969, was an unparalleled calamity for the Ngok and other Dinkas farther South. Ngokland suddenly ceased to be a secure bridge between the South and the North. The fear, despair, and surrender to the concept of a spoiled world that came with Deng Majok's death left no doubt in anybody's mind that a great leader and protector was dead.

We eyewitnessed this crucial phase in the history of the Ngok when we took his body from Cairo where he had died. . . . On landing at Abyei, we found a reign of terror. Deng Majok's absence had created a vacuum which the security forces were filling with arrests, torture, and murder. Just two nights before our arrival, they had shot and killed a brother of the Chief – a highly regarded and well-established person whom they had suspected of cooperation with the rebels. Among the many who had been tortured was the Chief's own sister because one of her sons was a rebel. Her arms had been rendered paralyzed. The Dinka, including their Chiefs and especially their educated, were under careful scrutiny and in constant apprehension. Abdalla

Monyyak de Deng, the son whom Chief Deng had left in charge and who was to succeed him, had tried to fill his father's position; but he had neither the legal authority nor as yet the personal influence to be effective. He was even suspected of cooperation with the rebels by the security forces. He succeeded his father without delusions about the size of the shoes he was inheriting. As though his father were to blame, he remarked with tears in his eyes, "We were all praying for him to return and bring an end to all this. Instead he returns as a corpse at the moment of our greatest need." [Deng 1972: 146]

It was the beginning of the end for the divine chieftaincy of the Ngok Dinka. Chief Abdalla Deng reportedly made some progress in becoming an effective leader and protector of his people under difficult circumstances. But then, one year later, he and several members of his family were assassinated by the police as they were strolling on the edge of the village. Where once the mark of chieftainship had been a calm and voluntary ritual death in old age, now a twenty-seven-year-old chief was shot in the back by a handful of security police.

The instrument of the modern state, which once reinforced the institution of chieftaincy, added to its traditional prominence, and made it pivotal, is now the instrument threatening its continuity. Chieftaincy being the backbone of Dinka society, its extinction also threatens the existence of that society. This is in essence the major crisis of the Ngok. [Deng 1972: 152]

Clearly, it has been many decades since an important Ngok chief has been buried alive. But the memory of the custom, the persistence of the belief, and all that it implies about the nature of Ngok chieftainship have implications for the death of every chief, however that death comes about; and the death of every chief has implications for the polity. One speculates that the Ngok chieftainship might have survived almost any emasculation of the authority of a living chief, but that the radical contrasts between each of these last two deaths and the ideal of chiefly death were decisive. For it is the death or, more precisely, the contrived death that allows images of immortality, that associates the chief with divinity and with the will of his people. The last two chiefs of the Ngok surely died in ways that left little room for images of immortality: one of a slow emaciating disease in a sterile hospital in a foreign land; the other by being gunned down in his own village.

Even a brief examination of the traditional customs will show how very great is the disparity between these two deaths and the ideal. Lienhardt presents the following account from a Dinka who had witnessed in his youth two ritual deaths of masters of the spear:

> The master of the fishing-spear Deng Deng was becoming very old, and when his years were finished and he was very old indeed, so that he could not see well and all his teeth had fallen out, he told his lineage that he wished to be buried alive, and that they should go and tell the people of the country and see if they agreed.
>
> They prepared the ground for his burial at a very ancient cattle-camp site called Malwal, which was also hard by the homestead of Deng Deng and near his cattle-byre. So it was at his very own original home. . . . The clan which cleared and dug the ground was Padiangbar; it is that clan which buries a master of the fishing-spear alive in my country.
>
> They dug a very big hole on the highest point of the cattle-camp site, in the middle of the cattle. Next to it were two bulls, a big white one and a red one . . . When the hole had been dug, they made two platforms (frameworks) of *akoc* wood, which had been fetched by the young men of Padiangbar from far away in the forest, as much as a day's journey distant.
>
> They worked for three days, and the old man was still above the ground. They honored the bulls with songs for two days, speaking invocations each day in the morning and the evening. Then the masters of the fishing-spear of Pakedang, along with those of Paketoi and Pagong, slit the throats of the bulls at about 10 o'clock. Deng Deng's mother was the daughter of a woman of Paketoi and his mother's father was of the clan Pagong. So they were all there together, to join together his father's and his maternal uncle's families.
>
> Deng Deng made invocations over the bulls, and the horns of the first bull, the white one, sank forwards to the ground. When the bull had been killed, they took its skin and cut it into strips,

and made a bed from it on the framework. And every day they made a feast and danced inside the cattle-byre during the day-time, and outside at night. And men slept in the byre with other men's wives, and everyone agreed to this (literally 'and there was no bad word').

They then placed a war-shield, made from the hide of a bull of the clan-divinity which had been killed in the past, on top of the bed. It was a war-shield which had for long been kept in the byre, and which the people had anointed with butter every spring and autumn, during the 'dividing months'. They placed Deng Deng on the shield and lowered him into the grave.

The red (brown) bull remained. When Deng Deng had been lowered into the hole, they made a platform over him, and so arranged it that the top of the platform was level with the sur-face of the ground. They sang hymns, and after the singing was finished, they made an enclosure of *dhot* wood around the grave. The enclosure was about twice the area of the surface of the grave, and of such a height that a man could just see over it if he tried. Then they took cattle-dung and partly covered over the top of the grave, leaving part uncovered so that his voice could be heard. From his grave, Deng Deng called the older men together outside the enclosure, and all the women and children, even his own wives, were sent away. . . .

Deng Deng had died at the time of the harvest. He said that in the following dry season, in the month of Akanythii, his tribe would fight with a neighboring tribe, and that he was distressed because his people were not brave enough in war.

Two months later, this fight took place, and eight of his people were killed and two from the neighboring tribe. That neighboring tribe soundly beat his tribe and drove them off as far as Agar Dinka country. Eventually, the Government forces came and prevented thefts of cattle. But even then that neigh-boring tribe made a feast near the river in the face of the dry-season pastures of his own tribe which had been so harried that they could do nothing about it.

While the master of the fishing-spear still speaks, they do not cover the grave with dung. But when he no longer replies when they address him, they heap up the dung over him. And when it has all sunk in, they make a shrine. Some people may then say "the master of the fishing-spear has died," but they will usually say "the master has been taken into the earth." And nobody will say, "Alas, he is dead!" They will say "It is very good." [Lienhardt 1961: 301–303]

There are a number of other accounts reported by Lienhardt of the burial alive of masters of the fishing-spear and rainmakers among the various groups of the large and sprawling Dinka population. There are certain variations that correspond to region: The rituals of the northern groups tend to be more elaborate due in part to the proximity of the Shilluk and in part to more centralized social institutions. Otherwise, Lienhardt reports that the wide variation in practice is not regionally based, but that each "performance" creatively draws on a common fund of symbols and practices. The ritual, as an institution, was flexible to the desires of the master, his people, and to the demands of the times.

In spite of the variety of the customs, several very important general points must be noted. First of all, burial was voluntarily initiated by the master himself when he was quite old and felt himself to be dying. But the burial of a living master against his will is not unknown among the Dinka. In legend, such is the fate of an evil master of the spear. In reality, such murder is rare and considered terribly wrong. On the other hand, the volition of the master is limited by the fact that he is expected under certain circumstances to request the ritual, and he has lived much of his life with the knowledge that such would likely be his eventual end.

Second, the people must consent. In all the reports, the master requests that the elders consult with the people to see if they agree. The act of burial alive is a collective act: It is neither suicide nor regicide. It is performed by the master and people in concert, for the well-being of the community and the honor of the master.

Third, the master of the fishing-spear is believed to die. The ritual is not performed out of any unsophisticated or erroneous belief on the part of the Dinka that their leader achieves real immortality. The ritual is expressed in the idiom of immortality, to be sure, but we must be careful not to accept their symbols more literally than do the Dinka themselves. Some of the expressions are

clearly euphemisms that "replace the involuntary and passive connotations of the ordinary verb for 'to die' (*thou*) by expressions
suggesting a positive act. Similarly . . . when we hear that the
people bury their master of the fishing-spear it is as an alternative
to 'letting him die'. In other words, the deliberately contrived
death, though recognized as death, enables them to avoid admit-
ting in this case the involuntary death which is the lot of ordinary
men and beasts" (Lienhardt 1961: 314).

The fact that the Dinka actually did bury their leaders alive
under certain circumstances does not eliminate the important role
of symbolic fiction or artifice. The Dinka symbol of burial alive
contains as much fiction as the English notion of the king's two
bodies, the French royal effigy, or the Shilluk spirit of Nyikang.
Lienhardt presents sound evidence that the Dinka recognized the
artificial and metaphorical quality of the ritual just as surely as
the French, English, and Shilluk were not entirely deceived by
their symbols. For example, the close kin of the deceased master
were permitted and expected to mourn in recognition that, in spite
of the idiom of renewed community vitality and joy, the death is
real. "For the rest of the master's people . . . the human symbolic
action involved in the artificial burial must be seen to transform
the experience of a leader's death into a concentrated public experience of vitality and, in the Dinka world, aggressiveness" (Lienhardt 1961: 317).

Burial alive stresses the dual nature of the master's life force in a
manner not unlike that of a European king of the Renaissance.
The reality of the perpetual communal life that the master represents and to which his burial alive makes the decisive contribution
is separable from his personal mortality. The immortal aspect of
the master of the fishing-spear is the spirit of communal solidarity
and experience created by the ritual.

Each of our "kings" – French, English, Shilluk, Dinka – possesses
a certain duality by virtue of being a living symbol. The dualities
are not entirely the same in every case, however. The English and
Shilluk dualities make a radical distinction between the individual
and corporate aspects of the leader and, as we noted above, ascribe
contrasting weights to these aspects. The French and Dinka make
a less clear-cut distinction, ritually mining the ambiguity of lead-

ership. In these two cases, the corporate kingship is subsumed to a certain extent within the individual representative. Whereas the French kings used this ambiguity to create an absolute dynastic and personal rule, the Dinka masters of the fishing-spear weld themselves to the needs of the community and meet death in a way that is also a "social triumph over death" (Lienhardt 1961: 317). The power of the Dinka master is largely dependent upon his personal morality and dignity. Such dignity in life implies personal dignity and unselfishness in the face of death, death which is as inevitable for him as it is for each Dinka. "Notions of individual personal immortality mean little to non-Christian Dinka, but the assertion of collective immortality means much, and it is this which they make in the funeral ceremonies of their religious leaders" (Lienhardt 1961: 319).

It seems that the most powerful natural symbol for the continuity of any community, large or small, simple or complex, is, by a strange and dynamic paradox, to be found in the death of its leader, and in the representation of that striking event. This would come as no surprise to Robert Hertz, who drew attention to the fact that the most instructive illustrations of regular aspects of funeral behavior are often those pertaining to the special case of the succession of kings and chiefs:

> The custom of not proclaiming the successor to a chief until the final ceremony . . . is reported from several peoples belonging to different ethnic groups. We may imagine the dangers of such an interregnum to the societies which are subjected to it. The death of a chief causes a deep disturbance in the social body which, especially if it is prolonged, has weighty consequences. It often seems that the blow which strikes the head of the community in the sacred person of the chief has the effect of suspending temporarily the moral and political laws and of setting free the passions which are normally kept in check by the social order. [Hertz 1960: 49]

Hertz's observation takes us beyond the political issues, beyond the corpse as symbol of the community. The death of a king or leader involves something more profound. Such an event becomes a symbolic paradigm for our own deaths and for the meaning of death itself. Whatever one may think of the leader's person or policies, one has a strong and vicarious personal identification with his death. Questions of political competition, social status, and constitutional stability aside, the royal funeral, effigy, and corpse become a highly condensed set of symbols directly representing every one of the deaths of all the people of the realm.

CONCLUSION
AMERICAN DEATHWAYS

Taking our cue from Hertz, we have tried to unravel the ideological and sociological implications of funerary rites by focusing attention upon the fate of the corpse. Our comparative examples ranged from Europe to Asia, from predynastic Egypt to contemporary Africa, and from the simplest acephalous societies to complex states. But even so, our survey is far from exhaustive. This is for four reasons.

First, a world survey of mortuary customs, given the central importance that such rites often have, would amount almost to an encyclopedia of world cultures. Instead, we have drawn many of our examples from those areas that we know best, namely Africa and Southeast Asia. Second, we are conscious of the risk of overburdening the reader with descriptions of funerals to the point where they all begin to look alike. This is rendered all the more likely by the very similarities that it has been our purpose to identify. Third, we have chosen comparative examples from among the classics of anthropology; from the work of Durkheim, Evans-Pritchard, Frazer, Radcliffe-Brown, Van Gennep, Wilson, and others. In this way, we have pointed out the importance of mortuary rites to the evolving study of religion and society. Fourth,

184

our emphasis on secondary treatment rites narrows the range of our examples.

The justification for our initial emphasis on rites of secondary treatment is that it represents an attempt to *extend* Hertz's analysis. We first, in Chapters 1 and 2, discuss the attractiveness and difficulties of trying to explain certain seemingly universal psychological and symbolic features of funeral rituals. Chapter 3 provides a validation of Hertz's central equation of secondary burial, bodily decomposition, and certain belief about the afterlife. Chapter 4 extends this analysis and relates the practice of secondary burial to the issue of transition from life. In the chapters on royal funerals, we go beyond the topic of secondary treatment but continue to pay attention to the details of treatment of the corpse.

In so doing, we begin to explore traits that have little to do with secondary treatment per se, but that have a global distribution and a fascination of their own. Two examples of such traits are the use of effigies and mummification. The former, which we saw in connection with French royal rituals, is a recurring feature of funerals. In Bali, an effigy can be substituted for, or used in conjunction with, the corpse in the final cremation. In Malekula, New Hebrides Islands, life-size clay effigies are made, incorporating the skull of the deceased (Guiart 1963: 230, 240). One wonders whether these three cases share any other similarities than the use of effigies. In other parts of Melanesia, a seemingly related practice is found: the preservation of the corpse itself (Pretty 1969: 36–43). Many years ago, Elliot Smith (1915) showed that techniques of mummification have a worldwide distribution, and attributed this to diffusion from ancient Egypt. Few would now agree with his explanation, but an alternative has yet to be framed. These questions show that the impetus of Hertz's ideas is far from spent.

However, we pursue no further comparative material here – with one exception.

A justification that is often claimed for the study of societies remote from our own is that they permit a level of objectivity that cannot be achieved close to home. Armed, it is argued, with the insights that this objectivity provides, we return to our own society with new powers of observation. In our introduction, we pointed out just how odd American mortuary practices can be made to appear. Now we examine American funerals in more detail, asking ourselves what the approach through ritual can reveal about them.

PROBLEMS IN THE STUDY OF AMERICAN DEATHWAYS

There are pitfalls in the way of the analysis of American mortuary rites. First, there is the problem of the comparability of our data. In contrast to many of the small-scale societies discussed above, America has a population of over 200 million, and great cultural diversity. Does the United States provide us with one case or several? If the latter, how many? The second pitfall is superficiality, due, ironically, to lack of data. We have more descriptive material about funerals in Indonesia than in America. As Sudnow remarked a decade ago: "Nowhere do we have an ethnography of death" (Sudnow 1967: 3).

These problems make it necessary to deal in generalities, creating a risk that a comparison with complex non-Western rituals will produce nothing more than a few bromides about the virtues or idiocies of American funerals. The risk is exacerbated by the literature on death in America, which is pervaded by value-laden and ethnocentric assessments. On the one hand are exposés of the American death industries, of which Jessica Mitford's *The American Way of Death* (1963) is the best known. An equally harsh critique, also of English origin, is Evelyn Waugh's satirical novel *The Loved One* (1948). On the other hand, there are numerous manuals combining, in different proportions, psychological insight with homely advice on how to approach one's own death and the deaths of those who are near and dear. A recent example is Elizabeth Kübler-Ross's *Death: the Final Stage of Growth* (1975). Dr. Kübler-Ross's title neatly conveys an areligious optimism appropriate to her profession as a psychiatrist. This partisan literature makes it hard to strike a balance between homily and sarcasm.

Our task is neither to criticize nor justify American deathways, but to explain them as they exist. We begin by focusing on some illuminating paradoxes.

THE FIRST PARADOX: RITUAL UNIFORMITY AND INDETERMINATE IDEOLOGY

Given the myriad variety of death rites throughout the world, and the cultural heterogeneity of American society, the expectation is that funeral practices will vary widely from one region, or social class, or ethnic group, to another. The odd fact is that they do not. The overall form of funerals is remarkably uniform from coast to coast. Its general features include: rapid removal of the corpse to a funeral parlor, embalming, institutionalized "viewing," and disposal by burial (see Plate 8).

According to a national census of morticians conducted by Pine, there are approximately 50,000 licensed funeral directors operating 22,000 funeral establishments, together taking care of "almost all" the dead in the United States (Pine 1975: 21). Embalming is nearly universal as a consequence of this reliance on death specialists. Contrary to common belief, embalming is not legally required, but funeral directors insist upon it on grounds of hygiene, in order to protect themselves (Pine 1975: 24). Even in rare cases where religious preferences disallow embalming, some other process of disinfection is substituted.

A study in Philadelphia revealed that 90 percent of burials were conducted directly from funeral homes. This does not mean that the participation of clergy has been eliminated, however, because the homes regularly provide their own interdenominational chapels (Dempsey 1975: 171). Regarding final disposal, over 92 percent of deaths result in earth burial (Pine 1975: 22). Cremation has never been as popular in the United States as it is in Europe, and accounts for less than 4 percent of deaths annually (Dempsey 1975: 180). Finally, with regard to the public "viewing," it seems that there is more variability, but that display of the restored corpse is still clearly the norm. In his census, Pine asked funeral directors to state how many of the funerals that they conducted were what he refers to as "total funerals," that is, having a public

Plate 8. An embalmed corpse lies in an American funeral home.
The photograph was taken by the grandson of the dead man,
whose own child appears in the foreground (Mark Jury).

viewing (and hence cosmetic restoration) and a religious service. Of his respondents, 78 percent reported that almost all their funerals were of this kind, 20 percent said that most were, and a mere 2 percent said that only some were (Pine 1975: 201).

This uniformity becomes all the more striking if we compare it to the variety found among the 1,600 Berawan of Borneo. They have two widely different death ritual cycles, an extended and an abbreviated one, plus a number of choices with regard to temporary storage, final storage, and processing of the corpse. As we saw, Berawan beliefs about the afterlife are at first sight inconsistent. A coherent eschatology only emerged after extended analysis. Because American funerary rituals are so much more uniform, one might reasonably assume that it would be correspondingly easier to deduce the ideology underlying them. But this is not so.

In the first place, Americans claim adherence to a number of different denominations, whose formal doctrines on the fate of the soul in death are dissimilar. The Roman Catholic notion of purgatory is not shared by Protestants; Mormons are unique in believing that it is possible to arrange the salvation of unconverted kin who are long dead; and so on (Grollman 1974: 81–141). But these are formal doctrines – we know little about the degree of faith that ordinary practitioners have in them. Even more opaque are the views of those who claim no affiliation to any organized religious sect. We certainly cannot conclude that they totally lack ideas about the nature and meaning of death. Just how Americans conceive of death therefore remains a thorny issue: Few seem able to adopt a thoroughgoing agnosticism, and yet the majority seem shaky in their faith in a Christian afterlife.

In reviewing the customs of Borneo, we noted that it was frequently the case that the rituals of death are clearly set out and known to all, whereas their rationale is less explicit. American funerals present an even more extreme example of this phenomenon. We are left with two interrelated questions: What accounts for the uniformity in American deathways? What do they express? At present, there are two sets of answers, both of which contain some truth, yet fail to provide a satisfying explanation for the form of the American funeral. The first relates to economic variables, the second psychological.

Conclusion

CRITIQUES OF THE FUNERAL INDUSTRY

The economic explanation sees the uniformity of American death-ways as a product of ruthless capitalism and their content as expressing only materialist values.

The emergence of the contemporary funeral parlor is the result of a process of accretion of functions over a period of two centuries. In colonial times, the undertaker was a part-time specialist only; his main skills were those of the carpenter. In addition to making coffins, he assisted in the laying out of the corpse. The first important abdication of function by church and congregation came about with the change in the location of graveyards. Partly as a result of increasing urbanization, and partly as a result of changing styles in mortuary architecture, the cemetery became separated from the church and was moved to an area peripheral to the residential area (Stannard 1974: 69–91). The undertaker now became a livery man as well, dealing in hired rigs. As factory-produced coffins became available, his premises also became a showroom.

Experiments with embalming began in the early part of the nineteenth century as a response to practical considerations. With the increasing mobility and spread of the population, it frequently became necessary to ship corpses long distances for burial by the close kin. During the Civil War, large numbers of young men died far from home, and professional embalmers appeared around the battlefields (Pine 1975: 16). At the conclusion of the war, the assassination of Lincoln brought further attention to the new techniques. The funeral cortege, with Lincoln's body on display, traveled from Washington across the Northeast and Midwest to Springfield, Illinois. In the 1880s methods of arterial injection were introduced, and for the first time effective cosmetic restoration became generally available; the funeral industry grew rapidly as a consequence (see Habenstein and Lamers 1955: 321–52, for a detailed account of developments in embalming).

The new techniques made possible the evolution of an old European institution, the wake, into a new and peculiarly American form. Traditionally, the wake occurs on the night immediately following death, when relatives and friends gather in the house where the corpse is laid out, either on a tabletop or in an open coffin. On the following morning, the sealed coffin is carried off for burial. Embalming allowed the period between death and burial to be extended, giving time for the deceased to journey home or for relatives to assemble. After restorative techniques were introduced, attention was focused upon the display of the corpse and a more sumptuous setting was provided for it. In this way the old elements of the wake – a gathering in the presence of the body of the deceased – were reworked into a new complex.

These developments strengthened the role of the undertaker in several ways. First, in the beginning of the nineteenth century states began to enact legislation for the licensing of competent embalmers. This move, designed no doubt to protect the public from charlatans, created a controlling professional elite. Second, the technical apparatus required for embalming now rendered it impractical to perform the operation in the deceased's home, making it necessary for the undertaker to provide premises for the "viewing." This trend was encouraged by two features. Many houses, especially those of the less well-to-do, were too small to contain the crowds that now gathered for these occasions. Moreover, neither Jewish nor Roman Catholic practice allows the funeral service to be conducted with the coffin open, and most Protestant churches discourage the practice (Dempsey 1975: 177). In this way, the church or synagogue became removed from an important ritual phase of the funeral. The final step in this accretion of function was the addition of chapels to the proliferating mortuary complexes.

As the critics have shown, funeral directors have not failed to exploit their position in order to make a profit. Harmer (1963) and Mitford (1963) are full of examples of such opportunism. For example, Mitford describes how funeral directors regularly play upon the emotional state of their customers in order to get them to purchase a more expensive coffin than they had intended. As she points out, the morticians' customers are almost by definition "impulse buyers" (Mitford 1963: 19–21). Again, cemetery landscapers are in a particularly favorable position vis-à-vis their customers: They collect payment on plots that they will not have to provide for perhaps many years, leaving themselves with interest-free capital in the interim (Mitford 1963: 97–118).

The National Funeral Directors Association has frequently exercised a powerful political influence. It maintains well-financed lobbies in Washington and the state capitals. Occasionally it has been able to secure legislation favorable to the business interests of its members. For instance, the association has steadily opposed cremation, and in some states has supported laws that make it unnecessarily expensive by requiring that a coffin be provided and burned up with the corpse (Dempsey 1975: 170).

However, in comparative perspective the proportion of available resources committed to death ritual does not seem exceptional: Certainly the Berawan and the Malagasy use up more. Moreover, the amount spent each year on funerals in the United States is considerably less than the amount spent on weddings, yet few condemn the materialism of weddings. Charges of exploitation are not leveled at the dressmaking industry, or the Brewers' Association of America on the grounds that they make a profit out of these festive events (Fulton 1965: 104). Presumably this is because the critics regard weddings as socially useful and funerals as useless. But who is to judge the value of a ritual?

The same kind of overstatement has occurred in connection with conspicuous consumption at American funerals. Certainly, commercialism is noticeable, but it is not unlimited. For example, sumptuous flower arrangements surrounding the coffin are a feature of the "viewing," and it could be argued that the mourners compete to display their affluence in such gifts. However, very nice distinctions of status govern the size of floral tributes. It would be entirely tactless for a mere acquaintance or a distant relative to offer too large a wreath. In general, the impression is of a striving to find the *correct* level of expenditure in funeral accoutrements, rather than the most *impressive* (Crocker 1971: 123).

The same tendency is noticeable in the funeral cavalcade. Although it is common for close relatives to request that the hearse drive past the deceased's former residence or work place, the display at such times is modest by comparison with, say, nineteenth-century England. Curl (1972) presents a remarkable photograph from England of a six-horse hearse, heavily draped in black crepe, the horses decorated with black-dyed ostrich feathers, and attended by a dozen or so equerries. The striking feature of the picture is the obvious poverty of the neighborhood to which this apparition has been summoned. By comparison, the dark American hearse and line of cars is positively spartan. In grave markers also, the prevalent trend is toward simple horizontal tablets. Clearly, wealth and social class *are* expressed in funerals, as they are in other phases of American culture, such as housing, clothing, and automobiles. However, there is little evidence of the manipulation of the dead for status-climbing purposes.

Considering the economic explanation as a whole, there is no doubt that the existence of a tightly organized group of specialists who control every phase of the disposal of corpses is the most significant single feature of American funerals. It explains why funerals cost what they do, and why nonspecialists, such as kin and clergy, appear only in passive roles.

But it does not explain everything about them. Why do they have the ritual form they do? There are other things that could be done to the corpse that would be just as expensive and therefore just as profitable. The very uniformity of funeral rites places limits on the economic explanation because merchandisers usually try continually to add new products to tickle the fancy of consumers. There has been, it is true, some gimmickry in the funeral industry – drive-in funeral parlors are a recent example – but the overall form of the rites has remained remarkably stable for several decades.

Moreover, it is clear that Americans are not just passive consumers of the only services available to them; they actively approve of them. A survey in several midwestern cities revealed that a majority of respondents felt that contemporary funerals are appropriate, and that the funeral director has an important role to play in comforting the bereaved (Kastenbaum and Aisenberg 1973: 213). Silverman (1974) reports that the widows she worked with in Boston received more help and comfort from the funeral director than from either physician or clergyman. This tacit approval is also manifest in the limited success of movements to reform funeral practices. Nonprofit funeral and memorial societies have had some success, and certainly provide much cheaper funerals, but their membership remains small. Some unions have established funeral plans for members, but their experience has been that the cheapest variety does not sell. Their blue-collar clientele still demands all the elements found in the commercial funeral (Dempsey 1975: 183, 187).

A final piece of evidence: Modern-style embalming, with its associated rites, has been practiced for nearly a century now. During that time, the United States has continued to receive immigrants from many different cultural backgrounds. The statistics quoted in the preceding section indicate that the majority have adopted American deathways, just as they have absorbed other aspects of national culture. Had it been otherwise, institutions would surely have sprung up to cater to their needs. This shows that funerals somehow fit into a peculiarly American ideology; that funerals express something. Economics is powerless to explain what.

FEAR AND GUILT: THE INADEQUACY OF PSYCHOLOGY

The second type of explanation for the form of American funerals has the advantage that, unlike the economic explanation, it deals directly with the content of the rituals. It sees them as expressing deep currents of fear and guilt, and points to the uniformity of the rites as evidence of the prevalence of such emotions. The widest extension of the theory is found in Becker's influential book *The Denial of Death*, in which he argues that "the idea of death, the fear of it, haunts the human animal like nothing else; it is the mainspring of human activity" – presumably of funerals in particular (1973: ix). A more specific application of the theory to funerals is found in Bowman's *The American Funeral: A Study of Guilt, Extravagance, and Sublimity* (1964).

The strongest argument in support of these views is provided by the elaborate avoidance, both in word and deed, of the brute facts of death. The majority of deaths now occur in hospitals, where the fiction of probable recovery is often maintained until a person is near the point of death. The corpse is then promptly removed without the aid of the bereaved, who see it again only under very special circumstances, after it has been primped up to appear as if asleep. Coffins are selected for their superior padding, as if comfort mattered to the corpse. We speak of the deceased as having "passed on"; we describe the premises of the death specialist with the cozy-sounding terms "funeral parlor" or "funeral home"; we comment how "well" the embalmed corpse looks lying in the "slumber room"; and so on.

This endless shying away from confrontation with mortality is undeniably a marked feature of American culture. However, we cannot conclude that this is solely or exclusively the result of a pervasive fear of death. Other causes may be involved. For example, the professional titles used by undertakers have grown increasingly euphemistic: "mortician," reminiscent of such medical specialists as optician; "funeral director," suggestive of business or perhaps the stage; and most recently "grief counselor," a kind of terminal marriage counselor. As a result of participant observation research in a number of Chicago funeral parlors, Kaut (1952: 7–35) suggests that these euphemisms may have less to do with the insecurities of the public over mortality than with the insecurities of the specialists over their professional status. These titles represent a desire to shake off their pallid public image and acquire more of the éclat of the medical profession.

Similarly, the process of embalming itself represents more than an illusory negation of death. If Americans really associated preservation of the corpse with perpetuation of life, would there not be a demand for true mummification, as there was in ancient Egypt? Current embalming practices generally only impede decomposition by a few weeks, because the use of high concentrations of preservative fluids evidently makes it harder to produce a lifelike appearance for display purposes. The techniques exist to do a much more permanent job, but they are not in demand. In one instance, a funeral director was obliged to move a coffin to allow a road expansion a year or so after interment. The corpse turned out to be perfectly preserved, and the undertaker, proud of his handiwork, invited the close kin to come and inspect it.

Conclusion

They emphatically refused (Kaut: personal communication). What this anecdote illustrates is that embalming is for a specific ritual purpose. Once the funeral was completed the family had no further desire to see or think about the lost member they had so carefully housed underground. The response of Americans to cryogenic suspension – the deep freezing of the body for later revival – validates the same point. It has now been available for a decade; it is promoted by an active Cryonics Youth Association; and it holds out the promise of a scientifically feasible immortality. Yet at the present time there is a grand total of just *fifteen* people in suspension (Dempsey 1975: 191).

What embalming clearly *does* prevent is the confrontation of the mourners with the processes of putrescence in the corpse. But this horror of corruption may be seen as a special case of the general aversion to body processes, of which the American stress on hygiene is a part. There are at least as many taboos on, and euphemisms for, defecation and copulation as there are on dying. In their horror of putrescence Americans resemble the Berawan of Borneo, but their reaction to it is different: The Berawan try to hasten the completion of the process; the Americans try to halt it.

The avoidance of death may have several contributing factors other than fear. But there is also a difficulty in specifying what exactly is feared. Choron (1964: 73–84) deals with this problem at some length. He shows that "fear of death" may be several things: fear of what happens after death, fear of the event itself, or fear of ceasing to be. It may even be the fear of being *unable* to die. Choron quotes the case of a young woman who found terrifying the idea of living with herself forever: "She worried most about it at the age of ten, but at twenty, she heard an address on immortality, and the feeling of unbearableness returned: it was as if she simply could not endure it – better total annihilation, anything, than this continual going on and on" (Choron 1964: 18). If there are all these different *kinds* of fear, and if the fear of death conditions the rituals of death, should there not be a corresponding variety of rituals?

This indeterminacy about the nature of the fear of death may explain the contradictory results obtained in psychological tests. In a volume edited by Fulton (1965) is a series of articles exploring unconscious attitudes to death among various populations, such as students, the aged, and the mentally ill, employing a variety of verbal and projective tests. As the editor points out (1965: 80), the results are confusing: Swenson reports an inverse correlation between fear of death and religiosity, whereas Christ finds no connection between the two. Rhudick and Dibner find that people in good health are more likely to have a "positive attitude" toward death, whereas Swenson reports that the healthy are more "evasive or defensive" on the topic than the sick. The researchers also differed on what influence an unstable ego structure had on morbid fears.

We do not doubt that morbid anxiety forms an important force in the psychodynamics of the individual, in our society and in others, as Becker has argued. But these private fears cannot provide us with a theory of public ritual. If the fear of death is indeed universal (and the anthropologist invariably views such claims with narrowed eyes), then it cannot explain the *variation* of mortuary rites from one place to another. The general cannot be used to explain the particular. To salvage the hypothesis, it must be argued that all funerals express fear of death, but that American ones do so more than others because Americans are more fearful than other people. This heightened fearfulness is usually attributed to the decline of organized religion in the West, with a consequent loss of faith in the old certitudes (Becker 1973: ix). But the problem of exceptions remains. In Britain church attendance has declined even more markedly, yet British funerals lack many of the death-denying rites found in American ones, notably embalming and public viewing. Attempts to market these services in Britain have largely failed (Mitford 1963: 161–76).

These are the hazards of reductionism. In Chapter 1, we showed how variable are the emotions, or more precisely the emotional expressions, that different societies regard as appropriate toward death. These differing views on what is proper do not control the feelings of the individual, which are sovereign. But the former condition the latter and provide a setting for them. Between ritual and emotion there is a subtle feedback, so that it is difficult at any moment to say whether the emotions are propelling the ritual or vice versa. In this circumstance, it becomes necessary to follow

Conclusion

Emile Durkheim's precept: *The determining cause of a social fact should be sought among the social facts preceding it and not among the states of the individual consciousness* (1938: 110).

COLLECTIVE REPRESENTATIONS
OF DEATH IN AMERICA

That the practices of embalming, display of the corpse, and earth burial are social facts is easy to demonstrate: They satisfy the twin criteria that they are perceived by the individual as originating externally (even where they have been internalized as personal values; see Parsons 1968a: 315) and are normatively sanctioned. The mourners do not think of themselves as inventing anew the rite of embalming in order to express or relieve their guilts and fears. Instead, they do what they think is proper, what is socially prescribed. Proponents of the economic explanation might argue that they only do what they must. But, as we have shown, the bereaved *do* have other alternatives if they truly consider that the standard rites lack moral authority. The fact that people are so easily led to believe that embalming is legally required – all the funeral directors have to do is fail to inform their customers otherwise – is interesting in itself. Americans feel that it is the sort of thing that *ought* to be enforced by law.

But these main elements of the ritual sequence are only the most obvious social facts governing the funeral, only the tip of the iceberg. American deathways comprise an extensive complex of social facts and associated collective representations. There are many other items of behavior or expression associated with death and funerals that turn out to be subtly governed by notions of propriety, notions that ordinary people are not in the habit of formulating in words yet that they regularly put into action in moments of crisis. For examples we turn to Sudnow (1967), whose own work in two large hospitals in California goes a long way toward alleviating that lack of an "ethnography of death" that he pointed out.

The first example concerns rules governing the transmission of the news of death. These cover both the *way* that people are told, and the *order* in which they are told. The immediate family have the right to know within minutes or hours, and expect to be informed in person or over the telephone. In choosing between these two, the greater speed of the telephone must be taken into account if there is a risk that the person will learn of the death in an improper way. The physician is often the first to know, and will try to impede the spread of the news until he or she has talked to those entitled to learn it directly. Other visitors who happen to be at the hospital are only told if the doctor is confident that they cannot "leak" it to close kin. Sometimes this requires delicate maneuvering. Thereafter, people should ideally learn from someone who stood in approximately the same degree of intimacy to the deceased, and in rough order of intimacy. Some little discussion is often necessary to decide who should telephone whom, since the urgency, or lack of it, with which the close kin contact friends and relatives constitutes an evaluation of the importance of the person in the life of the deceased and in the estimation of the survivors (Sudnow 1967: 154–5, 158–63).

After news of the death has spread, a second set of representations is called into play, having to do with the timing of encounters between sympathizers and the immediate family. Normal rules governing the privacy of the bereaved family are put aside, and new ones substituted during the course of the *rite de passage* that are both more and less restrictive than normal. Those less closely related to the deceased are embarrassed to offer their condolences too soon after the death occurs. Information is sought as to the propriety of a visit, in order to make sure of not intruding on an intimate family scene. On the other hand, the family, out of respect for the intent of such sympathizers, cannot reject them or show irritation. They are therefore open to receiving relative strangers as well as close friends in a more intimate and less controllable way than they normally would. This open-door accessibility is institutionalized in the Jewish custom of *shiva*, but is evidently found in many American communities. Under these circumstances, an organizer often emerges who is able to decide matters of protocol; someone close enough to the family to be aware of their desires, but not so close as to be more properly concerned in active grieving (Sudnow 1967: 156–7).

Conclusion

A third example concerns the obligation not only to view the corpse, but also to say the correct things about it. Friends and relatives of the deceased mingle freely at the viewing, and often there is considerable sociability. But, on entering, the mourner must first approach the coffin. There is little show of emotion, but afterward it is appropriate to make some brief remark about how well the deceased looks. This pattern is established with the immediate family, who are the first to view the restored corpse. Generally the reaction is relief and muted admiration. If the reaction of some close relative is other than expected, particularly if someone so forgets themself as to comment that the deceased looks dead, they will be gently coached by the funeral director. Often, he or she will ask the family to leave the viewing room while adjustments are made. It is hard to do much to the corpse at this stage, so the real changes are minimal. Yet when the family returns, they almost invariably say something to the effect: "That's just perfect now." Those less emotionally involved conform more easily (Pine 1975: 95–6).

These usages are rapidly acquired, even by those who have not had occasion to employ them previously, because they conform to collective representations that are found in everyday contexts, and not just in the situation of the funeral. That a close relationship exists between deathways and other ideological and social systems in a society is easily demonstrated by tracing the changes that occur in each over time. Even a casual glance at the history of funerals in the West, for which of anywhere in the world we have the best records, suffices to reveal a complex and sometimes remarkably rapid evolution in style. There is variation in the pace and direction of innovation from one country to another, indicating a dynamic interaction with other changing social factors. Interestingly enough, variation in the form of the death rites between classes within one nation (aside from sheer cost) is less noticeable than variation from country to country. This relative uniformity may indicate that, insofar as the nation is a solidary community, it needs to share a system of beliefs and practices concerning death.

The detailed history of Western deathways has yet to be written, although some interesting beginnings have been made, notably in the essays of Ariès (1967, 1974a) and in those contained in Stannard (1974). Ariès provides an overview of funerals in Europe from the Middle Ages to the present and shows that the medieval pattern has haltingly, and with occasional reversals, been made over into its complete opposite.

THE SECOND PARADOX: PUPPET DEATH

Ariès's argument is a striking one: Contemporary French and English people have been deprived of their own deaths, and of the right to mourn the deaths of others.

In the Middle Ages, people were expected to detect the imminence of their death. If they failed to do so, it was the duty of a friend to point it out so that they could prepare themselves. The preparations involved were partly spiritual and partly social, and on both counts the sick were well aware of what was expected of them. The drama took place in a room crowded with people – kin, workmates, neighbors, even casual passers-by. The dying person played the central role, striving for the same dignity that he or she had previously witnessed at similar scenes. Each visitor was bade adieu, asked for his or her forgiveness, and given a blessing. Final instructions were given with the authority that death invested, and the sacraments were taken. After the event, the close kin gave themselves over to uninhibited grief. With this cathartic release, they soon returned to normal life (Ariès 1974b: 3–4).

Today, the physician and the family conspire to keep all knowledge of impending death from the sick person. The truth is also kept from children, and indeed the terminally ill are reduced to the status of minors. Should they suspect the truth, they keep quiet about their fears so that the survivors can have the comfort of saying to themselves: "At least, he never knew." The doctor presides over the deathbed. Afterward displays of emotion are kept to an absolute minimum, and those who, it is feared, will "break down" in public are avoided. Such intense embarrassment surrounds loss of control that widows or widowers will often stay away from the funeral rather than risk it, thereby giving up whatever comfort they might have obtained from an extremely brief and otiose ritual (Ariès 1974b: 8–11).

As he himself notes, Ariès's account of contemporary practices mainly applies to Europe. In America developments have taken a somewhat different turn, not in terms of the secrecy about impending death, which Americans share, but in terms of the response when death has occurred. Let us compare the ritual sequence of medieval Europe with that of contemporary America, which is as much a descendent of the former as is that of present-day France and England.

The medieval sequence began with the deathbed scene that Ariès describes so movingly, and which is often portrayed in pictures of the epoch. It continued with the wake – indeed the wake was virtually a continuation of the deathbed gathering because it occurred in the same building as the death (if not in the same room), it involved the same people or a group much like them, and it was held on the evening following the death. The corpse was removed to the church for the funeral service the next day, or at most a day later, and buried nearby.

In the contemporary American sequence, the deathbed scene has all but been eliminated. Sudnow (1967: 85) reports that relatives were infrequently present when death occurred in the large county hospital that he studied, and very seldom asked to see the corpse before removal to the funeral home. Even when they are present near death, no moral authority is invested in the dying person. The wake, however, has increased in duration and function. Usually it extends over about three days, although even longer periods were common a few decades ago. Funeral directors have attempted to establish the norm that shorter wakes are sufficient, using the rationale that transport is now rapid enough that a mourner can arrive from any part of the country within a couple of days. Visiting is light during the morning, but heavy in the late afternoon and evening. Often close members of the family are there many hours a day, and sometimes wish to stay all night, although this practice was already declining in the early 1950s (Kaut 1952: 51). The funeral service, meanwhile, has become fused with the wake, because it is often held on the same premises.

Displays of emotion within the funeral parlor are perfectly permissible, and appear to have a cathartic effect. The wake or funeral is rarely held in the absence of the close kin, as happens in England; this is resented by the funeral director when it occurs because it compromises his position (Pine 1975: 99). The burial is not an important phase of the ritual: The close family may attend only briefly at the graveside and leave before interment occurs.

The comparison reveals a number of ironies. In contrast to medieval Europe, the nuclear family in America has been invested with enormous sentiment that was formerly dispersed over a wider group. Yet, in the country where "togetherness" is a national fetish, no phase of the most severe crisis of the family's existence takes place at home. But the oddest feature is that a society that provided harsh living conditions and little chance of mobility for its members stressed a positive role for them in death, whereas a country that emphasizes individual achievement allows only a passive role to the dying.

Since the fifteenth century, there has been in the West a continuous tradition of literature on how to die. The *Ars moriendi* instructed the individual on how to shrive his or her soul in preparation for death, and how to meet social obligations to achieve a "proper death" (Boase 1972: 119–20). A seventeenth-century version, Menston's *The Art to Dye Well* is phrased in equally muscular terms. But recent editions, such as *The Art of Dying* by Robert Neale (1973), stress an almost Buddhist resignation in the face of one's own death and the deaths of others. The earlier volumes urge that the sinner "look on death" in order to wake the fires of conscience; the latest writers advise a sidelong glance in order to avoid psychological maladjustment. In the Middle Ages, men and women made themselves masters of their own deaths. In America, the archetypal land of enterprise, self-made men are reduced to puppets.

AN INDIGENOUS AMERICAN RELIGION

The historical comparisons that we make here are crude, and the opportunity exists for more delicate analysis. For example, Douglas (1974: 49–68) describes a remarkable religious movement in mid–nineteenth-century America that (for social reasons that she convincingly explains) sought to promote a homely, even domestic, view of the world to come. This movement produced some of the most detailed eschatology on record, with descriptions of the "eating habits, occupations, lifestyles, methods of childcare and courtship current in Heaven" (Douglas 1974: 63). How, one wonders, did such views relate to ritual practice?

Ariès's own explanation for the inversion of death since the Middle Ages turns on the increasing sentimentalization of the nuclear family during that period, with a consequent loss of individuality. However, the inversion of ritual is less complete in the United States, where the process of sentimentalization is most advanced. Ariès accounts for this by positing a rediscovery or continuation in America of the "tone and style of the Age of Enlightenment" (1974b: 17). This is a difficult assertion to test, but we can perhaps break it down into more tangible variables.

Though it is not easy to specify how Americans conceive of their fate after death, there are attitudes toward death that are strongly held by them, and which distinguish their views from those of societies in other times and places. As Sudnow's work suggests, the place to begin looking for these attitudes is not in the representations of organized religion, but in something more pervasive – medicine. Americans have vast faith in medicine – a faith that is certainly in tune with the Enlightenment values of progress and humanism. The development of powerful new drugs, and of reliable and safe surgical techniques, together with improvements in diet, have enabled the "inevitability" of death to be redefined. Formerly, for instance in medieval times, death was everywhere, in all its ugliness and suffering. It might pick out anyone. In contemporary America it is removed to the hospital, or the television screen, so that it is sometimes suggested that Americans are simply "soft" and unable to face reality. But *reality* has changed. Modern medicine has not greatly increased the maximum lifespan that a person can hope for, but it has greatly improved the chances of reaching that age. Moreover, it has the power to alleviate pain, even in the incurably ill. With the exception of the specter of cancer, it is strongly felt that death is only a matter of resignation in the geriatric, and suffering never (Parsons 1963: 61–3).

These attitudes toward death frame a view of the proper life that confounds the medieval view of a proper death. The key notion is fulfillment. The life of the individual should rise in an arc through brassy youth to fruitful middle years, and then decline gently toward a death that is acceptable as well as inevitable. The practices of embalming and viewing express these collective representations: The point is to reveal the dead at peace. Because the last hours or days preceding death may have been marred with pain, which is inadmissible, the restored body provides a truer image of death. Because heavy sedation may have been necessary to alleviate suffering, deathbed scenes are precluded. Controversy has revolved around whether or not the viewing of the embalmed corpse helps the bereaved to recover from their grief by providing them with a pleasant "memory picture," as the Funeral Directors Association would have us believe. Psychiatric opinion is divided (Dempsey 1975: 175–8). What is clear is why the main actor in the rituals is dramaturgically passive (our "puppet death"), because peace and fulfillment are conceived of as passive conditions.

Views about the worth of medicine figure prominently in these attitudes toward death. But these views in turn derive from a world view that predates the rather sudden rise to efficacy of modern medicine in the last century. This world view is expressed in the Constitution, in concepts of the nature of social class, in aesthetic predilections, and in much else that is peculiarly American. Were an anthropologist from Borneo or Madagascar to visit the United States, we have no doubt that he or she would have little trouble in identifying a "solidary system of beliefs and practices relative to sacred things" (Durkheim 1965: 62) that constitute an indigenous American religion.

Robert Bellah highlights the public component of this religion in his essay on *Civil Religion in America:*

> While some have argued that Christianity is the national faith, and others that church and synagogue celebrate only the generalized religion of "the American Way of Life," few have realized that there actually exists alongside of and rather clearly differen-

tiated from the churches an elaborate and well-institutionalized
civil religion in America. This article argues not only that there
is such a thing, but also that this religion . . . has its own serious-
ness and integrity and requires the same care in understanding
that any other religion does. [Bellah 1967: 1]

Bellah explores the dimensions of this civil religion in the area
of national politics by analyzing the religiously charged language
of presidential inaugural addresses – which constitute a major rite
of the national religion. He outlines the changes that have occurred in these collective representations during the two centuries
of the nation's existence and what symbols have been mobilized to
express them. He shows that the trauma of the Civil War introduced new themes of death, sacrifice, and rebirth into the civil
religion. Abraham Lincoln came not only to express these themes,
but through his martyrdom to embody them in his own person
(see Plate 9).

In addition to the great rituals of state that Bellah points to,
there is another aspect of the civil religion, a domestic aspect,
which our study of funerals brings into focus. Here too, the death
of Lincoln was a highly significant event. His assassination riveted
public attention; his funeral continued to hold it. Lincoln's body
was returned to Springfield by almost the same route that he had
taken to Washington four years previously as president-elect. At
towns and cities along the way, the funeral procession was
repeated, amid crowds straining to catch a last glimpse of the man
that they now called "the Saviour of the Union." An observer
wrote:

> I saw him in his coffin. The face was the same as in life. Death
> had not changed the kindly countenance in any line. There was
> upon it the same sad look that it had worn always, though not so
> intensely sad as it had been in life. It was as if the spirit had
> come back to the poor clay, reshaped the wonderfully sweet
> face, and given it an expression of gladness . . . It was the look of
> a worn man suddenly relieved. [Quoted in Hamilton and Osten-
> dorf 1963: 234.]

In humbler rites across the country, a nation still grieving its war
dead tried to capture in their funerals something of the peace
written upon Lincoln's face. In this way, public attitudes were

Plate 9. Apotheosis picture of Lincoln. The martyred president
is shown ascending to Heaven, assisted by Washington. This
carte-de-visite is a composite of a photograph and a painting.
Such mementos helped turn Lincoln into an American folk
hero, and hardly a parlor in the North was without one in
the post–Civil War period (Library of Congress).

made ready to accept the new techniques of embalming then being perfected.

It would be wrong to suggest that funerals comprise the entirety of the domestic civil religion. There are numerous other family and community rites, of which Christmas, Halloween, and Thanksgiving are the most obvious. Nevertheless, since the Civil War, the standard rituals of burial have taken on the power of collective representations for all Americans, regardless of religious affiliation.

It may seem surprising that such a system of beliefs and practices exists alongside Christianity, to which a majority of Americans give at least nominal adherence. That it does is neatly illustrated by the dilemma of Jews at Christmastime. A large part of the Jewish identity in America is defined in opposition to Christianity. Yet Jews feel a strong pull to participate in Christmas, especially if they have children. The children's perception is more lucid that that of the adults: They perceive it as a rite of the national religion rather than a rite of Christianity. Occasionally the child's view prevails, occasionally the dogmatic, but frequently a compromise is reached in which the Jewish festival of Chanukah, which happens to fall conveniently close, is invested with the symbols of national-Christmas, such as gift giving and the tree.

But this duality is nothing new. For centuries, Christianity existed in Europe alongside the vestiges of tribal religions. As is well known, many of the trappings of Christmas itself are pagan in origin. Ariès cites a nice example from medieval Europe. The public gathering around a dying person was not a pious practice imposed by the Church. In fact, priests frowned upon it, because they saw it as distracting from the spiritual preparations and from their own role. Pious individuals sometimes took the church's advice and spent their last moments alone. More frequently, they responded to a different and independent set of mores, the power of which is demonstrated by the custom that anyone seeing a priest carrying viaticum should follow him to the dying person's bedside, even if that person were a stranger (Ariès 1974b: 4).

The only novel feature of the American situation is that the national religion germinated and grew under the nose, as it were, of a religious establishment that already commanded universal respect. What this demonstrates is the hardiness of such growths. It may be that no nation can emerge or persist without a belief system that encroaches to some extent upon the terrain of world religions.

Even allowing for the undoubted influence of the funeral industry, it is, in the last analysis, the existence of the civil religion that explains the uniformity of American death rites, and enables us to discuss them in general terms. Paradoxically, it is a death-centered religion. This is indicated by the sacred quality of funerals compared to that of other life crises, such as weddings. Marriages are often solemnized in registry offices without the attentions of a religious specialist. But death demands a full religious service, with clergyman and congregation, even for those with only nominal church affiliation, or even none at all. Despite the obligatory presence of an officiant of some organized religious group, the usual setting of the service is carefully interdenominational. Many take place in the chapel attached to the funeral parlor, which lacks all but the most generalized insignia. The most extended and important rite is the wake. The wake is largely social in content, emphasizing that the loss is a unit event, a happening of the group (Sudnow 1967: 165). Its most important icon, the embalmed corpse, presides in impassive benevolence.

The civil religion of America operates on every level between the state and the family. The national religion focuses upon the rituals of the presidency. Its hagiography features past presidents, such as the martyred Abraham Lincoln. As we have seen, it has a powerful effect on other phases of the civil religion, and may itself achieve poignancy by the borrowing of some small domestic rite. Another phase of the indigenous religion pervades the life of towns and cities. In *The Living and the Dead: A Study of the Symbolic Life of Americans*, Warner emphasizes that the local center of community ritual is the graveyard. In the New England town that Warner studied, Memorial Day is a solidary tribute to ancestors, with its parade to the cemetery, speeches, floral tributes, and gunshot salutes. It is the one event that unites all the residents of the town. We have stressed the most personal, though still social, level of the civil religion, which receives its most telling representation in the funeral of the average citizen. In the funeral parlor, basic values of life are condensed into the peaceful image of the embalmed body.

THE CORPSE ALONE

It is striking that the folkways of a society that scrupulously avoids death should center on funeral rituals, and especially on funeral rituals that require the visible presence of a corpse. But American society is not unique in this. As we have argued above, mortuary rites figure prominently in the religions of Bornean, Malagasy, and Nyakyusa people, yet none of them have a particularly ghoulish interest in the dead. Like Americans, they express at funerals the values of life. Nor is it surprising that the corpse itself should figure so prominently in the American rites: The very fact of avoidance makes the corpse an even more powerful symbol than it is for other peoples.

In the late 1940s, the New England artist Hyman Bloom completed a remarkable series of paintings. When they were first shown in Boston, his reviewer tells us:

> . . . one had to find ways to look at them. They were painfully difficult to face. Lifesize paintings of nude corpses confronted the viewer. . . . The single figures were lying on slabs, surrounded by sheets or shrouds; but set within a vertical format, they appeared to be standing, awkward and upright, against the wall. The shallow spatial backgrounds of the paintings contrasted strongly with the figures and tended to thrust them forward. The designing was simple and offered no obvious structural complexities . . . nowhere for the eye to wander, no way to avoid a direct confrontation with those dead men and women standing/lying in front of us. To make matters more difficult, the paintings were seductively beautiful, their physical presence, the color, and the paint itself extraordinarily sensuous. . . . There is no anger, no open moral attitude. Not even the message of *carpe diem*. There are no promises and no warnings. It was this non-homiletic celebration of the jewellike putrefaction of the

corpse itself, that most disturbed the audience. [Ablow, 1976: 9]

But, significantly, even the artist himself was unable to maintain so dispassionate a stance:

> Understandably, these painfully direct and unflinching images seem to have been difficult for the artist as well. Bloom, in the paintings that followed, retreated from his extraordinary confrontation. He turned the corpses into cadavers. . . . The bodies are no longer set parallel to the picture plane, pressing close to the surface, pushing into the viewer's world. They are removed to a deeper space and are seen in various complex foreshortenings. And now they have become cadavers, carcasses in dissecting rooms, they are fragmented, often hacked into parts. In many of the paintings and drawings the dead have lost their identities, sexual, or even human. [Ablow 1976: 9]

Bloom's approach to, and shying away from, the corpse in its simple reality is a measure of the power that it held for him as symbol. The power is one of evocation and association. At the sight of a corpse, emotions surge through the individual chaotically: fear, rage, curiosity, sympathy, even joy, for he or she is dead and you are not. In indirect confrontation, a verbal reference or ritual representation, the image is still potent, though modified. The vitality of a culture or ideology depends upon its ability to channel the power of such mordant symbols as the corpse.

BIBLIOGRAPHY

Abinal, R. P., and Malzac, R. P. 1888. *Dictionnaire Malgache-Français*. Paris: Editions Maritimes et Coloniales.

Ablow, J. 1976. "Hyman Bloom and the Uses of the Past." *New Boston Review*. Spring. Pp. 9–10.

Abrahamsson, H. 1951. *The Origins of Death: Studies in African Mythology*. Uppsala: Studia Ethnographica Upsaliensia 3.

Adams, M. J. 1971. "Work Patterns and Symbolic Structures in a Village Culture, East Sumba, Indonesia." *Southeast Asia* 1(4): 320–34.

⎯⎯ 1977. "Style in Southeast Asian Materials Processing: Some Implications for Ritual and Art." In H. Lechtman and R. Merrill (eds.). *Material Culture: Studies, Organization, and Dynamics of Technology*. Pp. 21–52. St. Paul: West Publishing Company.

Adriani, N., and Kruyt, Alb. C. 1912–14. *Der Baré'e Sprekende Toradja's van midden Celebes*. Batavia: Landsdrukkerij.

Ahern, E. 1973. *The Cult of the Dead in a Chinese Village*. Stanford, Calif.: Stanford University Press.

Aldred, C. 1961. *The Egyptians*. New York: Praeger.

Alexiou, M. 1974. *The Ritual Lament in Greek Tradition*. Cambridge: Cambridge University Press.

Althabe, G. 1969. *Oppression et libération dans l'imaginaire*. Paris: François Maspero.

Ariès, P. 1967. "La Mort inversée. Le changement des attitudes devant la mort dans les sociétés occidentales." *Archives Européenes de Sociologie* 8: 169–95.

1974a. *Western Attitudes Towards Death from the Middle Ages to the Present.* Baltimore: Johns Hopkins University Press.

1974b. "Death Inside Out." *Hastings Center Studies* 2: 3–18.

1978. *L'Homme devant la Mort.* Paris: Editions du Seuil.

Barnes, R. H. 1974. *Kédang: A Study of the Collective Thought of an Eastern Indonesian People.* Oxford: Clarendon Press.

Beattie, J. 1966. "C. A. Comment" on E. Leach. "The Founding Fathers." *Current Anthropology* 7(5): 570–1.

Becker, E. 1973. *The Denial of Death.* New York: Free Press.

Beidelman, T. O. 1966. "Swazi Royal Ritual." *Africa* 36: 373–405.

1974. *W. Robertson Smith and the Sociological Study of Religion.* Chicago: University of Chicago Press.

Bellah, R. N. 1967. "Civil Religion in America." *Daedalus* 96: 1–22.

Belmont, N. 1974. *Arnold Van Gennep: créateur de l'ethnographie française.* Paris: Petite Bibliothèque Payot.

Binford, S. 1968. "A Structural Comparison of Disposal of the Dead in the Mousterian and the Upper Paleolithic." *Southwestern Journal of Anthropology* 24: 139–54.

Bloch, M. 1971. *Placing the Dead: Tombs, Ancestral Villages, and Kinship Organization in Madagascar.* London and New York: Seminar Press.

Boase, T. S. R. 1972. *Death in the Middle Ages.* London: Thames and Hudson.

Boon, J. 1977. *The Anthropological Romance of Bali 1597–1972.* Cambridge: Cambridge University Press.

Bowman, L. 1964. *The American Funeral: A Study in Guilt, Extravagance and Sublimity.* New York: Paperback Library.

Braches, S. 1882. "Sandong Raung." *Jahresberichte der Rheinischen Mission.* Barmen: D. B. Wieman.

Breasted, J. 1912. *Development of Religious Thought in Ancient Egypt.* New York: Scribners.

Budge, E. A. W. 1911. *Osiris and the Egyptian Resurrection.* London: Medici Society. Reprinted in 1973. New York: Dover Press.

Bühler, A. 1972. "Hanfverarbeitung und Batik bei den Meau in Nordthailand." *Ethnologische Zeitschrift* 1: 61–81.

Butzer, K. W. 1976. *Early Hydraulic Civilisation in Egypt: A Study in Cultural Ecology.* Chicago: University of Chicago Press.

Choron, J. 1964. *Death and the Modern Man.* New York: Collier Books.

Bibliography

Covarrubias, M. 1937. *Island of Bali*. New York: Knopf.

Crawley, A. E. 1912. "Drums and Cymbals." *Encyclopedia of Religious Ethics* 5: 89–94.

Crocker, J. C. 1971. "The Southern Way of Death." In J. K. Morland (ed.). *The Not-so-Solid-South*. Pp. 114–29. Athens, Ga.: Southern Anthropological Society.

1977. "The Mirrored Self: Identity & Ritual Inversion among the Eastern Bororo." *Ethnology* 16(2): 129–45.

Cunnington, P. 1977. *Costume for Births, Marriages, and Deaths*. Atlantic Highlands, N.J.: Humanities Press.

Curl, J. S. 1972. *The Victorian Celebration of Death*. London: David and Charles.

Dahl, O. C. 1951. *Malgache et Maanjan: une comparaison linguistique*. Oslo: Studies of the Egede Instituttet 3.

Decary, R. 1958. *La mort et les coutumes funéraires à Madagascar*. Paris: G. P. Maisonneuve et Larose.

Delvert, J. 1961. *Le Paysan Cambodgien*. The Hague: Mouton.

Dempsey, D. 1975. *The Way We Die: An Investigation of Death and Dying in America Today*. New York: McGraw-Hill.

Deng, F. M. 1972. *The Dinka of the Sudan*. New York: Holt, Rinehart & Winston.

Douglas, A. 1974. "Heaven Our Home: Consolation Literature in the Northern United States, 1830–1880." In D. Stannard (ed.). *Death in America*. Pp. 49–68. Philadelphia: University of Pennsylvania Press.

Douglas, M. 1966. *Purity and Danger: An Analysis of Concepts of Pollution and Taboo*. New York: Praeger.

1970. *Natural Symbols: Explorations in Cosmology*. London: Barrie & Rockliff, Cresset Press.

Douglass, W. A. 1969. *Death in Murelaga: Funerary Ritual in a Spanish Basque Village*. Seattle: University of Washington Press.

Downs, R. E. 1956. *The Religion of the Baré'e-speaking Toradja of Central Celebes*. The Hague: Excelsior.

Driver, H. 1961. *Indians of North America*. Chicago: University of Chicago Press.

Dubois, H. 1938. *Monographie des Betsileo*. Paris: Institut d'Ethnologie.

Durkheim, E. 1938 (orig. 1895). *The Rules of Sociological Method*. Translated by S. Solovay and J. Mueller. New York: Free Press.

1965 (orig. 1912). *The Elementary Forms of the Religious Life*. New York: Free Press.

Durkheim, E., and Mauss, M. 1963 (orig. 1903). *Primitive Classi-*

fication. Translated and edited by R. Needham. Chicago: University of Chicago Press.

Dworakowska, M. 1938. "The Origin of Bell and Drum." *Prace etnologiczne* 5. Nakladem Towarzystwa Naukowego Waszawskiego.

Eckhardt, A. R. 1973. "Death in the Judaic and Christian Traditions." In A. Mack (ed.). *Death in American Experience*. Pp. 123–48. New York: Schocken.

Edwards, I. E. S. 1947. *The Pyramids of Egypt*. London: Penguin.

Emery, W. B. 1961. *Archaic Egypt*. Harmondsworth, England: Penguin.

Evans-Pritchard, E. E. 1948. *The Divine Kingship of the Shilluk of the Nilotic Sudan*. The Frazer Memorial Lecture of 1948. Cambridge: Cambridge University Press.

Fabian, J. 1973. "How Others Die – Reflections on the Anthropology of Death." In A. Mack (ed.). *Death in American Experience*. Pp. 177–201. New York: Schocken.

Faublée, J. 1947. *Récits Bara*. Paris: Institut d'Ethnologie.

    1954. *La cohésion des sociétés Bara*. Paris: Presses *Universitaires de France*.

Feifel, H. (ed.). 1959. *The Meaning of Death*. New York: McGraw-Hill.

Firth, R. 1967. *Tikopia Ritual and Belief*. Boston: Beacon Press.

Fortune, R. 1965. *Manus Religion*. Lincoln: University of Nebraska Press.

Fox, J. J. 1973. "On Bad Death and the Left Hand: a Study of Rotinese Symbolic Inversions." In R. Needham (ed.). *Right and Left*. Pp. 342–68. Chicago: University of Chicago Press.

    1977. "Chicken Bones and Buffalo Sinews." Ms.

Fox, R. 1959. *Experiment Perilous*. New York: Free Press.

Frankfort, H. 1948. *Kingship and the Gods*. Chicago: University of Chicago Press.

Frazer, J. G. 1963 (orig. 1890). *The Golden Bough*. New York: Macmillan.

French, S. 1974. "The Cemetery as Cultural Institution: The Establishment of Mount Auburn and the 'Rural Cemetery' Movement." In D. Stannard (ed.). *Death in America*. Pp. 69–91. Philadelphia: University of Pennsylvania Press.

Fulton, R. (ed.). 1965. *Death and Identity*. New York: Wiley.

Fulton, R., and Geis, G. 1965. "Death and Social Values." In R. Fulton (ed.). *Death and Identity*. Pp. 67–75. New York: Wiley.

Gardiner, A. 1961. *Egypt of the Pharaohs*. Oxford: Clarendon.

Bibliography

Geertz, C. 1960. *The Religion of Java*. New York: Free Press.

1973. *The Interpretation of Cultures*. New York: Basic Books.

1974a. "Symbol, Status, and Power in the Classical Balinese State." Institute for Advanced Studies, Princeton, N.J. Ms.

1974b. "Centers, Kings, and Charisma: Reflections on the Symbolics of Power." Institute for Advanced Studies, Princeton, N.J. Ms.

Genet, J. 1953. *Pompes Funèbres*. Paris: Editions Gallimard.

1969. *Funeral Rites*. New York: Grove Press.

Giesey, R. E. 1960. *The Royal Funeral Ceremony in Renaissance France*. Geneva: Librairie E. Droz.

Gluckman, M. 1937. "Mortuary Customs and the Belief in Survival After Death Among the South Eastern Bantu." *Bantu Studies* 11: 117–36.

1954. *Rituals of Rebellion in South-east Africa*. Manchester: Manchester University Press.

(ed.) 1962. *Essays on the Ritual of Social Relations*. Manchester: Manchester University Press.

Gomes, E. H. 1911. *Seventeen Years Among the Sea Dyaks of Borneo*. Philadelphia: Lippincott.

Goody, J. 1962. *Death, Property and the Ancestors*. Stanford, Calif.: Stanford University Press.

Gorer, G. 1965. *Death, Grief, and Mourning*. New York: Doubleday.

Goris, R., and Dronkers, P. 1955. *Atlas Kebudajan*. Jakarta.

Grabowsky, F. 1884. "Der Distrikt Dusun-Timor in Süd-Ost Borneo und seiner Bewohner." *Ausland* 57: 444–9, 469–75.

1889. "Der Tod, das Begräbnis, das Tiwah oder Todtenfest bei den Dajaken." *International Archives of Ethnography*, Leiden. Vol. 2: 177–204.

Grollman, E. A. 1974. *Concerning Death: A Practical Guide for the Living*. Boston: Beacon Press.

Guiart, J. 1963. *The Arts of the South Pacific*. New York: Golden Press.

Habenstein, R. W., and Lamers, W. M. 1955. *History of American Funeral Directing*. Milwaukee: Bulfin Printers.

Haddon, A. C. (ed.). 1908. *Cambridge Anthropological Expedition to Torres Straits, Reports*. Cambridge: Cambridge University Press.

Hall, D. G. E. 1968. *A History of South East Asia*. Third Edition. London: St. Martin's Press.

Hamilton, C., and Ostendorf, L. 1963. *Lincoln in Photographs: an*

Bibliography

Album of Every Known Pose. Norman: University of Oklahoma Press.

Hardeland, A. 1858. *Versuch einer grammatik der dajakschen sprache. Bearbeitet und herausgegeben im auf-frage und auf kosten der Niederlaendischen bibelgesellschaft.* Amsterdam: F. Muller.

Harmer, R. M. 1963. *The High Cost of Dying.* New York: Crowell-Collier.

Harrison, T. 1962. "Borneo Death." *Bijdragen Tot de Taal-, Land- en Volkenkunde* 118: 1–41.

Hertz, R. 1907. "Contribution à une étude sur la représentation collective de la mort." *Année sociologique* 10: 48–137.

1909. "La Prééminence de la main droite: étude sur la polarité religieuse." *Revue philosophique* 68: 553–80.

1922. "La péché et l'expiation dans les sociétés primitives." M. Mauss (ed.). *Revue de l'histoire des Religions* 86: 5–53.

1928. *Mélanges de sociologie et de folklore.* M. Mauss (ed.). Paris: Alcan.

1960. *Death and the Right Hand.* Translated by R. and C. Needham with an Introduction by E. E. Evans-Pritchard. New York: Free Press.

Hicks, D. 1976. *Tetum Ghosts and Kin.* Palo Alto, Calif.: Mayfield.

Hocart, A. M. 1954. *Social Origins.* London: Watts.

1970 (orig. 1936). *Kings and Councillors: An Essay in the Comparative Anatomy of Human Society.* R. Needham (ed.). Chicago: University of Chicago Press.

Hoffman, M. In Press. *Egypt before the Pharaohs.* New York: Knopf.

Hooykaas, C. 1973. *Religion in Bali.* Leiden: Brill.

Hubert, H., and Mauss, M. 1899. "Essai sur la nature et la fonction du sacrifice." *Année sociologique* 2: 29–138.

1964. *Sacrifice: Its Nature and Function.* Translated by W. D. Halls. Chicago: University of Chicago Press.

Hudson, A. B. 1966. "Death Ceremonies of the Padju Epat Ma'anyan Dayaks." *Sarawak Museum Journal* 13: 341–416.

Huntington, W. R. 1973. "Death and the Social Order: Bara Funeral Customs (Madagascar)." *African Studies* 32(2): 65–84.

1978. "Bara Endogamy and Incest Prohibition." *Bijdragen Tot de Taal-, Land-en Volkenkunde* 134: 30–62.

Jackson, C. O. (ed.). 1977. *Passing: The Vision of Death in America.* Westport, Conn.: Greenwood.

Bibliography

Jensen, E. 1974. *The Iban and their Religion*. Oxford: Clarendon Press.

Jung, C. 1964. *Man and his Symbols*. New York: Doubleday.

Kantorowicz, E. 1957. *The King's Two Bodies: A Study in Mediaeval Political Theory*. Princeton, N.J.: Princeton University Press.

Kastenbaum, R., and Aisenberg, R. 1973. *The Psychology of Death*. New York: Springer.

Kaut, C. 1952. "The Treatment of the Dead Body in Contemporary American Society." M.A. Thesis. University of Chicago.

Kopytoff, I. 1971. "Ancestors as Elders in Africa." *Africa* 41(2): 129–42.

Kübler-Ross, E. 1975. *Death, the Final Stage of Growth*. Englewood Cliffs, N.J.: Prentice-Hall.

Kurtz, D. C., and Broadman, J. 1971. *Greek Burial Customs*. London: Thames and Hudson.

Leach, E. R. 1958. "Magical Hair." *Journal of the Royal Anthropological Institute* 88(2): 149–64.

1961a. "Golden Bough or Gilded Twig?" *Daedalus* 90(2): 371–87.

1961b. *Rethinking Anthropology*. London: University of London, Athlone Press.

1966. "On the Founding Fathers." *Current Anthropology* 7(5): 560–7.

Lévi-Strauss, C. 1963. *Totemism*. Translated by R. Needham. Boston: Beacon Press.

1969. *The Raw and the Cooked*. New York: Harper & Row.

1973. *From Honey to Ashes*. New York: Harper & Row.

Lienhardt, R. G. 1954. "The Shilluk of the Upper Nile." In Forde, C. D. (ed.). *African Worlds: Studies in the Cosmological Ideas and Social Values of African Peoples*. Pp. 138–63. Oxford: Oxford University Press.

1961. *Divinity and Experience: The Religion of the Dinka*. Oxford: Clarendon Press.

1966. *Social Anthropology*. London: Oxford University Press.

1970. "The Situation of Death: An Aspect of Anuak Philosophy." In M. Douglas (ed.). *Witchcraft Confessions and Accusations*. Pp. 279–92. London: Tavistock.

Lloyd, G. E. R. 1966. *Polarity and Analogy in Early Greek Thought*. Cambridge: Cambridge University Press.

Lopatin, I. 1960. *The Cult of the Dead Among the Natives of the Amur Basin*. The Hague: Mouton.

Bibliography

Mack, A. (ed.). 1973. *Death in American Experience*. New York: Schocken.

McLennan, J. 1970 (orig. 1865). *Primitive Marriage: An Inquiry into the Origin and the Form of Capture in Marriage Ceremonies*. P. Rivière (ed.). Chicago: University of Chicago Press.

McLeod, N. 1964. "The Status of Musical Specialists in Madagascar." *Ethnomusicology* 7(3): 278–389.

Malinowski, B. 1929. *The Sexual Life of Savages in North-Western Melanesia*. New York and London: Harcourt Brace Jovanovich.

Mauss, M. 1921. "L'expression obligatoire des sentiments (Rituels oraux funéraires australiens)." *Journal de Psychologie* 18: 425–34.

— 1922. Introduction et conclusion à Robert Hertz: "Le péché et l'expiation dans les sociétés primitives." *Revue de l'histoire des Religions* 86: 1–4, 164–5.

— 1926. "Effect physique chez l'individual de l'idée de mort suggestée par la collectivité (Australie, Nouvelle-Zélande)." *Journal de Psychologie* 23: 653–69. Reprinted in Mauss, M. 1960. *Sociologie et anthropologie*. Paris: Presses Universitaires de France.

— 1938. "Une catégorie de l'esprit humain; la notion de personne celle de 'moi'; un plan de travail." *Journal of the Royal Anthropological Institute* 68: 263–81.

Mendelssohn, K. 1974. *The Riddle of the Pyramids*. London: Thames and Hudson.

Metcalf, P. A. 1976. "Who are the Berawan? Ethnic Classification and the Distribution of Secondary Treatment of the Dead in Central North Borneo." *Oceania* 47(2): 85–105.

— 1977a. "Berawan Mausoleums." *Sarawak Museum Journal* 24: 121–36.

— 1977b. "The Berawan Afterlife: A Critique of Hertz." In Appell, G. (ed.). *Studies in Borneo Societies*. Pp. 72–91. Dekalb, Ill.: Northern Illinois University.

Meyers, E. 1971. *Jewish Ossuaries: Reburial and Rebirth*. Rome: Biblical Institute Press. Biblica et Orientalia No. 24.

Miles, D. 1965. "Socio-Economic Aspects of Secondary Burial." *Oceania* 35(3): 161–74.

Mitford, J. 1963. *The American Way of Death*. New York: Simon & Schuster.

Moody, R. A. 1975. *Life After Life*. New York: Bantam.

Morley, J. 1971. *Death, Heaven and the Victorians*. London: Studio Vista.

Bibliography

Neale, R. 1973. *The Art of Dying*. New York: Harper & Row.

Needham, R. 1954. "The System of Teknonyms and Death-Names of the Penan." *Southwestern Journal of Anthropology* 10: 416–31.

1964. "Blood, Thunder, and the Mockery of Animals." *Sociologus* 14: 136–49.

1967. "Percussion and Transition." *Man* N.S. 2: 606–14.

1970. "Editor's Introduction." In Hocart, A. M. *Kings and Councillors*. Pp. xii–xcix. Chicago: University of Chicago Press.

1972. *Belief, Language and Experience*. Chicago: University of Chicago Press.

1973 (ed.). *Right and Left: Essays on Dual Classification*. Chicago: University of Chicago Press.

Neher, A. 1962. "A Physiological Explanation of Unusual Behaviour in Ceremonies Involving Drums." *Human Biology* 34: 151–9.

Parsons, T. 1963. "Death in American Society – A Brief Working Paper." *American Behavioral Scientist* 6: 61–5.

1968a. "Emile Durkheim." In *International Encyclopedia of the Social Sciences*. Vol. 4: 311–20. New York: Macmillan.

1968b. *The Structure of Social Action*. New York: Free Press.

Pelzer, K. J. 1945. *Pioneer Settlement in the Asiatic Tropics*. New York: American Geographic Society.

Perham, J. 1896. "Iban Religion." in H. L. Roth (ed.). *The Natives of Sarawak and British North Borneo*. Pp. 168–213. London: Truslove & Hansen.

Pine, V. R. 1975. *Caretaker of the Dead: The American Funeral Director*. New York: Wiley.

Pretty, G. 1969. "The Macleay Museum Mummy from Torres Straits: A Postscript to Elliot Smith and the Diffusion Controversy." *Man* 4: 24–43.

Rabibhadana, A. 1969. *The Organisation of Thai Society in the Early Bangkok Period, 1783–1873*. Cornell University South East Asia Program Data Paper No. 74.

Radcliffe-Brown, A. R. 1964. *The Andaman Islanders*. New York: Free Press.

Reisner, A. 1936. *The Development of Egyptian Tombs to the Accession of Cheops*. Cambridge: Cambridge University Press.

Renault, M. 1958. *The King Must Die*. New York: Pantheon.

Riffert, G. R. 1932. *Great Pyramid: Proof of God*. Haverhill, Mass.: Destiny Publishers.

Rivers, W. H. R. 1926. *Psychology and Ethnology*. London: Kegan Paul.

Bibliography

Rosenblatt, P. C., Walsh, R., and Jackson, A. 1976. *Grief and Mourning in Cross Cultural Perspective*. New Haven: Human Relations Area Files Press.

Saum, L. 1974. "Death in the Popular Mind of Pre-Civil War America." In D. Stannard (ed.). *Death in America*. Pp. 30–48. Philadelphia: University of Pennsylvania Press.

Schärer, H. 1963 (orig. 1946). *Ngaju Religion: The Conception of God among a South Borneo People*. Translated by R. Needham. The Hague: Marinus Nijhoff.

Schebesta, P. 1929. *Among the Forest Dwarfs of Malaya*. Translated by A. Chambers. London: Hutchinson.

Silverman, P. 1974. "Another Look at the Role of the Funeral Director." Paper presented at a conference of the Foundation of Thanatology, March 1974.

Smith, G. E. 1929 (orig. 1915). *The Migrations of Early Cultures*. Manchester: Manchester University Press.

Smith, R. B. 1967. *Siam, or The History of the Thais from 1569 A.D. to 1828 A.D.* Bethesda, Md.: Decatur Press.

Smith, W. R. 1889. *Lectures on the Religion of the Semites*. Edinburgh: A. and C. Black.

Stannard, D. (ed.). 1974. *Death in America*. Philadelphia: University of Pennsylvania Press.

Steiner, F. 1967. *Taboo*. Harmondsworth, England: Penguin.

Sudnow, D. 1967. *Passing On: The Social Organization of Dying*. Englewood Cliffs, N.J.: Prentice-Hall.

Swellengrebel, J. L. 1969. "Nonconformity in the Balinese Family." In *Bali: Further Studies in Life, Thought, and Ritual*. Pp. 199–212. The Hague: Van Hoeve.

Tambiah, S. J. 1970. *Buddhism and the Spirit Cults in North East Thailand*. Cambridge: Cambridge University Press.

   1976. *World Conqueror and World Renouncer: A Study of Buddhism and Polity in Thailand against a Historical Background*. Cambridge and New York: Cambridge University Press.

Tellefsen, O. 1975. "A New Theory of Pyramid Building." In D. Hunter and P. Whitten. *Anthropology: A Contemporary Perspective*. Pp. 151–6. Boston: Little, Brown.

Thomas, L. V. 1968. *Cinq essais sur la mort africaine*. Dakar: Université de Dakar.

   1975. *Anthropologie de la mort*. Paris: Payot.

Toynbee, J. M. C. 1971. *Death and Burial in the Roman World*. London: Thames and Hudson.

Bibliography

Traube, E. 1977. "Ritual Exchange Among the Mambai of East Timor: Gifts of Life and Death." Ph.D. thesis. Harvard University.

Turner, V. 1953. *Lunda Rites and Ceremonies.* Occasional Papers of the Rhodes-Livingstone Museum, No. 10.

1967. *The Forest of Symbols.* Ithaca, N.Y.: Cornell University Press.

1968. *The Drums of Affliction.* Oxford: Clarendon Press.

1969. *The Ritual Process.* Chicago: Aldine.

1975. "Death and the Dead in the Pilgrimage Process." In M. West and M. Whisson (eds.). *Religion and Social Change in Southern Africa.* Pp. 107–27. Capetown: David Philip.

Tuzin, D. 1975. "The Breath of a Ghost: Dreams and the Fear of the Dead." *Ethos* 3(4): 559–78.

Van Gennep, A. 1904. *Tabou et totémisme à Madagascar.* Paris: Ernest Leroux.

1909. *Les rites de passage.* Paris: Emile Nourry.

1960. *The Rites of Passage.* Translated by M. B. Vizedom and G. L. Caffee with an Introduction by S. T. Kimball. Chicago: University of Chicago Press.

Vizedom, M. B. 1976. *Rites and Relationships: Rites of Passage and Contemporary Anthropology.* Beverly Hills, Calif.: Sage.

Wagner, R. 1972. *Habu: The Innovation of Meaning in Daribi Religion.* Chicago: University of Chicago Press.

Wales, H. G. Q. 1931. *Siamese State Ceremonies: Their History and Function.* London: Bernard Quaritch.

Warner, W. L. 1959. *The Living and the Dead: A Study of the Symbolic Life of Americans.* New Haven: Yale University Press.

Waugh, E. 1948. *The Loved One.* Boston: Little, Brown.

Westermann, D. 1912. *The Shilluk People, Their Language and Folklore.* Philadelphia: United Presbyterian Church of North America.

Wilson, G. 1939. "Nyakyusa Conventions of Burial." *Bantu Studies* 13: 1–31.

Wilson, J. 1946. "Egypt." In Frankfort, H., Wilson, J., Jacobson, T., and Irwin, W. *The Intellectual Adventure of Ancient Man.* Pp. 31–123. Chicago: University of Chicago Press.

1951. *The Burden of Egypt.* Chicago: University of Chicago Press.

Wilson, M. 1951. *Good Company: a Study of Nyakyusa Age Villages.* London: Oxford University Press.

Bibliography

1957. *Rituals of Kinship among the Nyakyusa*. London: Oxford University Press.

Wirz, P. 1928. *Der Totenkult auf Bali*. Stuttgart: Strocker and Shroder.

Wittgenstein, L. 1971. "Remarks on Frazer's 'Golden Bough'." *Human World* 3: 18–41.

Wolf, A. P 1970. "Chinese Kinship and Mourning Dress." In Freedman, M. (ed.). *Family and Kinship in Chinese Society*. Pp. 190–207. Stanford, Calif.: Stanford University Press.

Wood, W. A. R. 1926. *A History of Siam from the Earliest Times to the Year A.D. 1781*. Bangkok.

Zandee, J. 1960. *Death as an Enemy, According to Ancient Egyptian Conceptions*. Translated by Mrs. W. F. Klasens. Leiden: Brill.

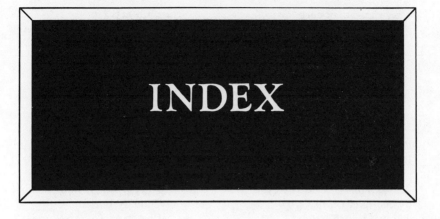

INDEX

Adams, Marie, Jeanne, 51–5, 57
Adriani, N., 83, 85
Africa, 16, 66, 172, 184
afterlife, *see* eschatology; soul
Aldred, C., 151
American funeral rites, 2–4, 15, 16,
    20, 96, 187–210
    death specialists, 187, 190–1, 193,
    195, 200, 202, 203
    wake, 190–1, 202, 209
    see also embalming; corpse,
    display of
ancestors, *see* soul, spirits of the
    dead
Andaman islands, 24–8, 43
Année sociologique, 7, 16, 61
archaeology, 5–6, 143, 144–5
Ariès, Phillippe, 4, 201–2, 204, 208
Ars moriendi, 203
Australia, 30, 43

bade tower, 131–2
Bali, 85–7, 89, 130–2, 185
Bara, 98–118
    boisterousness and sexual license,
    98, 103, 105

burials, 100–5
    contrasted to Berawan, 110, 111
    "gatherings," 105–7
    generation of vitality, 99–101,
    109–15
    legends, 112–13, 118
    life as transition, 116–17
    notions of conception, 99
    ritual weeping, 27, 102, 118
    secondary treatment rites, 95,
    107–9
    see also *faha*; cattle wrestling
Becker, Ernest, 194, 197
Bellah, Robert, 205–6
Berawan, 67–82, 89, 92, 110, 111,
    133–41, 150
    boisterousness and sexual license,
    46–8, 50, 52–3, 58, 76, 111
    death songs, 70–2, 74
    migrations of, 72, 137
    notions of death and afterlife, 69,
    70–3, 74–7, 79, 80
    privations of widow, 77, 78, 79,
    83
    rank among, 133–5, 139–40

Index

Egypt, 6, 19, 141–52, 184, 185, 195
embalming, 3–4, 187, 190–1, 194,
    195, 198, 205
Emery, Walter, 144
emotions at funerals, 18, 23–43, 44,
    62–5, 74, 99, 170, 171, 176, 197,
    200, 201, 203, 211
endocannibalism, 57
England, 20, 35, 160–5, 173, 181,
    193, 197, 201–2
eschatology, 33, 67, 74, 80, 87, 97–8,
    133; see also soul
Europe, 154, 173, 184
Evans-Pritchard, E. E., 15, 61–2,
    155, 158–9, 173, 174, 184
evolutionism, 6–7, 10, 150

faha, 111
flesh and bone, *see* bone and flesh
Fox, James J., 89
France, 20, 165–73, 181, 201–2
Frankfort, H., 144
Frazer, Sir James, 6–7, 155, 173,
    174, 184
Fulton, Robert, 165
funeral director, *see* American
    funeral rites, death specialists
funerals, 8, 18, 25, 28, 29, 31, 35, 42,
    46, 58, 78, 98, 115, 189, 200, 202
    processions, 103–4, 108, 118, 127–
    8, 131, 170, 192–3
    and the social order, 96, 129,
    138–9
    and social status, 63, 85, 130–2,
    133–41, 145, 192–3
    see also American funeral rites;
    corpse; dancing at funerals;
    death; drinking at funerals;
    economic aspects of funerals;
    secondary burial; sexual license
    at funerals; myths associated
    with funerals

Geertz, Clifford, 42, 130–2
ghosts, *see* soul, spirits of the dead
Giesey, Ralph, 159, 165, 170, 173

Goody, Jack, 16, 66
Gorer, Geoffrey, 4
grave goods, 87, 108, 145–6, 148
Greece, 15, 27

"hall of grief" (*salle de deuil*), 169
"hall of honor" (*salle d'honneur*),
    168, 169
Harmer, R. M., 191
Hertz, Robert, 13–17, 61–8, 77, 78,
    81, 83, 85, 87, 89, 122, 182, 184,
    185
    and metaphor of secondary
    burial, 13–14, 57, 63, 73, 92,
    141
    and Van Gennep, 8, 13, 14, 19,
    97, 101, 102, 116
Hicks, David, 89
Hocart, A. M., 153
Hoffman, Michael, 151
"house of many tears," 102–3, 112,
    115
Hudson, A. B., 82

Iban, 87–9, 91
incest, 114
Indonesia, 13, 19, 88, 89, 93, 101,
    172, 186

jar burial, 68, 125
Java, 42–3
Jews, 15, 191, 199, 208

Kantorowicz, Ernst, 159–60, 164,
    173
Kaut, Charles, 195
Kayan, 138
Kenyah, 138, 139–40
kin, at death, 90, 107–8, 117, 199, 203
    mourning usages of, 25, 30, 32,
    35, 41, 64, 74, 77–8, 79, 83, 84,
    109
    see also incest
kings, 19, 122
    coronations of, 127, 128, 157
    divine kings, 67, 123, 151, 153–9,
    177

227

Index

funeral rites of, 19, 85, 122–3, 150, 163, 168–72, 183
powers of, 123–4, 130, 152, 155–6
royal corpses, 144, 163, 167, 183
royal cults, 125, 151, 153, 157
succession of, 124, 129, 172
see also symbolism, involving power
Kruyt, A. C., 83, 85
Kübler-Ross, Elisabeth, 186

legends, *see* myths
Lévi-Strauss, Claude, 9, 32, 46, 50
Lienhardt, Godfrey, 175, 180
Lincoln, Abraham, 190, 206, 209
LoDagaa, 66
"loss of breath," 70, 74
Lubbock, J., 6

Ma'anyan, 82–3, 85, 86, 91, 94
McLennan, J., 6
Madagascar, 2, 19, 27, 65, 93–8, 170, 172, 192, 205, 210
Malay, 138
Malaysia, 49
Mambai, 89–92
mastaba, 146–148
"master of the fishing spears," 175, 179–82
mausoleum, 68, 135–40, 79; *see also* tomb; mastaba
Melanesia, 15, 19, 185
memorial societies, 194
Merina, 16, 65, 95, 97
metaphor, 67, 78, 81, 90, 97
Miles, Douglas, 16, 78
Mitford, Jessica, 3, 4, 20, 186, 191
mock battles, 11, 137, 157
Morgan, Lewis Henry, 6
mourning, *see* kin, mourning usages of; weeping, ritualized; wounds, inflicted during mourning
mummification, 185, 195
myths associated with funerals, 72, 92, 112–13, 118, 115

National Funeral Directors Association, 192, 205
Needham, Rodney, 16, 48–9, 53, 58
noise, 46–50, 52–3, 76, 103
Nuer, 156
nulang, 68, 70, 72, 73, 78, 80, 135; *see also* secondary burial
Nyakyusa, 2, 34–43, 96, 210
Nyikang, 157–8, 164, 173, 181

Olo Ngaju, 64, 82, 83
"owner of the death," 36, 104

Parsons, Talcott, 32
Petrie, Flinders, 144, 145
pharoah, 19, 143–52
Pine, Vanderlyn, 187
pollution, 17, 64–5, 77
psychic universals, 18, 49, 58, 185, 194, 197
pyramids, 141–52

Radcliffe-Brown, A. R., 18, 24–8, 31, 34, 184
Rajah Brooke, 134
regicide, 19–20, 154, 155–6, 158, 162, 166, 173–4
relics, *see* corpse, relics of
rites of passage, 8, 19, 97, 98, 99, 118, 172, 199
ritual
   and belief, 62, 74, 78, 99
   and daily actions, 51–3, 55–7
   as display, 105, 129, 130–2, 139–40
   function of, 27, 30–1, 33, 66
   inversion, 164, 204
   native exegesis of, 73–4, 78, 98, 176
   nature of, 81, 103, 164, 166, 173, 180, 193
   of power, *see* kings; symbolism, involving power
   and sentiment, 23–43, 44, 197–8
   and solidarity, 23–33, 138, 181, 209

228

Index

Tylor, E. B., 6–7, 33

undertaker, *see* American Funeral Directors Association; American funeral rites, death specialists

Van Gennep, Arnold, 8–13, 14, 19, 50, 54, 67, 98, 101, 102, 116, 169, 184; *see also* rites of passage
"viewing," *see* corpse, display of

wake, *see* American funeral rites, wake
Wake, C. S., 6
Wales, H. G. Quaritch, 124

warfare, 38–9, 114, 124, 130, 137–8, 150
Warner, W. Lloyd, 209
Warramunga, 29
Waugh, Evelyn, 186
weeping, ritualized, 24–8, 33, 36, 39–40, 74, 102
widow, widower, *see* kin, mourning usages of
Wilson, Godfrey, 34–7, 184
Wilson, John A., 144, 150–1
Wilson, Monica, 35, 36
witchcraft, 36, 41, 106, 117
Wittgenstein, Ludwig, 174
wounds, inflicted during mourning, 29–30, 32